Spartacus and Rome's Servile Wars

About the Author

Sotirios F. Drokalos holds three Master's degrees, in International Relations, Military History, and International Antiterrorism, from the University of Bologna and the Niccolò Cusano University of Rome. He is the author of several books and articles published in English, Greek and Italian, including contributions to peer-reviewed journals such as the *British Journal for Military History*.

His book *The Wars Between Greeks and Carthaginians* was published in 2025 by Pen & Sword.

See more at www.drokalos.com

Spartacus and Rome's Servile Wars

Sotirios F. Drokalos

Pen & Sword
MILITARY

First published in Great Britain in 2026 by
Pen & Sword Military
An imprint of Pen & Sword Books Limited
Yorkshire – Philadelphia

ISBN 978 1 03619 534 2

A CIP catalogue record for this book is available from the British Library.

Typeset by Mac Style
Printed in the UK by CPI Group (UK) Ltd, Croydon, CR0 4YY.

MIX
Paper | Supporting responsible forestry
FSC www.fsc.org
FSC® C013604

The Publisher's authorised representative in the EU for product safety is Authorised Rep Compliance Ltd., Ground Floor, 71 Lower Baggot Street, Dublin D02 P593, Ireland.
www.arccompliance.com

For a complete list of Pen & Sword titles please contact:

PEN & SWORD BOOKS LIMITED
47 Church Street, Barnsley, South Yorkshire, S70 2AS, England
E-mail: enquiries@pen-and-sword.co.uk
Website: www.pen-and-sword.co.uk
or
PEN AND SWORD BOOKS
1950 Lawrence Road, Havertown, PA 19083, USA
E-mail: uspen-and-sword@casematepublishers.com
Website: www.penandswordbooks.com

Again, to my kittens, always.

Contents

List of Illustrations

18. Mosaic from the third century CE, found in a private house in Curium, Cyprus, depicting two gladiators and a referee, with their names inscribed in Greek.
19. Statue of Spartacus at the Louvre, created by French sculptor Denis Foyatier in 1830.
20. Ancient Roman temple dedicated to Bacchus in Baalbek, Lebanon. Dionysian worship remained relatively distinct from the official religion of Rome and the Greek cities.
21. Detail from the 'Mosaic of the Gladiator' (*c.* 320 CE), Villa Borghese, Rome.
22. Relief depicting Roman legionaries from the time of Emperor Trajan.
23. The impressive Roman aqueduct Pont du Gard, spanning the Gardon River in southern France. One of the best-preserved Roman aqueducts.
24. The Roman bridge over the Tagus River at Alcántara, Spain – an enduring example of Roman engineering and provincial development.

Introduction

The final century of the Roman Republic, from the murder of Tiberius Gracchus in 133 BCE to the victory of Octavian Augustus at Actium in 31 BCE, was one of turbulence and transformation. During this period, the older political and social structures were tested by objective structural pressures and altering conditions. Eventually, they gave way to new ones, more functional and adapted to the new circumstances.

In this period, the reform movement of the Gracchi, the Social War, the bloody political conflict between *optimates* and *populares*, and finally, the large-scale civil wars with famous Romans such as Pompey Magnus and Julius Caesar, culminating in the rise of the empire, marked a century of intense upheaval and change. In the context of this explosive process, a multitude of other political, social and ethnic conflicts took place. These included three slave revolts, the most famous in our time being that of Spartacus.

Specialists in Roman history tend to focus their research and writing on the major and decisive events of that period, and usually find little interest in the specific revolts. Consequently, the approaches to the subject in historical essays, novels and, of course, films and TV series are primarily ideological, often resulting in distortions of historical reality. In particular, the two most important ideological currents of modern times, liberalism and socialism/Marxism, have frequently used the figure of Spartacus as a symbol of a liberation struggle against oppression, denouncing the ancient world as 'slave-owning' and subtly claiming their own supposed superiority in terms of respect for human dignity and freedom compared to Greco-Roman civilisation.

This attitude is not only adopted at the theoretical level but also primarily at the level of popular culture and propaganda. Thus, communists in the Soviet Union and its satellites in the twentieth century gave the name 'Spartacus' to many sports clubs, such as Spartak Moscow, Spartak Trnava, Spartak Sofia and so on, while in Germany, they used it to name their revolutionary movement – the 'Spartacus Union' of Karl Liebknecht and Rosa Luxemburg. On the other hand, in the liberal democratic world, popular Hollywood films, TV series and novels have been produced that present Spartacus as a hero of freedom, most famously, Stanley Kubrick's film of the same name with Kirk Douglas in the title role.

Karl Marx, in a famous letter to Friedrich Engels dated 27 February 1861, praised Spartacus as the 'most capital fellow' in all ancient history and a great leader of the ancient proletariat.[1] On the other side, US President Ronald Reagan, during his famous speech at the Palace of Westminster in London on 8 June 1982, mentioned the revolt of Spartacus as one of the historic examples of the struggle for freedom.[2] It is ironic to see an author who wrote a PhD in Philosophy on Democritus and Epicurus calling a gladiator mob leader the most capital fellow of antiquity, and ignoring that the actual proletariat filled the lines of the legions who fought against Spartacus. And a prominent Republican president praising bandit rioting and the stealing of private property at the expense of the original Republicans as an exemplary act of freedom.

Most importantly, both sides overlook the fact that the Spartacus uprising did not promote any new political or social concept but instead behaved like any other barbarian invasion in history, destroying and plundering at the expense of the people of the Italian peninsula. They also disregarded that Roman society, which suffered from the rebels' actions before it suppressed them, possessed one of the most developed and sophisticated political and social organisations of the ancient world. Moreover, it was precisely ancient Greek and Roman political concepts and practices that initiated or inspired most of the institutional and moral principles that modern ideologies invoke as proof of their alleged humanistic and progressive character. More scholarly approaches to the issue, free from the preconceived views of modern regimes and ideologies, are therefore necessary.

In the following pages, I examine the Servile Wars and the Spartacus uprising not as separate events, but as integral parts of a broader era of transformation. Unlike what often happens, the right way to understand them is as constituents of an intense and troubled period during which the Roman state evolved to address the new conditions created as a result of its spectacular expansion. From the mid-fourth century BCE to the mid-second,

Rome evolved from a city fighting to dominate Latium[3] to the hegemon of the entire Mediterranean, while its political institutions remained essentially the same. There is no emergence from such enormous increase in size and extent, as well as matters to address, without the need for profound reform in the political structure of an international actor, as modern political science can assure.

This is why I have not exclusively covered the slave wars, but have tried to present them within the context of that transformation of the Roman state. Even historians, alongside novelists and filmmakers, who try to talk about Spartacus or the slave wars in general and neglect or ignore this crucial point are doomed to present simplistic and biased views of these events, even if that wasn't their intention.

The Servile Wars were not episodes within an eternal struggle between freedom and oppression, or between social classes. They were one of the symptoms of an evolving political and social entity. It is evident that no events of a similar magnitude occurred for centuries before or after in ancient history. All this will become clear in the following chapters, as we unfold the history of those crucial developments.

Chapter 1

The First Servile War and Its Era

The famous revolt of Spartacus was not an isolated event but the last and probably smallest of three major slave uprisings that took place during the period of crisis and decline of the Roman Republic. These revolts assumed the dimensions of actual wars and are therefore known as the First, Second and Third Servile (or Slave) Wars. In the following pages, I will examine the First Servile War (135–132 BCE) in the historical context in which it happened, beginning with slave revolts that preceded it, and the initial conflicts inside the Roman Republic around the central figure of Tiberius Gracchus. Then follows an extended presentation of the First Servile War in Sicily.

Slave Revolts Before the Great Servile Wars

The First Servile War was not the first slave revolt of the Roman era. As often happens, conventional terms might not be perfectly accurate on closer examination. Before the First Slave War there had been a few slave revolts worth noting. Those revolts do not share the same underlying causes with the later major slave wars, but they do share some characteristics, eespecially the most basic: all of them relate to the great and triumphant expansion of the Roman Republic. Indeed, an earlier slave rising erupted a few years after the crucial victory against Hannibal at Zama in 202 BCE. The other subversive story of the early second century BCE, which we'll see in the following pages, is again connected to a crucial event of the Roman rise, during largely the same period – the annexation of the Italian and Sicilian Greeks to the Roman Federation.

After the end of the Second Punic War, with the Roman victory over Hannibal at Zama, the Romans held noble Carthaginians as hostages. It was common at this time, after a victory in battle, to keep the nobles of the enemy as hostages, treat them well and demand ransoms from their households, and sell the common soldiers who were prisoners and did not have wealthy families to pay for them in the slave market. In another function, keeping the upper-class members of the enemy as hostages was guaranteed to make them think twice before turning against you again. Polybius, one of our primary sources of ancient history, would be such a hostage from the Achaean League a few decades later, around the middle of the second century BCE.

Back in 198 BCE, the Carthaginian hostages, all of whom were sons of important and wealthy families in Carthage, had their own slaves with them. Moreover, as Titus Livy informs us, the inhabitants of the town of Setia, near Rome, bought large numbers of the common soldiers who were prisoners of war to have as their slaves. The sudden growth in the number of slaves drawn from soldier prisoners, who had once been free and were warriors, resulted in many of them conspiring to revolt. They also incited the slaves living in the countryside of Setia, as well as those in the towns of Norba and Cerceii, to join them. Then, they launched a surprise attack on the day when some spectacles and games were scheduled to take place in Setia. The unexpected, sudden revolt was successful as the rebel prisoners and slaves killed several people and managed to capture Setia. However, they failed to take over Norba and Cerceii.

The praetor Lucius Cornelius Lentulus learned about the bloody uprising in Setia during the night, when two slaves, along with a freedman from the town, came to Rome asking to see him. They gave Lentulus details of the revolt and the insurgents' subsequent plans. The praetor immediately summoned the Senate, presumably early in the morning, and told the senators about what had happened and what he had learned during the night. The Senate ordered an investigation into the conspiracy, and its suppression, and Lentulus departed for Setia, accompanied by a force of 2,000 men and five legates.

It was the insurgents' turn to be surprised, as they had not expected such a swift mobilisation from Rome. Lentulus' men arrested the leaders of the revolt and hunted down the slaves, who, upon noticing the Romans' arrival, had fled to the countryside surrounding the town. The operation was almost a complete success; however, some of the slaves managed to escape, and a little bit later, they tried to occupy another town in the area, Praeneste (modern-day Palestrina). The Roman response was again immediate, as the praetor Lentulus arrested and executed around 500 men who had participated in the conspiracy.

Yet, the attempted revolt alarmed the Roman authorities, who worried that the Carthaginian hostages and their slaves could have participated in these plots and attempts. Thus, they became much more attentive and strict in patrolling and guarding them. The noble hostages would no longer be free to go around in public as they wished and would have to stay under surveillance in private estates, while Carthaginian prisoners of war would be bound with leg irons. The leg irons would weigh at least 10 pounds, which was also the specification for those used in state prisons.[1]

Moreover, the Senate rewarded the two slaves who informed the praetor about the bloody insurgence in Setia with 25,000 asses each, and the freedman received 100,000 asses. Livy mentions the freedman who provided information only when he mentions the rewards, although he doesn't mention him alongside the slaves when they were telling Lentulus what had happened in Setia. Moreover, he doesn't explain why the freedman was paid so much more than the two slaves were, even though they appear in the text as the main informers.

However, Livy does inform us that another dangerous conspiracy of slaves happened in Etruria two years later, in 196 BCE. The praetor Manius Acilius Glabrio quickly entered the region with one legion to crush the revolt. Some of the slaves were apparently arrested, but many others had indeed arrived in time to form armed groups, and the Roman army had to fight a battle to eliminate them. The Romans killed many of the insurgent slaves and took as their prisoners those who survived. Glabrio ordered that the leaders of the conspiracy should be whipped and then crucified, but he spared the rest of the prisoners, sending them back to their masters.[2]

The Bacchanalia Conspiracy

During the same years, there was a much more famous occurrence of subversion and lawlessness, which perhaps does not qualify as a revolt or a slave revolt *stricto sensu*, but it still put the Roman state and order to the test, and probably included slaves and outsiders. This was the Bacchanalia conspiracy. A murky and mysterious movement that could inspire sensual, dark novels and film noir, it introduced into Etruria and Latium a Dionysian cult of orgiastic celebrations and rites, evidently derived from the Greek regions of southern Italy, which took bizarre form and spread rapidly. Based on Greek festivals honouring the god Dionysus, also called Bacchus, it seems that the Bacchanalia evolved into something even more orgiastic and raving in central Italy, causing great alarm amid Roman society.

Livy mentions in his account of the Bacchanalian conspiracy that everything began with a low-class Greek who had come to Etruria. He explains that this Greek man did not possess any of the qualities that the 'most learned of all peoples bring for the education of our minds and bodies', but instead was one of those 'little sacrificers' and fortune tellers. The Roman historian adds that the mysterious low-class Greek, unworthy of his origin, was not even the type of religious leader who fills people's minds with false beliefs, preaching openly in daylight hours. On the contrary, he established and conducted secret rituals during the night. As time passed, more people were initiated into these nocturnal rites, and sensual pleasures were added in order to make the cult even more compelling. Under the intoxication of food, wine and darkness, males and females, younger and older, had their desires inflamed and shame extinguished, says Livy, and 'every kind of lewd behaviour began to be practised'.

However, libertine sex was not the main problem with the cult. Livy mentions murders and poisonings committed by members of the sect, organised in such a way that it was impossible to identify the murderers or even the dead bodies. They left false and misleading evidence, confused the law enforcement and judges with lying witnesses and fake signatures, which aimed to draw money illegally through scam testaments and wills. The murders were accompanied by orgies to the sound of drums and cymbals and the raving behaviour of the cultists. Livy says that the rising cult and its practices began in Etruria and spread until it reached Rome itself. Then, the consul Spurius Postumius received evidence of what was happening. Eventually, the Senate and the public assembly (Comitia Centuriata) discussed the matter, and the authorities started to dismantle the Bacchanalian cult in Rome and the rest of Italy. According to the prevalent opinion, it was believed that around 7,000 people had joined the cult. Livy describes how many were arrested and some committed suicide, both men and women.[3]

In 185 BCE, there was one more slave revolt, this time in Apulia (modern-day Puglia). About 7,000 slaves, including a number of herdsmen, plundered the roads and common fields of the area, attacking and robbing travellers. The praetor Lucius Postumius, who governed the province of Tarentum (the Latin name for the city that Greek colonists called Taras), intervened and suppressed the bandits' activities, punishing many of them.[4] In the following year, the praetor relentlessly confronted and repressed the criminal activities of the herdsmen, and also pursued the remaining cases of conspirators related to the Bacchanalia and arrested them.[5]

Tiberius Gracchus

The series of victories and the expansion of the limits of the Roman Republic's sovereignty continued in the second century BCE, with the final subjugation of Macedonia (171–168 BCE) and the destruction of Carthage at the end of the third Punic War (149–146 BCE), as well as that of Corinth (146 BCE) during the annexation of the Achaean League to the Roman hegemony. At the same time, Rome's wars against the Celtic tribes for the control of Spain were raging in various phases, with the last one breaking out in 143 BCE.

In 137 BCE, the 26-year-old Tiberius Sempronius Gracchus was sent to Spain, having been elected quaestor, to serve under the command of the governor, Gaius Hostilius Mancinus.[6] Tiberius belonged to the upper Roman aristocracy and was an example of an aristocrat of both plebeian and patrician descent. He was a member of the *nobilitas*, which had been created after the patricians accepted the plebeian elite into the Senate and the highest state offices as early as the fourth century BCE. His father was descended from a plebeian family and had enjoyed a brilliant political career, even serving twice as consul, while his mother was descended from one of the oldest and most intimate families of patricians, the Cornelii Scipiones.[7]

This mission was to have a profound effect on Tiberius Gracchus and his political stance in the years to come. In 135 BCE, Publius Cornelius Scipio Aemilianus, the triumphant victor of the Third Punic War and the destroyer of Carthage, who was a cousin of Tiberius Gracchus, was elected consul.[8] The difficulties that Scipio encountered in trying to recruit new soldiers for the war in Spain, as well as the situation he faced there, made Tiberius understand that a major problem had arisen in the functioning of the Roman army.[9]

The problem was the significant reduction in the availability of men to take up the Roman arms. This was a result of the decrease in the number of free peasants that had occurred in the previous decades, as only citizens owning private property were allowed to be called up to the legions. Landless people, the so-called proletarians, could not be called up to serve in the Roman army (*proletarii* were those who possessed only *prole*, i.e. descendants, but no property). From the expansion during the third century BCE, and especially during and after the second great war against Carthage, two interrelated reverse processes had begun. On the one hand, the amount of land at the disposal of the Roman state was increasing, and on the other, the number of free small farmers was constantly decreasing.[10]

This trend emerged through specific socio-economic processes that evolved even further during the territorial expansion of the second century BCE. Some of the new lands incorporated into Roman territory as Rome expanded its sovereignty, especially those seized by the state as punishment against cities in Italy that had sided with Hannibal, were considered public (*ager publicus*) and were rented to private individuals for cultivation. However, although legally, the ownership of the estates remained public, in practice, the private individuals who farmed them, who were often already large landowners, did not pay the rental fee that they formally owed to the state and treated them as their own property, while also transferring their 'ownership' to their descendants.[11]

This tolerance of large landowners was complemented and compensated for by the fact that the authorities also tacitly allowed the illegal encroachment of public land by small farmers, who in this way supplemented their incomes and managed to survive.

However, the latter condition was to be reversed precisely because of the development of extensive land ownership. The renting and exploitation of ever-larger portions of public land by the large landowners interrupted the illegal exploitation of the land by small farmers. At the same time, the new rich who emerged from the political and economic expansion of Roman power, who, as a rule, were merchants, bankers, tax collectors, artisans producing equipment for the army, and moneylenders, invested their profits massively in the acquisition of land. That was natural in an economy largely dominated by agriculture, with a more minor role for other productive sectors, and also because owning land was a key element of aristocratic prestige.

As a result, a massive demand for land was created, which was not only met by public land but also by private transactions. Many small farmers voluntarily sold their fields and, with the profits, attempted to turn to commercial activities or urban occupations, as they preferred city life to rural life, while many others were effectively forced to abandon their estates since they faced insurmountable difficulties in trying to survive as farmers next to the huge farms that had been created.[12]

Small agricultural production could not compete with large landownership, not only because the latter was able to increase its productivity more easily but also because the large workforce employed by the rich landowners put a particular burden on the estates of the poorest, which were consequently undermanned. The destruction of the Italian countryside by Hannibal's invasion was also an important factor in these developments.[13] The damage caused by Hannibal to the technical infrastructure of many agricultural production units was often so severe that their owners were unable to cover the cost of restoration.

Therefore, for a variety of reasons, during the second century BCE there was a strong tendency for many agricultural production units to be transferred to large landowners. At the same time, many small farmers fled to the cities, including Rome itself, seeking work in the artisanal sector of the economy. And while the number of autonomous small farmers was steadily decreasing, the availability of slaves was growing by leaps and bounds as the numbers of prisoners of war were immense, which in addition lowered the prices of slaves in general.[14]

Consequently, the big landowners at that time in Italy met the increased need for labour on their farms by using ever-larger numbers of available slaves – a very convenient source as they could not be called to arms or seek work elsewhere. The result was that by the middle of the second century BCE, small-scale autonomous agricultural production in Italy had been mainly replaced by mass slave labour on oversized farms, which Tiberius Gracchus observed in a speech.[15]

This process continued until it became clear that things had been brought to a standstill. In the mid-130s BCE, two critical issues arose in parallel: the lack of sufficient men for the legions fighting in Spain, as already mentioned, and the outbreak of a major slave revolt in Sicily.

The Attempted Reform and the First Civil Conflict

Tiberius Gracchus had, during his service in Spain, seen at first hand the difficulties that had arisen in the Roman army. On the same trip, he had the opportunity to observe the state of agricultural production in the Italian countryside. Much of the latter was now carried on in extensive latifundia, in which numerous slaves were employed, while the countryside had been cleared of free peasants.[16]

Returning to Rome, Gracchus had a clear view of the steps that needed to be taken to stimulate the prosperity of small rural property, and thus restore Roman military power. Having the support of a section of the aristocracy who had come to the same conclusions and believed that immediate reforms were needed regarding agricultural policy, he chose to run for the office of tribune of the plebeians,[17] capitalising on the plebeian side of his ancestry. There were ten tribunes who presided over the plebeian council. In addition to proposing laws for enactment, they also had the power to veto laws proposed to the assembley by their fellow tribunes as well as those proposed by the Senate.[18]

Gracchus' candidacy was voted for, as his intentions had become known and had made him very popular with the small farmers.[19] His plan primarily provided for the reactivation of an earlier law that had fallen into disuse, which stipulated that no private individual could receive for usufruct more than 500 *iugera* (approximately 311 acres) of public land. According to Gracchus' proposal, in cases of estates exceeding this limit, the extra land was to be taken from the tenant's disposal and distributed to a number of poor Roman citizens. To compensate the large landowners, the proposal provided that the 500 *iugera* remaining in their possession would cease to be public land and become their private property, as well as that an additional

250 *iugera* (156 acres) would be allocated to each of the first two potential sons of the family. Thus, the maximum area of public land that could remain in the hands of a landowning family would be 1,000 *iugera* (623 acres).[20]

The latest predictions failed to appease the opposition of the majority of the aristocrats, which was sharp. On the other hand, Gracchus had the support of the consul Publius Mucius Scaevola and his brother, Publius Licinius Crassus Dives Mucianus, who was at that time the *pontifex maximus* and probably the richest Roman. Some senators also supported Gracchus, but the majority of the Senate strongly opposed him.[21] In the face of such opposition, Gracchus decided to put the proposed law directly to a vote in the plebeian council without first presenting it to the Senate, as was usual political practice. In Rome, there was no written constitution, but a set of principles and customary practices had been established over time, according to which the political process was conducted. While a politician's violation of these principles did not constitute an offence in the formal sense, it was, in fact, an indication that he did not fully respect the existing framework of legitimacy and was therefore inclined to oppose the constitution.

Nevertheless, Gracchus, trusting in the support of the landless and small farmers, submitted the bill directly to the plebeian council in the spring of 133 BCE. The unprecedented response of the poor citizens seemed to vindicate his choice, as large masses of people flocked from the countryside and the outskirts of Rome to participate in the vote and advocate in favour of the proposal. However, Gracchus had not counted on meeting the opposition of one of the tribunes of the assembly, Marcus Octavius, whom the reform-negative wing of the Senate had approached since he was a landowner who possessed large tracts of public land. The result was that Octavius vetoed Gracchus' proposal, as was his right.[22] Determined not to yield, Gracchus denounced Octavius' action as contrary to the interests of the people, which he was bound to serve. He proposed that the assembly vote to remove Octavius, which they did.[23] The law was then passed and put into effect.

This is a complex political and legal case, as it is true that the tribune Octavius acted contrary to the universal will of the assembly he was supposed to represent. However, on the other hand, the veto was a fundamental power of his office, akin to that of the consuls, and served as the supreme guarantee against any arbitrary and authoritarian actions. In combination with the previous bypassing of the Senate, Gracchus' action constituted an unprecedented breach of the institutional framework.

The anxiety of the aristocracy and the hostility towards Gracchus intensified even more when, sometime later, in Asia Minor, the king of Pergamon, Attalus III, died. Pergamon had been a loyal ally of Rome for many decades, and in his will, the dead ruler had named the Roman Senate as his successor in power, believing that this was best for the future of his kingdom. Gracchus then proposed that the plebeian council vote that at least part of the lands coming under the jurisdiction of Rome in Asia Minor should be given to poor citizens, again ostentatiously bypassing the Senate, which generally had the first say in matters of foreign policy.[24]

The tolerance of the aristocrats was finally pushed to its limits when, in the early summer of 133 BCE, Gracchus stood for election to remain tribune in the following year[25] in order to promote the implementation of the agrarian law and maintain the immunity of the higher offices. However, this was again in stark contrast to the institutional framework of Roman politics up to that time, which did not authorise a person to remain in the same office for two consecutive years. Thus, on the day of the elections, many senators denounced Gracchus for staging a coup d'état. Then, despite the opposition of the consul Mucius Scaevola, armed with their sticks and accompanied by their followers and supporters, they moved against Gracchus and his own supporters in the assembly area. A scuffle ensued, in which Tiberius Gracchus and some of his followers lost their lives.[26] It was the first bloody clash in the history of the Roman Republic,[27] and the beginning of a period of conflict that would lead to large-scale civil wars.

Sicily in Flames: The Causes of the First Servile War

While Tiberius Gracchus was about to rise to political prominence, the First Servile War broke out in 136 or 135 BCE in Sicily. This slave war was the earliest indication of systemic social crisis in the Roman Republic's dominions. Being the first doesn't mean it was a mild introduction to future conflicts, though. On the contrary, it was an extremely violent, large-scale event, perhaps even more so than those that followed.

Having long been one of the granaries of the Mediterranean, and especially of Rome, Sicily experienced intense forms of exploitation that grew under the veneer of Roman rule. The big Mediterranean island was annexed by the Romans following the First Punic War in 241 BCE and the conquest of Syracuse in 212 BCE. Eight decades later, much of its countryside had become primarily a vast latifundium economy, dominated by usually absentee Roman landlords and worked by many thousands of slaves imported from conquered regions or purchased in the various slave markets.

There is no doubt that these developments created a social environment of intense stratification, which, in collaboration with the legal and institutional limitations of Rome's early phases of imperial domination of the Mediterranean, produced an explosive mix. Studying it helps us better understand the imbalances and limitations that future political reforms would address, often after more tension and conflicts had arisen. Our primary narrative source, as in several other cases, is Diodorus Siculus, who provides a detailed account of the First Servile War, albeit sometimes confusing in its structure, as there are essentially two versions of the story. Other ancient sources include Appian of Alexandria, Paulus Orosius and Lucius Annaeus Florus, while Livy's account, now lost, is known only through the Periochae (summaries), and brief references to it survive in the works of the aforementioned historians.

After centuries of Greek predominance, contested by Carthaginian attempts to seize control,[28] and home to earlier local tribes, Sicily by the second century BCE was organised as a Roman province. It was certainly Rome's first and most important overseas possession, and it remained one of the wealthiest regions in the ancient world. As for its fertile interior, it was now the primary supplier of grain to Rome.

In this way, the Sicilian countryside was transformed into pretty much a patchwork of large agricultural estates, known as latifundia. These estates often belonged to Roman senators or knights and were managed by overseers, with the majority of labour being performed by imported slaves. Sicilian and Italian Greeks, as well as other Italians, also had their fair share of agricultural estates and slaves. At the same time, the latter predominantly came from the Hellenic and Hellenistic East to Sicily. As we'll see, almost all the names of the protagonists, both slave owners and rebellious slaves, were Greek, except the Roman officers.

Diodorus, a Sicilian Greek himself, emphasises that the number of slaves in Sicily had grown enormously during that initial period of Roman rule, and that many slaves worked under brutal conditions,[29] revealing the scale and tension within that socio-economic structure. This was the initial period of significant growth and enrichment for many people under Roman rule, characterised by a widespread accumulation of wealth in which not only landowners but also state officials participated. Roman, Greek and other Sicilian and Italian landowners had amassed large numbers of slaves, who worked in the fields under very harsh conditions at excessive rates and were often subjected to brutal behaviour by their masters. Florus confirms this broader picture, noting that Sicily was very fertile and a leading producer of cereal crops, so it was divided into vast agricultural estates owned by Roman citizens.[30] There was an extended amassing of slaves, who sometimes were in chains, and others were enclosed in slave barracks.

The enslaved population would seem diverse in origin to a modern reader, comprising Syrians, Cilicians, Phrygians, Thracians and others, who were imported in massive numbers through the expanding slave trade that followed Rome's conquests. In reality, at the time, the apparent diversity indicated a quite homogeneous, albeit multifaceted, world created in the previous centuries: the Hellenistic East. This fact is crucial for understanding the First and Second Servile Wars better, as well as their differences from the Third, led by Spartacus, as we will see. It helps explain the relative cultural cohesion of the first two great revolts, including their shared language world, religious symbolism and tendency to reproduce Hellenistic forms of leadership and legitimacy.

The slave owners frequently used violence with impunity, which created outrage and pushed many slaves towards a violent reaction. Moreover, many of them were not born into slavery but had been captured in war or through piracy during their lives, meaning they retained cultural memories of freedom or even of wealth and power of their own.

The combination of huge slave numbers, unrestricted exploitation and brutality, lack of solid institutions, and ingrained heritage brought increasing rural disorder in the Sicilian countryside. Armed slave bands were formed, and they began to commit robberies and even murders.[31] Diodorus gives a systematic explanation of the causes of the First Servile War, stating that it occurred for the following reasons. After the fall of Carthage, Sicily experienced a period of peace that allowed it to grow even more prosperous, which in turn enabled the Sicilians to acquire a large number of slaves. The slaves were brought in droves and were treated cruelly. For instance, they were branded with marks burned on their bodies, as they came from many different places, like herds of cattle.[32] The younger ones were used as shepherds, and the older ones for 'such services as they had occasion'. Diodorus adds that not only was the behaviour of the slaves' masters severe and strict, but sometimes they did not even provide enough food or clothes for the slaves' survival. So, Diodorus says, the slaves were forced by their living conditions to begin robbing and stealing. That was how murders and robberies came to be committed daily all around Sicily, as if, in Diodorus' words, an army of murderers and thieves had filled the island.[33]

The lack of solid institutions and mechanisms of control emerges not only from the unchecked exploitation of the slaves to the point of social disruption, but also from the absence of quick and efficient Roman intervention after the disorders began, leading to the outbreak of the main rebellion. Indeed, Roman magistrates in Sicily, either unwilling or unable to intervene, allowed slave owners to establish their own armed squads for protection, formed from labourers. This contributed to intensifying the climate of impunity and latent violence, since the distinction between the agricultural workforce and private militias was blurred.

The surprising element in Diodorus' account is that all those criminal behaviours and activities didn't elicit opposition from the large slave owners. Diodorus reports that the Roman authorities actually did whatever they could to address the issue of violence committed by slaves throughout Sicily. However, this did not include actual suppression by force and punishment. They tried to prevent crimes from being committed, rather than punishing criminals after they had committed them. How did this come about? The wealthy and powerful slave owners were often Roman knights who, by then, had the authority to judge the cases of governors accused of misconduct in the provinces. The governors seem to have wanted to avoid friction with the knights[34] and perhaps with the wealthy and influential slave owners in general, regardless of whether they were Romans, and had direct involvement in politics and the legal system, or they could have had indirect influence through their fellow owners of many slaves who were Roman officials. Yet, the most striking fact that emerges from Diodorus' statement is that the wealthy and powerful slave owners were perfectly fine with their slaves committing crimes against other free people of Sicily, including robbing them and killing them. There emerged a scheme, according to which, many wealthy land and slave owners ultimately exploited the free local population instead of just exploiting their slaves, as the latter were protected by their masters against the authorities and the law – the same masters who wouldn't give them the necessary means to survive. Prominent slave masters encouraged their slaves to abuse the rural Sicilian population, essentially rolling over to the free population the effects of their own conduct towards their slaves. Obviously, the slaves were not particularly happy with this arrangement, since the abuses at their expense continued, and they were 'vilely beaten and scourged beyond all reason'. Hence, they began to meet up when they could and discuss how to get themselves out of this situation.[35]

Sicily was an unstable province, on the verge of social explosion. All that was needed was leadership and opportunity. It seems the event that sparked the riots was the conduct of a couple of Sicilian Greek slave owners. Diodorus mentions Damophilus and his wife Megallis as examples of administering excessive cruelty at the expense of their household slaves.[36] Wealthy and arrogant, they reportedly treated them with sadism and disdain. One day, the slaves' hatred and animosity for their masters erupted, and after an aggression, they arrested them and kept them hostage.

However, that was just the beginning. The revolt against Damophilus and Megallis did not quell their household slaves' fury and settle the situation. Instead, it functioned as a signal for similar acts of defiance that ignited the tense atmosphere and clashes around the Sicilian countryside into a massive slave insurrection. These elements would converge in the city of Enna, and the discussions about shared grievances would bear fruit through an enigmatic magician called Eunus.[37]

The Uprising

Damophilus of Enna was very wealthy and also haughty and arrogant. His attitude towards his slaves went beyond severity and was particularly cruel. His wife Megallis matched and even exceeded his cruelty, subjecting their slaves to inhuman and sadistic treatment. After being treated like this for a long time, the couple's slaves were furious like 'wild beasts', says Diodorus, and they desired to kill their masters. Posidonius condemns Damophilus for the eruption of the first Sicilian slave war, talking about his extravagant lifestyle, and calling him a 'slave of luxury and evildoing'. In accusing him, Posidonius gives us, though, a brilliant image of ancient Greek and Roman luxury lifestyle, saying that Damophilus went out in the Sicilian countryside in four-wheeled carriages drawn by magnificent horses and with him there were handsome young slaves and a 'coterie of boys in livery'.[38]

At a certain point, the outraged slaves approached Eunus, who had made a name as a fortune teller, and asked him whether the gods would be favourable to them if they moved violently against their suppressive masters. Eunus, recognising the opportunity to gain more leverage over the local slave community and affairs, promptly responded with an enigmatic and suggestive approach, encouraging them to proceed with their plans, ensuring they would execute them quickly and efficiently.

Eunus was a slave from Hellenistic Syria and his native city was Apamea, which had been founded in 300 BCE by Seleucus I 'Nikator' (winner), one of Alexander the Great's generals and then founder of the Seleucid Empire. Apamea was an important city, as it was a major military centre of the Seleucids. Additionally, it was the native city of the Stoic philosopher Posidonius, who several consider to be the greatest polymath among Greek philosophers, alongside Aristotle. Coincidentally, Posidonius was born in 135 BCE, precisely when his compatriot Eunus was beginning to lead the big servile rebellion in Roman-dominated Sicily.

Eunus' master was a wealthy man from Enna called Antigenes, who indirectly promoted Eunus to receive his high-status position among slaves, which allowed him to emerge as a leader. Indeed, Eunus became the leader of the first big slave rebellion after being already famous in the surrounding areas as a magician and a prophet. He breathed fire and chanted exciting and promising oracles, allegedly channelling the Syrian goddess Atargatis, promising liberation and divine favour.[39] Eunus claimed that he was able to predict the future due to the gods appearing to him and revealing events that were going to happen. Diodorus immediately makes clear that he considered the whole thing a fraud, mentioning that Eunus 'deceived many people' with those claims and practices of supposed foreseeing the future. As he made an impression and a name for himself as a fortune teller, Eunus went even further, claiming that now the gods appeared to him not only during sleep but also while he was awake, giving him even more direct information about future events.[40] Rationalist Diodorus comments that some of Eunus' predictions were coincidentally confirmed and celebrated as proof of his divine inspiration and prophetic ability, whereas many other predictions failed but were ignored.[41] Of course, this is a mechanism we are familiar with from our own time as well, where not only fortune tellers and astrologers but also analysts of politics, wars, finance and sports, plus many more amateur commentators, keep reminding people of the few times they got it right, while neglecting the numerous times they got it wrong. Statistically, a percentage of predictions will come to pass even though there is often no real knowledge or understanding behind them, and even less future foreseeing ability.

However, one should give credit to Eunus as he used to put on a real show. He made excellent use of his abilities as a magician, breathing flames out of his mouth as from a 'burning lamp', and then giving his prophesies, claiming that he was inspired by Apollo. We can imagine the wonder created by a talented magician and actor throwing flames out of his mouth as he invoked the god of light and recited oracles with bombastic and theatrical verse and tone. As Diodorus explains, to create fire, Eunus put combustible matter into a nutshell or something similar, which had little holes on both sides. In this way, he fed the fire and put the nutshell in his mouth, making it spark flames from both sides with his strong breath. That kind of impressive show enabled Eunus to become more convincing to the populace with his claims of divine inspiration, and openly declare his ambitions of becoming king, as a Syrian goddess revealed to him that it was his destiny, even before the initial slave revolt.

Florus confirms the theatrical and religious dimension to Eunus' behaviour, writing that he tossed about his hair like a mad prophet and claimed to speak under divine inspiration from the Syrian goddess. He pretended that a divinity prompted him, inciting the slaves to armed revolt to gain their freedom. Florus also confirms that Eunus put in his mouth a nutshell with holes, filled with sulfur and embers. So, when he exhaled, flames came out of his mouth as he spoke.[42]

However, it seems that not many took Eunus seriously, and instead, those claims made him a laughing stock.[43] This was especially so with his master, Antigenes, who was so entertained by the 'jest and the ridiculous conceit of the man', as Diodorus puts it, that he began to take Eunus with him to dinners and feasts, presenting him as a charlatan so that the other wealthy guests could have a good laugh and be entertained during the event. A usual way to entertain themselves was by asking questions of the clown oracle destined to be king about his future kingdom, and in particular, how he was going to treat those present at the dinners. Eunus responded that he would be kind and magnanimous as a king, and used weird expressions with magical and monstrous nuances, making them laugh and have fun. In this way, he earned their favour and received generous portions of food, instructing him to remember them when he became king. Of course, the great irony is that a short time afterwards, Eunus found himself in a real position of power, and reportedly, he was indeed kind to those who had treated him well during those feasts and dinners.[44]

It's thus clear that the rebellion of the slaves that erupted in 135 BCE in Sicily was led by a religious leader, rather than what we would call a social revolutionary. This should not be taken for granted, given the historical era, which would have still been inclined towards myths rather than rationalism. A similar interpretation would be erroneous because there had already been movements and revolutions with predominantly political and social characteristics rather than mystical ones centuries before that point, including those in Athens and Rome. Eunus was instead a conscious bearer of Eastern religiosity and Hellenistic charisma.

In Diodorus' account, it becomes immediately evident that the Damophilus and Megallis case was only the sparking point of much larger and broader developments. As he writes, after the slaves consulted with Eunus, they raised a force of 400 from amongst them, ready to attack, appointing the same Eunus as their leader. Then, they stormed the city of Enna. Diodorus provides an image that would make an amazing film scene, writing that Eunus used his signature trick as a magician, entering Enna breathing flames of fire out of his mouth.

However, the next scenes are anything but amazing, and instead, they would be too much even for the most brutal horror movies. The insurgent slaves entered the houses and committed a horrible slaughter, killing even suckling infants, tearing them from their mothers' breasts and dashing them against the ground. Mass rapes were also committed by the rebels, and it cannot be expressed, says Diodorus, how vilely and filthily those people behaved in satisfying their lusts using wives in front of their husbands. That sequence of crimes during the monstrous savage attack felt appealing to many more slaves of the city, who joined the rabble of the insurgents, murdered their masters with fury, and then began killing anybody else.[45]

The only admirable thing in these passages is Diodorus' integrity and directness as a historian. Even though earlier he had justified the slaves' revolt as caused by the masters' oppressive and cruel behaviour, and he would do it again in later parts of his writings, he does not embellish or neglect the insurgents' monstrous brutality and inhumanity. That's a great example of intellectual honesty and detachment, so crucial for a scholarly historical approach, as opposed to the political and ideological biased propaganda passed off as journalism or even history, in several cases.

During the Enna massacre, Eunus came to know that Damophilus and Megallis were not inside the city but in a nearby orchard. So, he ordered some of his men to find them, and they arrested them and brought them back to Enna. The rebel slaves tied their hands behind their backs, and the mob taunted them as they passed along. The rebellious slaves guided them into the city's theatre, claiming that they had the intention of putting them to a popular trial. All the insurgent slaves were assembled to attend, and the rebels initially pretended they gave Damophilus the right to defend himself in front of the crowd. The wealthy slave owner spoke, and apparently things did not go as planned, since, as Diodorus reports, Damophilus pleaded fervently for his life, and the things he said moved many of the people attending the trial in the theatre. Then, two of the rebels, Hermeias and Zeuxis, responded, denouncing him with bitter charges for his behaviour, accusing him of being a fraud and a hypocrite. After that, dispensing with the facade, they rushed on Damophilus and attacked him with no less than a sword and an axe, passing the former through him and cutting his head off with the other, before the crowd could render a verdict.[46]

As for Megallis, she was given to the women slaves to do with her as they wanted. Their revenge was terrible and more cruel than Damophilus' execution, as they whipped her and tormented her, and then gave her the final blow, throwing her off a sheer cliff.[47]

Another fact from the initial uprising, reported by Diodorus and worth mentioning, is that the rebellious slaves did not kill, ill-treat or abuse Damophilus and Megallis' daughter. Instead, they were eager to defend her honour and chastity, and they brought her alive and well to her relatives who lived in Catana. That was because she had always been kind and helpful to the household's slaves, showing pity and compassion, and even taking care of their wounds after her parents' sadistic abuses. That suggests a capacity for an advanced moral and political sense. Diodorus, at this point, comments that this fact shows that the savage behaviour of the slaves did not arise from them having an innate cruel nature, but from a dark hate and desire to get revenge for the sufferings they had experienced due to their masters' behaviour.[48]

Could the event that happened at Enna's theatre cast doubt about the accepted version of the story and what had really happened? The fact that the armed insurgents appeared to be uncertain of their own followers' decision may suggests that the charges against Damophilus and Megallis were not perfectly accurate. Perhaps the entire story of the couple's brutality and sadism was an exaggeration or a fabricated propagandistic lie of the rebellion, to justify their own later atrocities? The fact that the rebels reportedly were kind to the couple's daughter could indicate a strange contradiction, since although not impossible, it's also not so easy to see how such a loving person was the daughter of two sadistic monsters as the ones described. Similar doubts could be heightened by the fact that Eunus killed both his master Antigenes and his former master Python, with his own hands,[49] despite the high society events he frequented thanks to them and the fame he gained as a fortune teller and showman through his performances there. Moreover, Posidonius mentions that Damophilus and his whole family met their fate in a suitably humiliating way, killed by their own slaves.[50] This version contradicts the story relating that the slaves didn't harm Damophilus' daughter, and could indicate that it was manufactured to portray a more humane image of the insurgents. We do not have a way to verify the issue, and we must trust the fact that other primary sources available on the matter agree on the basic judgement about the slave-owning couple. It's also certain that the slaves in Sicily in general were not that happy with their masters' attitude and routines, as the revolt grew more extensive in the following period.

Birth of a 'Slave Kingdom'

In what was clearly a staged performance of vengeance, Eunus and his men executed Damophilus and Megallis before a public gathering, delivering theatrical justice. The fact that they didn't just kill them on the day of the uprising, but kept them hostage and opted for that popular trial, is a sign of political acumen and actions driven not solely by rage, but also by political calculation and propagandistic skill.

According to Diodorus' account, at this point, Eunus was proclaimed king by the insurgents, not because of his military skills and valour, but rather because of his magician tricks that brought him to the leading position of the revolt in the first place. Also, his name itself perhaps helped with that, as 'Eunus' in ancient Greek means something like 'bearer of favour', or the 'favourable'. [51] Eunus put a diadem on his head and made sure to acquire all the symbols related to royal status,[52] and named his wife, who was from Apamea as well, a queen.

His first actions as 'king' were to call for another gathering of the people and execute all the prisoners. He spared only those who knew how to produce weapons, and he effectively enslaved them and put them to work for the rebellion. It was then that he also gave Megallis to the female rabble for them to kill her as described above.[53]

The notion of people who knew how to make arms among the prisoners could again raise questions about who was taken prisoner, since it's unlikely that wealthy aristocrats were blacksmiths, especially in an era with so many slaves around.

Eunus' political acumen is evident by the fact that he quickly assumed the classic royal name of the Seleucid dynasty, 'Antiochus'. In this way, Eunus styled himself as a king, not just a rebel, and invoked the Seleucid monarchy, attempting to lend legitimacy and a clear historical and political reference to the rebellion. The vast majority of the slaves in Sicily originated from the Hellenistic East, whose great part had belonged to the Seleucid Empire.

Succeeding in seizing control of Enna gave the rebellious slaves a capital and an inaccessible fortified citadel, marking the passage from scattered riots to a coherent and coordinated insurrection. Strabo mentions that Enna was situated at a high altitude, and around it were mountains with arable and fertile plains below them.[54] Eunus' self-proclamation as King Antiochus and his charismatic leadership with the religious framework offered the rebellion a strong momentum, which Eunus and his collaborators knew how to capitalise on. So, the uprising rapidly began to spread across the interior of Sicily. The new rebel state, based in Enna, began expanding to central Sicily through systematic raids, with the goal of capturing several towns and agricultural estates, and it succeeded in doing so. Its success prompted more and more slaves to join it. Other groups on society's margin found the opportunity to expand their activities. Strabo mentions that in earlier times, the Romans had settled people who herded horses, sheep and cattle to empty highlands in Sicily. However, those men sometimes became bandits, and eventually, by the time Eunus and his slave rebellion had taken control of Enna, these groups had become widespread and well organised.[55] Moreover, Livy mentions that Eunus and his men liberated slaves by breaking open the barracks where they were held. In this way, Eunus-Antiochus soon commanded a force of 10,000 men, or, according to Livy, a force that had the number of men of a regular army.[56]

Eunus surrounded himself with a court composed of advisers and proceeded to issue coinage, which is again impressive as it becomes clear that he consciously emulated the Hellenistic rulers of the East, possessing a financial understanding as well as political, with people around him who could give advice on complex issues.

Shortly afterwards, a second major slave revolt broke out near the city of Akragas, under the leadership of another slave who originated from the Hellenistic East with a Greek name, Kleon from Cilicia. The emergence of another rebel leader was a crucial development at the time, and precious for the historical understanding of the nature of the revolt, as it further indicates that the causes of the rebellion were structural and not strictly local, such as the brutal behaviour of certain slave owners like Damophilus and Megallis.

Instead of a mystical and wonder-worker background, Kleon had a more martial one. Diodorus describes him as physically powerful and experienced in warfare.[57] Kleon initially led his own independent rebellion in the central part of southern Sicily, around the countryside north of Akragas, raising a force of 5,000 armed slaves. Perhaps the Roman authorities and wealthy inhabitants of Sicily hoped that those two slave forces, which seemed like groups of gangs, would clash with each other, trying to establish control over the largest territory possible, and end up slaughtering and destroying each other.[58] However, they were wrong. Kleon accepted a subordinate position to Eunus-Antiochus, recognising his kingdom and settling as a military chief, while Eunus would remain the king and religious leader. This merger consolidated the revolt as an emerging reality and brought greater military magnitude and coherence. Kleon was able to lead campaigns in various parts of Sicily, while Eunus retained political and religious leadership, which further solidified the rebel state's resemblance to a real kingdom, with a division of roles that included a king, a court, priests, generals and armies.

From that point, the rebellion gained still greater momentum, reaching its height, according to Diodorus Siculus, with 200,000 people, likely including women and children. Other ancient sources, though briefer, corroborate the scale and threat of the rebellion. Orosius notes that the slaves 'infested Sicily with fire and sword',[59] and gives the number of 70,000 armed men, while Florus calls it a war 'more serious than a foreign enemy',[60] and claims that Eunus initially managed to gather 2,000 men with his tricks, but later the insurgents broke open the slave barracks and the slave army reached more than 60,000 men.[61] According to Livy, Kleon alone had gathered around 70,000 slaves before the merge.[62]

The revolt continued with the occupation of large parts of Sicilian territory. The rebels proved adept at guerrilla tactics, striking isolated targets and retreating into the rugged terrain of the Sicilian interior. They captured weapons, food and fortified positions. However, the slaves' limited equipment and the strong fortifications kept the insurgent forces away from the larger cities of the island, such as Syracuse and Akragas. Moreover, the rebellion could not surpass its limitations as a rural-based slave movement. The slaves of the major urban centres did not join the rebellion, remaining loyal to their masters, and the people of the free population were even less willing to join it. Apparently, despite Eunus' adoption of Hellenistic royal imagery, the rural slave movement could not rise to the level of an ethnic anti-Roman revolution in Sicily.

Contest with Rome

Initially, the Romans were not particularly alarmed and they underestimated the potential of the uprising. Even when their small forces stationed in Sicily were annihilated by the rebellious slaves and the revolt spread, with the rebels entrenching themselves across central Sicily, the Roman response was not that massive. They dispatched praetors with limited resources to recruit troops from Roman citizens resident in Sicily, as well as local allies, to suppress the slave rebellion.

However, Rome finally began to understand that a more serious involvement was needed when one of those commanders, Lucius Hypsaeus, and his militia were defeated in open battle.[63] Then, other praetorian militia troops were defeated by the slave army, which proved to be stronger than expected. That unexpected outcome, where Roman forces, however small, lost battles to what back in Rome they perceived as a slave mob, revealed that those rebel forces had discipline and that the provincial Roman command was rather inadequate for the task.

At that point, the Romans began to understand that the rebellion in Sicily had the scale of a real war. In 134 BCE, the consul Gaius Fulvius Flaccus arrived in Sicily,[64] and after the end of his term, the new consul, Lucius Calpurnius Piso Frugi, continued the war in Sicily the following year. However, although larger, the consular armies were again inexperienced, as the best and most experienced Roman troops were still engaged in the prolonged and difficult Numantine War in Spain. The Sicilian servile war remained a secondary theatre of operations, and this strategic distraction likely helped the rebellion endure for longer than it might have otherwise.

Nevertheless, the rebels' conduct of the war was remarkable. The two consuls achieved a few successes, such as the capture of the town of Mamertium by the consul Piso, where, according to Orosius, the Romans killed 8,000 rebels and crucified those who survived the battle and were unable to escape.[65] Perhaps those successes limited the activity of the slave forces somewhat, but they did not quell the rebellion.

The Roman leadership was not happy to confront such serious problems and delays in a war against rebel slaves. Valerius Maximus mentions that the consul Lucius Calpurnius Piso, during the war in Sicily in 133 BCE, inflicted a humiliating punishment upon one of his officers, Gaius Titius. Titius commanded a cavalry unit and had given way because of being surrounded by slave forces, fleeing the battlefield after throwing their weapons. After that, somehow Titius and his men were back in the Roman army, but they didn't get a very warm welcome. Piso made Titius dress in a toga cut into pieces and covered with a tunic without a belt, and stay barefoot outside Piso's headquarters all day long. He also banned him from interacting with the other men in the army and even from using the camp's baths. Moreover, Piso punished the entire cavalry unit for their shameful flight from the battlefield after throwing their arms away by removing them from the cavalry and downgrading them to slingers. Valerius Maximus closes the passage with a rather strong paragraph, saying that although what had happened was very humiliating for the Romans, those guilty of that shame were punished with equal humiliation. They were 'soldiers of ours', he says, who allowed rebel slaves, worthy only to be crucified, to 'celebrate victories at our expense', only because they wanted to live. They were free men, yet they had agreed to pass under a shameful yoke of slaves. 'Piso made these men feel the mere light of day in which they lived as bitter, so that those who had feared death like a bunch of women would now actually hope for it like real men.'[66]

On the other hand, Piso rewarded his son, who had fought bravely and managed to hold specific positions during the war. Piso's son received a gold crown, but Piso would cover the cost privately, without making the state pay for it, since he considered that an official should not spend state money on something that would generate income for his own family.[67]

On his part, Florus emphasises the Roman humiliation in this phase of the war, as the rebels defeated a number of praetors – Manlius, Lentulus, Piso and Hypsaeus – and also captured their camps. Praetors ended up fleeing and being pursued by fugitive slaves – people whom hunters of fugitives should have arrested, Florus says.[68]

Given the Roman uncertainty in the conduct of the war, taking advantage of the opportunity, Eunus and his followers had made significant progress in establishing an entity that truly resembled a new kingdom in Sicily. As already mentioned, they had cut their own currency, minting bronze coins featuring the figure and name of the king, 'Antiochus'. They established a royal council composed of the most learned and intelligent among the insurgents. Moreover, a slave named Achaeus emerged as another military leader of the rebellion.

Achaeus was wise and able as a soldier, Diodorus says, and within three days, he managed to gather more than 6,000 men. They were only roughly armed with what they could find, but more insurgents joined them in the following days, and they had axes, hammers, slings, bills and spits, and stakes with one sharpened and burnt end to make them more lethal. They plundered and gained spoils from around the countryside, and always more slaves joined them. At one point, Achaeus commanded more than 10,000 rebels, and he could confront Roman officers and their forces openly in battle, which he did with success thanks to the superior number of his men.[69]

Achaeus, which means 'Achaean', was indeed an Achaean, which at the time meant from the Achaean League or the Peloponnese in general. Diodorus writes that Eunus' adviser and military leader was Ἀχαιὸς καὶ τοὔνομα καὶ τὸ γένος, i.e. Achaean in name and heritage alike. I emphasise 'Achaeus', which means 'Achaean', to play with words, because it offers a useful opportunity to inform the English-speaking reader about something important in approaching ancient history, and in particular the Hellenistic and Roman eras. Often, ancient history is not fully understood because translations fail to convey the nuances that can alter the meaning of events. Notes help with that, of course, but a closer look is still needed. In this case, the Latinisation of the Greek 'Ἀχαιὸς', 'Achaeus', was adopted in the English language, where it is translated as 'Achaean' in its ethnic or regional sense. So, in English, there appear to be two similar but different words in the text, while in the original Greek, there is only one, and the identification of the person's name with the ethnic-regional name of the Achaeans is immediately clear. Other cases are more complicated and require greater knowledge to grasp what the ancient author actually says. A non-specialised English-speaking reader today could not understand immediately that, for instance, 'Eunus from Apamea in Syria' indicated a person who was an integral part of the Hellenistic world, and that a contemporary reader of Diodorus would probably have understood this as referring to a Greek or Hellenised person, since neither Eunus, nor Apamea, nor Syria bring to mind what we know as 'Greece' in our time. Another example regarding Diodorus' text is his use of the terms Σικελιῶται and Ιταλιῶται, which are translated as 'Sicilians' and 'Italians', or 'Siciliots' and 'Italiots', to be closer to the original. These are the exact terms Diodorus uses to mention the Greeks of Sicily and Italy in previous books of his – for instance, those referring to the wars between Greeks and Carthaginians.[70] Given that we are now referring to a long time later, during the First Servile War, and within the era of Roman dominion, one could suppose that those terms also include non-Greeks. Nevertheless, their core meaning couldn't be anything but the same as that of their previous use by the same author, as all the names mentioned, both of slaves and slave owners, are again Greek, except for the Roman officers.

The Revolt Grows Stronger

The rebellious slaves continued the war by systematically targeting and destroying the farms of the wealthy landowners. However, although Eunus and the other leaders cleverly tried to promote the policy of not harming the small farmers, mobs of slaves, criminals, adventurers and bandits were indiscriminately looting and destroying the farms and houses they encountered. The result was that the small farms of Sicily suffered equally significant damage and destruction.

In parallel, the rebels, under Kleon's military command, began laying siege to major cities, including Akragas, Tauromenium (modern-day Taormina) and Catana. According to Diodorus, rebel forces attempted to storm fortified towns. They even constructed siege engines,[71] which demonstrates a substantial growth in the efficiency and logistical capability of the insurgents, as well as their confidence and ambition. If Eunus' aim to found a kingdom of Sicily felt comical in the beginning, now the Romans had no choice but to take it seriously.

Still, for all its unexpected success, the slaves' insurrection had the limitations of a rural-based rebel movement, and these became increasingly apparent over time. The rebels could not control ports and had no naval power, nor did they have extended and sustainable supply lines. Those weaknesses would prove decisive, as the insurgents failed to gain significant victories that would enable them to control urban centres, and their cohesion began to strain under the weight of prolonged warfare.

The war continued in Sicily, with atrocities from both sides. Florus records that captured Roman citizens were tortured and mutilated by the rebellious slaves, while Diodorus mentions ruthless Roman reprisals on the other side, but also that the rebels occupied entire cities and made their inhabitants slaves, as turmoil continued to grow and intensify in Sicily.

Roman Counter-offensive

In 133 BCE, Scipio Aemilianus decisively ended the long Spanish war by destroying the city of Numantia.[72] With this victory, Rome's strategic focus shifted towards suppressing the slave rebellion, as the Senate was now able to deploy experienced commanders and more substantial forces to Sicily. At the head of the troops sent to the island was appointed the consul Publius Rupilius, entrusted with the counter-offensive against the slave rebellion. Rupilius' campaign would indeed mark the final phase of the First Servile War. Rupilius pursued a methodical strategy, isolating and besieging the rebels' strongholds one by one.[73] In this way, the Roman consul concentrated his forces against a specific target each time, rather than dispersing them across different theatres simultaneously. At the same time, he exploited the rebels' overextension of their forces and their lack of urban support.

After some initial successes of Rupilius' troops, the turning point of the war came with the siege of Tauromenium, which the rebels used as a military base, and it marked a notable victory for the rebellion's early phases. The importance of that defeat for the Romans becomes more evident thanks to a passage by Valerius Maximus, where he writes that the consul Rupilius dismissed his son-in-law Quintus Fabius when he failed to defend Tauromenium, and it fell into the hands of the slaves because of his negligence.[74]

Now it was time for Roman redemption and vengeance. Rupilius and his forces starved the city into submission with a prolonged blockade, a tactic commonly employed in antiquity during sieges. At this point, Diodorus gives us another horrible image, saying that the siege brought the besieged to such a point of famine and desperation that they became cannibals. Parents began eating their children, and husbands their wives. In the end, apparently, even men killed each other to eat.[75]

A force of rebels attempted to break through the Roman blockade and escape, but their desperate exit met the prepared Roman troops, who massacred them. Kleon's brother Komanos, who apparently led the rebels' forces in Tauromenium, was one of the rebels who tried to escape, but he was captured. Valerius Maximus praises Komanos, saying that he had an honourable death when, caught by the Romans and brought in front of Rupilius, he preferred to kill himself with his own hands rather than give the Roman consul the information he wanted about the number of armed slaves Komanos had under his command and what their plans were.[76]

Eventually, according to Diodorus, a Syrian named Sarapion opened the gates of Tauromenium's citadel, betraying the rebels who remained there, and they were arrested by the Roman forces. Then, Rupilius ordered his men to throw them off a cliff, after whipping them.

The seizure of Tauromenium was a crucial blow. Diodorus mentions that the course of the war started to change when the Romans reoccupied the city of Tauromenium. Nevertheless, even with Tauromenium lost, Eunus and the insurgents continued to fight with the desperation of people whose destiny could only be death or slavery if they didn't win.

After capturing Tauromenium, Rupilius and his troops marched towards Enna, the capital of the slave kingdom. There, he put up another heavy and pressing siege, ensuring that there would be no chance for any of the besieged to escape either.

The final battles of the First Slave War occurred during the siege of Enna, the capital of the rebellion and the short-lived slave kingdom of Eunus in Sicily. The siege lasted for a considerable time, and the fall came after fierce fighting and, reportedly, again the betrayal of internal defectors, who likely hoped that by doing so, they would save their lives and escape a doomed situation. Kleon fought bravely and was killed during an attempt to break the Roman blockade around Enna and escape. Rupilius made the other rebels look at the dead body of their leader, adding to their desperation and fear.

Soon after, someone betrayed the city, just as had happened at Tauromenium. Diodorus writes that the strong defensive position of the fortified city would have rendered it impossible to capture if somebody hadn't betrayed it.[77] On the other hand, that was precisely the goal of this kind of siege: to bring the besieged to such a desperate position that at least some of them would have no choice but to surrender or try to escape. Strabo mentions that when the rebel slaves were under siege by the Roman forces, the city suffered greatly before the Romans eventually defeated them with considerable difficulty. Strabo also mentions that Catana and Tauromenium, and several other Sicilian cities, faced similar misfortunes during the slave wars.[78] Orosius writes that the number of slaves killed during the capture of Tauromenium and Enna was 20,000.[79]

Then, Diodorus depicts Eunus in a highly negative light. The slave king is shown desperately trying to escape, fleeing like a coward with about 600 of his followers, and trying to hide on some cliffs. However, Rupilius and his troops pursued them and blocked them again, with no way out. Understanding their fate was to be captured and probably tortured and killed, Eunus' men, according to this version of Diodorus, preferred to kill themselves by cutting each other's throats. Eunus did not participate in the collective suicide, and instead tried to hide in some caves in the cliffs, along with 'his cook, his barber, the man who rubbed him in the bath and the jester at his banquets'.[80] However, the Romans soon discovered them and arrested them. Interestingly, they didn't execute Eunus immediately. Instead, they threw him into a prison in the city of Morgantina, where the self-proclaimed prophet and slave king died, reportedly consumed by lice. Diodorus depicted Eunus' end as unheroic, showing all his contempt and disgust for the 'coward', 'conjuring king'[81] 'of the robbers'.[82] He wrote that Eunus had a death worthy of the 'wickedness of his life', offering a pathetic impression that was in stark contrast to the charismatic and bombastic images he had projected as prophet, magician and king,[83] and more suitable to the fact that, as Florus wrote, there was no evil that Eunus didn't do, bringing disaster and destruction upon cities, towns and villages.[84]

In contrast, Diodorus seems to praise Rupilius, who, after eliminating the main rebel force, swept Sicily with a smaller section of his troops and cleared the country of 'thieves and robbers'.[85] The historian's views are very interesting, as he condemns the rebellion and praises the Roman order, even though he considers the ill-treatment of slaves by many slave owners to be the cause of the revolt. In this way, Diodorus demonstrates a sober judgement that injustice does not justify savagery and further injustice. We could also see through his words an accusation towards the 'Italians', which could also mean Italian Greeks in great part, who acquired large estates in Sicily during those early decades of Roman dominion. Their brutal exploitation of the slaves sparked a disaster for the Sicilian populations, as they were the ones who bore the brunt of the rebels' savagery. In this way, Rupilius and the Roman troops' restoration of order and peace on the island becomes a gift instead of a burden on the Sicilian Greeks, such as Diodorus. On the other hand, the First Servile War demonstrates that Roman institutions were unable to manage the provinces effectively, thereby compromising prosperity and peace at the time.

In a different version, Florus attributes the final defeat of the slaves not to Rupilius but to Perperna, writing that eventually, Perperna forced them to retreat into Enna and laid them under siege, bringing them to the brink of famine and ultimately destroying them. He punished the survivors by crucifying them, putting them in chains, and in leg irons. Rome honoured Perperna with an *ovatio* (a lesser type of triumph), as a victory over slaves could not earn a complete triumph.[86]

Orosius, writing centuries later as a Christian author based on Sallust and Livy's largely lost accounts of the matter, adds some interesting thoughts. He points out that the situation of the slaves in Sicily was worse than elsewhere, because it was an island that had been often under the rule of tyrants and, at other times, slaves. There was no just law of its own. The tyrants were evil dominators of the others, and the slaves inverted freedom and slavery in an act of perverted arrogance. He reflects on the geographical limitations, as Sicily's island status means it is closed off by the sea on all sides, making it challenging to externalise its internal issues. Sicily 'nourished a viper conceived for its own destruction, a viper that grew very large because of Sicily's compulsive lusts and was destined to live at the cost of Sicily's destruction'. Orosius also specifies that the slaves who lived in the city of Messene did not join the rebellion, because their masters treated them fairly. That's another clue in favour of the interpretation our ancient sources give, from Diodorus to Posidonius, that the root cause of the rebellion was the cruel way many slave owners of that time in Sicily treated an increasing number of slaves.

Orosius indeed says that the war against the slaves in Sicily was severe and savage because the number of insurgent slaves was huge, and they also had many supplies and equipment. To show once more the magnitude of the events, he adds that praetors were destroyed, and even consuls were extremely preoccupied by the events. Orosius concludes that the war was great and long, and its causes deplorable, but so was the slaves' behaviour after they revolted. The slaves became increasingly insolent and cruel, and the masters had no choice but to fight them with the 'blade of a sword'. However, Orosius claims that the winners of that war lost just as much as the defeated.[87]

In 132 BCE, the first major slave rebellion in ancient history was crushed. Still, its temporary success appears to have had a lasting impact across the Roman dominions, inspiring further unrest and risings in other regions as well. News from Sicily and the initial successes of the slave revolt there spurred uprisings in various other parts of Italy and the Mediterranean. Diodorus refers to less extensive slave revolts that erupted in different parts of the Mediterranean world during or shortly after the major Sicilian insurrection.[88]

Orosius gives more details, mentioning that at the port of Latium, Minturnae, a slave revolt took place, which was immediately suppressed, and about 450 of the rebellious slaves died on the cross. At the port of Sinuessa, between Latium and Campania, a large number of slaves, reported to have reached 4,000, revolted, but their movement was crushed in a bloody manner by Roman troops led by Quintus Metellus and Gnaeus Servilius Caepio.[89] Even in Rome, it is reported that 150 slaves were gathered with the intention of starting a revolt. None of these attempts had any effect, as all of them were promptly dealt with and put down by the Roman authorities. Nevertheless, their appearance in different locations suggests that there were shared structural tensions across the area under Roman rule. A revolt also took place in the quarries of Laurion in Attica. Orosius says that it was 'praetor' Heraclitus who suppressed it, but we know that the Heraclitus mentioned was not a Roman magistrate but a local Athenian official.[90] Moreover, in the Greek island of Delos, where the largest slave market in Roman territory existed, some slaves were also preparing a revolt; however, the island's citizens took notice of it and repressed the attempted uprising with pre-emptive actions, as Orosius reports.[91] These two pieces of information are important because they show that the aversion to the slave revolts and the mobilisations for their suppression were not initiated solely by Roman authorities, but also by local communities and citizens, in this case, Greeks.

Diodorus' previous descriptions can better explain why, and also Orosius' claim that the slave uprisings, although rare, are the most dangerous of all, because free people revolt prompted by their will to see their homeland stronger. In contrast, a mob of slaves desires only to destroy it.[92]

Aftermath

Rome had initially underestimated the magnitude of the rebellion, but after facing great difficulty in addressing it, its response extended beyond the military and even political level. Diodorus records that the Senate, alarmed by the scale of the slave uprising in Sicily, consulted the Sibylline Books.[93]

The Sibylline Books were a collection of oracular hexameter verses written in Greek and kept in a temple in Rome. According to the legend, the last Etruscan king of Rome, Lucius Tarquinius Superbus, had purchased them from a Sibyl, possibly near Cumae, and they included divine advice for the Roman religion and the sound administration of the state.

The Sibyls were female oracles, prophetesses of the Greek world, and as philosopher Heraclitus wrote, 'The Sibyl raves, speaking solemn words without laughter, without adornment, without perfume, yet her voice reaches over a thousand years, thanks to the god.'[94]

In periods of great crisis and war, the Roman authorities visited the temple and read the oracles, seeking guidance and inspiration in the verses given from the Sibyl to the last king. The fact that the Senate consulted the Sibylline Books demonstrates that the Roman leadership was deeply shocked by the magnitude and severity of the events that occurred in Sicily.

After consulting the Sibylline Books, the Romans ordered special sacrifices to Zeus Aetnaeus, that is, the temple and festival of Zeus on Mount Aetna (Etna) in Sicily. They also continued with mop-up military operations and likely tried to develop a broader political response, which included the establishment of new provincial statutes. Publius Rupilius, as mentioned by

Cicero, introduced the *Lex Rupilia* later,[95] which established a legal framework to reorganise the administration of the province of Sicily. However, those reforms did not address the structural causes of the First Servile War, as the history that unfolded during the following decades proves.

The First Servile War took on immense proportions, revealing the depth of the crisis caused by Rome's reckless reliance on slave labour in agriculture. The impression of structural imbalances and dysfunction in the early Roman Empire is intensified by another significant insurrection of those years, although with different traits, which erupted in Pergamon, in Asia Minor, in 133 BCE.

The War of Pergamon

The War of Pergamon took place concurrently with the First Servile War and the other crucial events of that time, such as the war in Spain and the first civil conflict within Rome.[96] The revolt and the war of Pergamon do not belong to the slave wars, as it was in great part a national revolution rather than a slave revolt. Nevertheless, it is related to the slave wars not only chronologically but also due to its specific characteristics.

As mentioned, in 133 BCE, the king of Pergamon, Attalus III, had left his kingdom under the complete control of Rome in his will, thereby making it a proper Roman province rather than a client state, as it had been up to that point.[97] However, his half brother Aristonikos,[98] taking advantage of the fact that a significant part of the kingdom's population hated the Roman and Italian tax collectors, moneylenders and merchants who lived in the region and exploited its wealth, declared a revolt against Roman rule.[99] The movement was primarily made up of poor citizens and slaves, mainly from the countryside. On the contrary, most of the urban poor and slaves did not join the rebellion, as the authorities and the rich made a series of concessions precisely to prevent the movement from becoming more powerful.

For the next two years, Pergamon would be in a civil war, the outcome of which remained uncertain. In the initial phase, Aristonikos managed to gain the support and control of a part of the fleet, but the rest of the fleet prevailed against him at the Battle of Cyme,[100] on the north-west coast of Asia Minor in 132 BCE. As a consequence, Aristonikos was forced to abandon his coastal positions since they were exposed to the opposing fleet and could not be supported by his own naval forces. He retreated and settled inland, but there, he further increased his forces and organised them, creating a formidable army. As a result, although rulers of neighbouring kingdoms that were also clients of Rome, such as those of Pontus, Bithynia and Cappadocia, sent military reinforcements to the government of Pergamon, Aristonikos' forces were not bowed down and retained the territories they had occupied.

Aristonikos did not confine himself to continuing the revolution to seize power in Pergamon but proclaimed the establishment of a new state. He took the royal name of Eumenes III and ordered a new currency to be minted for the new state, which would have a radically different political and governmental structure. Unlike the slave revolt in Sicily, which was still raging at the time, the political programme Aristonikos presented, which persuaded many poor slaves to follow him, was not a typical imitation of the Hellenistic kingdoms but was aimed at creating a utopian society of equality. He designated his state as the 'State of the Sun', referring to its citizens as 'Sun Citizens' (*heliopolitae*). The god Helios was seen as the god of justice in the Hellenistic East, and Aristonikos' choice was an appeal to this belief.

An important contribution to the formulation of Aristonikos' programme was made by the Stoic philosopher Gaius Blossius, a Greek philosopher from Cumae in southern Italy.[101] Blossius came from the entourage of Tiberius Gracchus and had also influenced, along with other Greek philosophers associated with the Roman statesman, the aspiring reformer's views and political positions. When Gracchus was assassinated in 133 BCE, and many of his supporters were executed or imprisoned, Blossius fled Rome to Asia Minor, where meanwhile Aristonikos' rebellion had just broken out.

Stoic philosophy was prevalent in Roman times, as was Epicurean philosophy. Stoicism was in keeping with the Roman national tradition, which promoted the model of the man of integrity, who is not at the mercy of his excitements and circumstances, his hopes and fears, but who bases his existence and his attitude to life on the concept of duty. Unlike the Platonic and Aristotelian philosophical traditions, Stoicism and Epicureanism did not focus on political and sociological study and thought, but addressed themselves to the individual and how it was most beneficial to deal with life and its challenges. This partly explains their widespread appeal, regardless of political and social classes. Characteristically, two of the most important and famous Stoic philosophers are the Roman emperor Marcus Aurelius (161–180 CE) and the Greek slave Epictetus.

Rome did not intervene in the first phase of the civil war in Pergamon, as it was busy with the war in Spain, which at that time was culminating in the siege of Numantia, as well as the war against the rebellious slaves in Sicily. Consequently, initially, only a group of five officers was sent to Pergamon, with the task of surveying the situation, directing the local pro-Roman forces, and preparing for the Roman intervention. This committee was headed by Publius Cornelius Scipio Nasica Serapio, grandson of Scipio 'Africanus' and former consul, who had also led the aristocrats against Tiberius Gracchus a few months earlier.[102] It is possible that the Senate sent him to Asia Minor to protect him from the followers of Tiberius Gracchus or a charge of his murder, as the situation in Rome remained extremely tense. However, his mission was probably not enough to save him from their vengeance, as he later died of poison in Pergamon.

After the Roman forces had sacked Numantia in 133 BCE and suppressed the slave revolt in Sicily the following year, the Senate now turned its attention to the East, aiming to crush the third source of opposition to its rule that had emerged. In 131 BCE, an expeditionary force was formed and sent to Asia Minor under the command of Publius Licinius Crassus Dives Mucianus, who had now been elected consul.

With the arrival of the Roman troops, the war became much more difficult for Aristonikos and his 'Sun Citizens'. Conversely, the oligarchic pro-Roman factions and the citizens of the state of Pergamon were encouraged. Pergamon and the other cities of the kingdom gladly opened their gates to the Roman forces. Then the consul Crassus Mucianus exerted intense pressure on Aristonikos' army. Some months later, the latter was forced to take refuge and fortify himself in the city of Lefkae, which was situated on the Asia Minor coast of the Aegean. The Romans laid siege to the city, but Aristonikos and his forces managed to successfully carry out a surprise and well-planned exit, during which the Roman troops were disorganised and retreated, and the consul lost his life.[103]

The Senate responded by sending reinforcements to Asia Minor, led by the consul Marcus Perpena, who took command of the Roman forces. In the following period, the consul pushed Aristonikos and his army from the coast inland, finally succeeding in blocking him and surrounding him in the city of Stratonicea in Caria. Aristonikos' forces defended the city for some time behind its fortifications, but this time, the Roman general was cautious, and his forces were highly organised and diligent in the conduct of the war, ruling out any new attempts at surprise on the part of the besieged. The remarkable strategic skill that Aristonikos had shown from the beginning of the rebellion was not enough to free him again from the suffocating Roman grip. Consequently, the besieged were eventually forced to surrender due to a lack of supplies and an inability to continue the resistance.

Aristonikos was captured and led in irons to Rome, where, according to Strabo, he died in prison. According to Orosius, Aristonikos was indeed imprisoned in Rome but was executed by strangulation.[104] At the same time, the philosopher Blossius had committed suicide, wanting to avoid a similar fate. In 129 BCE, the new consul, Manius Aquilius (or Aquillius), arrived in Pergamon. In the following months, he eradicated the last remnants of the rebellion, completely wiping out the state Aristonikos had founded, and finally restored Roman control over the region. Velleius Paterculus writes that Aristonikos actually died during the triumph of Manius Aquilius in Tullianum, as he was dragged by the consul's chariot.[105]

Chapter 2

The Second Servile War and Its Era

The pacification of Sicily after the First Servile War was meant to be only temporary. Less than thirty years later, a new massive slave rebellion and war erupted, with similar magnitude and even similarities in its development with the previous one, though also with important differences. The structural problems of latifundium economy and the broader systemic crisis of the Roman Republic were not addressed in the meantime, ending up in further conflicts. In this chapter, we'll examine the Second Servile War (104–100 BCE) in the historical context in which it happened, beginning with the second attempt of socio-economic reform by the Gracchi movement, led this time by Gaius Gracchus, and the rise of Gaius Marius and his wide military reform. We will also see minor slave revolts that preceded it, and then, the extended presentation of the Second Servile War.

Gaius Gracchus and Gaius Marius

Back in Rome, in the years that followed the wars in Sicily and Pergamon, the agrarian law introduced by Tiberius Gracchus remained in force despite his assassination, and the commission appointed to distribute the land continued to function, albeit with difficulty. One of the members of the committee was Gaius Gracchus, the brother of Tiberius, younger by nine years, who, after being elected quaestor and serving in Sicily for two years, also stood for election as tribune of the plebeians.[1]

He was elected for two consecutive years, in 123 and 122 BCE, as obviously this had become legally permissible in the meantime,[2] during which he continued and deepened his brother's efforts. Gaius Gracchus further intensified the confrontation with the Senate, promoting the position that the role of the popular assemblies should be strengthened and made sovereign.[3]

He also proposed a new agrarian law, according to which not only the state land located in Italy but also that of the provinces should be distributed to the poor Roman citizens, which, of course, was damaging to the provinces. To overcome the opposition of the Italians to Tiberius' law, he proposed that they should be given Roman citizenship, but the plebeian council rejected this proposal.[4] The poor Roman citizens were opposed to the dissemination of Roman citizenship, as they wished to retain the privileges that this status afforded them over the other inhabitants of Italy, as well as reap the benefits of the agrarian reform themselves.

Another of Gaius Gracchus' important initiatives was the proposal and enactment of the law on feeding (*lex frumentaria*), which required the sale of wheat to the citizens of Rome at a price below the market price.[5] This measure again harmed the provinces, as it reduced the profits they could derive from wheat exports to Rome. Gracchus attempted to compensate for this damage with another fundamental law, which was likely aimed primarily at harming the Senate. It was a law that took away from the senators the jurisdiction of the courts that considered matters relating to the provinces and transferred it instead to the order of the knights, as well as the collection of taxes.[6] The knights or equestrians (*equites*) were the second upper class of Roman society and were more closely associated with artisanal, commercial and banking business activities.

These arrangements, however, instead of improving the situation of the provinces, led to deterioration, as the newcomer equestrians found opportunities to exploit the provinces in collaboration with the senators since there was still no central control mechanism. Finally, to gain even more popular support, Gracchus proposed the establishment of new colonies, to be inhabited by poor Roman citizens, in Italy and the provinces. He even suggested that one of them be built on the ruins of Carthage.[7]

The aristocracy, this time, faced the challenge with greater composure and more intelligent tactics than a decade earlier. Its new ally among the tribunes, Marcus Livius Drusus, did not veto Gracchus' proposals but began to promise and propose measures even more favourable to people with low incomes than before. Bubbling over with promises and thrilling the masses thanks also to his rhetorical skill, without explaining how it would be possible to realise what he promised (and indeed, it was never realised), he won the support of a large part of the plebeian council. He removed it from the influence of Gaius Gracchus.

Moreover, when Gracchus later raised the issue of Roman citizenship again, at least for the rest of the Latins, he met with the opposition of both the Senate and the plebeian council, which voted against the proposal.[8] These developments significantly reduced his popularity, and when he ran for tribune for a third consecutive year, he failed to be elected.[9] Things turned out even worse for him when, shortly afterwards, news arrived from Carthage that one night, some hyenas had dug up the foundations of the city he was building. The soothsayers decided that the incident was an evil omen and the establishment of the colony should be called off. The Senate took advantage of the event by putting to a vote in the assembly, through a tribune ally, the annulment of the law that had established the colony.[10]

On the day of the vote, there was much tension, and one of Gracchus' supporters clashed with a Senate supporter and murdered him. The result was a general clash in which Gaius Gracchus and many of his supporters were killed.[11]

In this way, the Gracchi reforms were thwarted in 121 BCE, but the disputes over the issues involved were far from over. The distinction between the *populares* and the *optimates* would be central for Roman politics. The difference had nothing to do with origin, as both were usually made up of aristocrats, but with the attitude towards popular demands that the Gracchi brothers had stirred up.[12] The turn of events and the increasing intensity of violence would gradually favour the emergence of leaders with more prominent military than political characteristics. The first of these would be Gaius Marius.

Marius had distinguished himself as a young soldier in the Spanish war. He came from a popular family without political credentials and wealth, lacked the education and culture of members of the aristocratic class, and had a rough character. However, he was also intelligent, organised, and decisive,[13] attributes that contributed to his emergence as the leading military figure of his generation and leader of the popular faction.

The opportunity to become a protagonist in his political life arose with the war in Africa against Jugurtha, who had usurped the throne of the kingdom of Libya, an ally of Rome. The war broke out in 112 BCE and was fought without success until 109 BCE, when Caecilius Metellus departed for Africa as consul and commander of the Roman troops there. Metellus was a capable military leader who brought discipline and efficiency back to the Roman forces in Africa.[14] He was also an exemplary aristocrat, but he chose Marius as his second-in-command,[15] which demonstrates that political and class divisions were not always decisive in Roman society.

The rest of the war was positive for the Roman arms, with a significant contribution from Marius, who had also gained the sympathy of the soldiers, as he was seen as one of them and shared the difficulties they were experiencing.[16]

Having gained the favour of the army, he then made sure to use it by encouraging the soldiers to write to their relatives and friends in Rome that he had to become consul in order to win the war, while undermining Metellus as incapable of bringing the war to an end.[17] Gradually, a positive atmosphere was created for Marius in Rome, and as the elections approached, he ran for consul and returned to the city.

On the election days, Marius constantly extolled his popular origins. He disparaged the aristocrats – an attitude that certainly pleased the masses.[18] He stressed that he had bled and struggled to reach his current position while the aristocrats occupied the highest offices thanks to the fame of their ancestors. He also noted that he possessed real experience, whereas they merely studied the teachings of others.[19] The aristocrats, on the other hand, despised him as uneducated and particularly censured the fact that he was the only senior Roman official who did not know Greek and had not received a Greek education. Marius replied that he thought it was ridiculous to learn Greek and study the wisdom of the Greeks since they had come to submit to Rome, and therefore, any wisdom they had had failed to help them too.[20]

Marius was elected consul for the year 107 BCE and continued the war against Jugurtha. He, too, faced the problem of a scarcity of recruits and responded in a more straightforward way than the Gracchi had proposed. Instead of trying to give property to the landless so that they could be called up into the army, he effectively abolished the ban on conscription for landless people, calling them to arms as standard, as it was for their landowning compatriots.[21] Also, in addition to the rewards provided for the duration of service, Marius introduced the distribution of land lots to each legionary when his service was concluded. With this change, the Roman army and Roman society as a whole entered a phase in which the personal bond between troops and commanders was significantly strengthened, further encouraging loyalties that could rival devotion to the state. Leaders promised to reward men who had served under them, and so the men tended to support and follow them faithfully in every choice, no longer caring more about the constitution, the institutional framework, or even the state itself.

The war in Africa was victoriously concluded, and the victorious Marius triumphed in Rome. However, a peer rival was already beginning to emerge. This was Lucius Cornelius Sulla, who distinguished himself as Marius' second-in-command and took some of the glory from his commander as it was he who contributed more to the capture of Jurgurtha.[22] Sulla belonged to the high aristocracy and at the same time was as capable and effective a soldier as Marius. In the following years, Sulla served successfully in the Alps and Asia Minor, becoming a leading member of the aristocratic faction and a key rival of Marius.[23]

At the same time, Rome already faced the threat posed by the Cimbri and Teutonic tribes in the north, two barbarian tribes of Germanic origin. Populations of hundreds of thousands of people from these two tribes, many of whom were hardy warriors, were moving southwards. Their movement had caused great trouble in Gaul but also threatened Italy itself after repeated defeats of Roman troops sent against them.[24] Faced with the danger, the Romans put aside their differences and jointly appointed Marius as supreme commander. From 104 to 100 BCE, Marius served as consul for five consecutive years, a feat that had never been achieved before as consecutive consulships had previously been excluded from Roman political norms. In this particular emergency, however, there was no reaction.[25]

Marius and his legions eliminated the threat of the northern barbarians with two sweeping victories in 102 and 101 BCE,[26] but at the moment of triumph, Marius' star began to wane. Being a great general but not as skilled as a statesman, he was less successful in peace as he had been in war, and his political influence began to diminish. Lacking a fundamental understanding of the issues and possessing no skills suitable for civil life and intercourse,[27] he attempted to please the people by demagoguing without plan or restraint, with the result that he lost the lustre his military successes had secured for him and he became unreliable. Thus, after the historic victories and the end of his sixth term, he was rather marginalised politically.[28]

That was not the end of Marius' career, as we will see in Chapter 3. However, there is no doubt that its peak was the final years of the second century, during which the second major slave revolt erupted in Sicily. Thus, by the opening years of the first century BCE, Rome faced not one isolated crisis but a convergence of agrarian tension, military transformation, provincial exploitation and weakening institutional restraint.

Slave Revolts before the Second Servile War

Diodorus narrates the Second Servile War (104–100 BCE) in his thirty-sixth book, beginning with minor slave revolts that preceded the great one in the previous years. These revolts happened in Italy. One of them occurred in Nuceria, where thirty slaves tried to plan an uprising but were immediately discovered and suppressed. Another one took place in Capua, and it was somewhat bigger, with 200 armed slaves taking part. However, the Roman authorities soon eliminated this attempted uprising as well.[29]

Then, Diodorus gives us yet another wild ancient story. He writes about a Roman knight whom he initially calls Titus Minutius, but later Titus Vettius. We'll go with Titus Vettius, as this is the name used more often and in the later parts of the story.

Whatever the name, the boy was the son of a very wealthy man. He had an intense encounter with a beautiful maidservant, with whom he became infatuated due to her attractiveness. The problem was that the girl was not his own maidservant, but belonged to another man. So, young Titus tried to buy her freedom to keep her with him. Even though her master initially refused to liberate her, after Vettius pushed and insisted, he managed to acquire the man's agreement, but for the very high price of seven Attic talents.

Vettius went with the girl to one of his father's estates and, without having to worry that someone could take her away, satisfied his lusts with her, as Diodorus mentions. However, when the payment day arrived, he couldn't pay, as his father was wealthy but apparently not to the point of being able or disposed to cover such a cost for a girl. Vettius requested a one-month delay, but it expired without him managing to pay what he had promised.

Things had become messy for the young guy in love. Instead of asking for an arrangement, like giving some money now and paying the rest in due time, Vettius opted for a drastic solution to the problem. He might not have had seven Attic talents at his disposal, but apparently he had enough money to buy 500 full armours, good enough to arm all of his 400 slaves, and he incited them to revolt after he went with them to a secret location. In other words, he made them his personal army. After that, he proclaimed himself king and put on some appropriate attire, including a purple cloak and a diadem on his head. So, after the expiration of a second postponed payment date, which he had asked for in order to delude the other party, he launched a campaign of violence. He first had his creditors whipped and executed. But he didn't stop there. It seems that, enjoying his newfound power, Vettius began, according to Diodorus, occupying and looting towns of the area with his army of slaves, killing anyone who tried to resist and accepting the slaves who wanted to join. After a while, his force reached 700 men and grew with more slaves who abandoned their owners. Vettius obviously found a way to train and organise his men, as Diodorus states that he divided them into centuries, following the standard Roman army structure.

The Roman Senate reacted to this news by appointing the praetor Lucius Lucullus to lead a force against the rebels and suppress them. Lucullus left Rome with 600 men and entered Capua, where he added 4,000 infantry and 400 horsemen, creating a considerable army. Then, he marched fast towards Vettius and his rebels, who had reached the impressive number of 3,500 men. Even though the Roman troops were more numerous, Vettius' strange rebellion managed to hold out, as he had positioned his men on high ground that gave them the advantage. However, Lucullus, preferring to avoid having severe casualties, tried and managed to approach and bribe Apollonius, who was a leader of Vettius' rebel army. Apollonius indeed betrayed Vettius, turning against him and attacking him with the rebels he had under his command, putting him in a very disadvantageous position. Soon, the Romans had total control of the battlefield, and Vettius decided to end his life rather than suffer the punishment that awaited him for his bloody rebellion. The rebel army was dissolved, while Apollonius probably lived happily ever after, since he was given a pardon from the state for his valuable services, negating any responsibility he had for the crimes commited during the revolt.[30]

Diodorus, in a second version of the story, which includes only the introduction to the events, immediately highlights the atypical and unusual nature of Vettius' rebellion, noting that it was distinctly different from any other and from what typically occurred in such cases. The historian calls Vettius' actions bizarre, childish and stupid, as they were driven by the fact that he had become a slave to his passion and was ashamed that he couldn't keep the agreement he had made. Instead of accepting that he couldn't keep his girlfriend, he devised an elaborate conspiracy to eliminate his creditors, which then spiralled out of control.[31]

There is no doubt that the story seems more of an urban legend than an accurate account of historical events, since we have a boy not capable of elementary reasoning under the heat of his passion transformed into a ruthless rebel and military commander who gathers and leads hundreds, or even thousands, of armed grown men in calculated terrorist attacks and rough fights against Roman praetors and troops. On top of that, the attractive girl for whom supposedly all that turmoil started disappears from the story and we never hear anything about her again. Even though I certainly won't exclude the possibility of erotic passion having had something to do with all that, as we can find it almost everywhere, the story seems like a romanticised fiction, either of a slave revolt or of a conflict that included criminal activities and perhaps a crime organisation with the participation of slaves, which created the need of massive intervention by the Roman authorities.

The New Uprising in Sicily

The Second Servile War in Sicily is indirectly related to Marius and his war against the Cimbrians in the north. Facing the threat we saw in the previous chapter, and wanting to raise as powerful an army as possible, the Senate gave Marius the commission to recruit soldiers from Rome's client states. Marius sent emissaries to the king of Bithynia, Nicomedes, and asked him to recruit as many soldiers as possible to join the Roman army as auxiliaries. However, King Nicomedes responded that, unfortunately, sending soldiers was impossible, as Roman tax collectors had enslaved many, and he had no men available.[32] Then, the Senate decreed that the enslavement of free men from Roman allies was from now on forbidden, and on top of that, even the free men from those countries that had been previously enslaved should be liberated.[33]

Receiving this order from the Senate, the praetor of Sicily, Licinius Nerva, began to review cases of allied persons who had been enslaved, and after only a few days, 800 of them had recovered their liberty. The hearings continued, and Nerva received many more slaves with the request that their freedom be granted. However, that wave of liberations and applications for liberty alarmed several wealthy and influential people in Sicily, who then visited the governor Nerva and asked him not to grant more slaves their freedom.

Either persuaded by the money they offered him, or simply obeying their political influences, as Diodorus notes, Nerva rejected all further applications of liberation and ordered the slaves who had visited him to return to their owners.

Cassius Dio agrees that Nerva had declared he was disposed to receive any slave and hear their accusations against their master, but he doesn't connect that decision with Marius and the war in the north. Dio comments that Nerva may have done this with sincerity to help the slaves because he had learned that they were often mistreated, or because he hoped to make some money out of his clemency, as he was not the type of man who was immune to bribery. Whatever the true reasons for Nerva's declaration to the public, many slaves began to visit his office and put forward charges against their owners for unfair treatment. Nevertheless, the freeborn slave owners, as Dio specifies, did not agree to satisfy their slaves' demands and recognise they had wronged them. Nerva, facing these contradictory stances, was afraid that whoever considered his decisions unfair could become hostile and create havoc and turmoil. Thus, he interrupted the hearings and stopped receiving the slaves and their petitions. However, this decision ended up provoking the very thing the Roman governor had attempted to avoid. The slaves who had already accused their masters were clearly hesitant to return to them and, discussing the matter amongst themselves, they decided to become bandits.[34]

Diodorus says that after Nerva's rejection, the outraged slaves formed a group and left Syracuse, finding refuge at the sanctuary of the Palici, two indigenous chthonic deities of Sicily, near the city of Leontini.

Then, one night, thirty slaves who belonged to two wealthy brothers killed their masters while they were sleeping. They were led by a man named Varius. This happened in the countryside of Halicyae, which was a city of the Elymians tribe in the western part of Sicily. That action sparked a more widespread revolt as the slaves fled to other farms in the area, and other slaves joined them in their quest for freedom. Before that same night ended, the rebels had reached 120 in number. Then, they occupied a natural strongpoint and further fortified it. In the following days, eighty more slaves joined them, and they were all armed.

These events immediately preoccupied Nerva, who led a Roman force to the strongpoint, aiming to crush the revolt at its inception, obviously aware of the history of the First Servile War, which had occurred thirty years prior. However, his force was not capable of besieging the defensive position, which had already become a fortress for the insurgents.

Under these circumstances, Nerva thought of another way to undermine the position of the insurgents and crush them by occupying their fortress. He came in contact with a bandit who had been committing raids around the countryside. During his criminal activities, the bandit had murdered several free people, but not slaves. Two years earlier, he had been arrested and condemned to death, but he had managed to escape. His name was Gaius Titinius, but he was known as Gadaeus.

Titinius approached the slaves' fortified position at the head of a group of other rebel slaves he had with him. The insurgents accepted him as a friend and ally. Moreover, given his fame from the years of raids and his criminal record, they thought it would be wise to trust him with the command of the revolt and their fortress, due to his experience, bravery and obvious skills. They didn't know that Titinius had previously reached an understanding with the Roman governor, obviously on mutually satisfying terms. His part of the agreement was that he would surrender the fortress, betraying his supposed companions, and so he did.

Some of the slaves fought the Romans and died, while others jumped down the cliff and ran to escape being killed or arrested. That initial revolt was soon effectively eliminated by the Roman authorities.[35]

However, turmoil in Sicily was far from over. As soon as the soldiers who participated in the previous operation returned to their homes, released from service, another similar revolt erupted. In what we would call a terrorist attack, eighty slaves assassinated a Roman knight named Publius Clonius. Moreover, they continued to riot and loot, and their numbers steadily increased over time.[36]

Yet, when governor Licinius Nerva was informed of all this, he chose not to act immediately, as he had the previous time. Diodorus mentions that the advice given to him by his collaborators played a role in this. Another reason could be that most of the soldiers were discharged after the previous operation, and there wasn't a force ready to move against the new subversive actions.

Failing to respond again right away would quickly prove to be a mistake. More and more slaves joined this new uprising, and eventually, Nerva was forced to act. He decided to mobilise the forces that he had at his immediate disposal, but he didn't engage the rebels. He went to the city of Heraclea, while the insurgents had occupied an area on the mountain Kaprianos.

Nerva's move ended up helping the rebels instead of hurting them, because his hesitation was perceived as weakness by many other slaves, and the insurgents incited them to join the rebellion. Many of those slaves were armed and ready to fight. Within seven days, the number of rebels had reached 800, and soon it surpassed 2,000.

Nerva, upon learning the news, finally decided to attack, and assigned a force of 600 soldiers from the garrison of Enna to a commander named Marcus Titinius (not mentioned to have anything to do with the other Titinius), to attack the rebels on the mountain. However, the slaves' numerical advantage and their strong defensive position proved to be insurmountable for Titinius and his men, who were defeated. Those who weren't killed ran away, abandoning their weapons and barely surviving.

The victory gave the rebels even more confidence and momentum. They collected the weapons the Romans had left behind, and even more significant was the fact that the news sparked the idea of the insurrection among the slaves in Sicily. This created a new wave of people who came to join the rebels, even more diverse than the previous ones. As Diodorus writes, within days, the rebels had reached 6,000 in number.

The newfound size of the rebels' forces necessitated a centralised leadership. The rebels formed a popular assembly, which decided that a slave named Salvius would be the king of what they intended as a new kingdom. Salvius in many ways resembled Eunus of the original slave revolt in Sicily. He was also a fortune teller, and he played the flute in women's religious festivals. So, we are discussing a charismatic spiritual leader again, not our typical social revolutionary. Nevertheless, his policies were extremely pragmatic and ruthless. First of all, he ordered his followers not to visit cities, as he had a bad opinion about them. They weren't any good, as they prompted effeminacy, laziness and vices. Second, he created three distinct groups of the same size and appointed the same number of officers to command each of them. Then, he gave them precise missions, which were anything but calm and innocuous. They would have to conduct raids throughout the countryside and gather at a specific location at a particular time. The primary objective was to acquire weapons and horses, enabling the creation of an army comprising 20,000 infantry and 2,000 cavalry. The people were there, ready and trained. All that was still missing were the arms and equipment.

Then, the slave army suddenly attacked the city of Morgantina. The slaves' attacks were savage and unceasing, as Diodorus reports. However, Morgantina was a strong and fortified city, making it difficult to conquer. Moreover, the Roman governor Nerva moved quickly to bring help to Morgantina, having now at his disposal 10,000 troops from Italy and more forces from Sicily. Acting cleverly, he did not immediately attack the bulk of the slave army, but instead, as they were focused on besieging Morgantina, he assaulted their fortified camp in the middle of the night, which was guarded by only a few men who had stayed there. Nerva's forces had no problem occupying the place, and then they plundered it, taking booty. The slave camp was also full of women whom they had taken prisoner.

Then, Nerva and his men marched towards Morgantina itself to engage with the main army of the rebels. Nerva hoped to surprise them as they were besieging the city. However, the insurgents took notice of the Roman movements and quickly turned around to face the approaching enemy army. Not only were they not surprised, but they also launched an attack themselves. Indeed, as the Romans approached Morgantina, Salvius ordered his men to abandon the siege momentarily and turn to confront the enemy from an advantageous position, as they were on the higher ground. In this way, the battle began favourably for the rebels while the Roman troops faced adversity.

The rebels launched their attack with confidence. The Roman forces, composed mainly of auxiliaries and allied soldiers, rather than battle-hardened legions, found themselves under pressure. As they were not experienced and exceptionally well-trained soldiers, and finding themselves in a disadvantageous position, Nerva's men lost their composure and soon began to retreat, many of them fleeing away from the battlefield, throwing down their weapons in order to run faster. The rebels' forces blocked another major part of the Roman force, leaving them in a challenging situation. Had they been an army made of legions, things would undoubtedly have been different, as there were still margins to resist and attempts to break through the slave army's block, given the numbers of the Roman troops. However, in this case, they had no tactical or operational skills to allow them to address a similar challenging position.

Then, seeing the enemy's difficulty, Salvius used a clever proclamation to further dissolve the Roman ranks with psychological warfare. Diodorus records that the slave king announced that the Roman troops who threw down their weapons and fled would be spared. This apparent act of mercy succeeded in ending any possibility of the Roman force bouncing back from the initial repulsion and retreat, as it had a profoundly electrifying effect. We can guess that at least some of the Italians who composed Nerva's army there had little loyalty to the Roman cause to begin with; some had likely been conscripted or were troops from regions indifferent to Sicily's fate. In any case, probably none of them was an experienced legionary, and certainly they were not legionary units. When faced with the dangerous prospect of retreating with thousands of desperate and relentless insurgents following them, the promise of safety if one surrendered their arms proved too tempting. A cascade of shields and swords fell to the ground as the Roman line disintegrated.

Weaponising clemency, Salvius secured the capture of the Roman troops' arms and supplies, effectively replacing the losses of his own forces due to the capture of their camp earlier. The sizeable booty added greatly to the rebels' resources. Moreover, the shameful surrender of Nerva's troops demoralised Rome's military presence in central Sicily. According to Diodorus, only 600 of the Roman-allied forces were killed in the fighting, while a staggering 4,000 men were taken prisoner.

Salvius and his men's success spread greater enthusiasm among many slaves in Sicily, and the rebels' numbers kept growing, as more and more slaves escaped their masters and joined them. At this point, Diodorus says that Salvius' forces became double what they were before, and he tried to capture Morgantina again.

However, the defence of Morgantina proved an insurmountable obstacle for the slave army for the time being. Salvius attempted to win over the city's slaves with further psychological warfare by inviting them to join the rebels and gain their freedom. Yet, the city authorities responded to the challenge by offering freedom to the slaves who remained loyal to their owners and the city. It's meaningful that the slaves of Morgantina preferred to take the side of the city rather than that of the army of rebellious slaves. Their choice, combined with the latter's inability to penetrate the strong fortifications, brought about the failure and the breaking of the siege.

The event is significant, as it highlights that for the urban slaves of Morgantina, it was preferable to remain members of the city and the Roman state rather than join a revolt led by other slaves aimed at creating a local kingdom. However, the attitude of the authorities and citizens of Morgantina is also indicative as, after the withdrawal of the besiegers, they refused to keep their promise to free the slaves, with the result that some of them eventually left the city and indeed joined the rebellion.[37] This, in turn, we can perhaps see as an event that exhibits some of the negative characteristics of much of the nouveau riche classes of the time, namely greed, gluttony and immorality.

The dishonest behaviour of Morgantina was soon to be punished. With the Roman legions still busy in the north, fighting the Cimbrians and Teutons, and the slave rebellion growing in Sicily, Salvius soon found himself at the head of an army of 30,000 men. With such a force in his hands, he attacked Morgantina again, succeeding this time in conquering it. Then, he also captured the fertile lands of the city of Leontini.

Revolt's Peak

In the same period, a second, parallel slave revolt broke out in Sicily. In the rural areas of Segesta and Lilybaeum's countryside, and near other cities close to them, many slaves began to move in a similarly rebellious direction.

Another leader with a Hellenistic profile emerged, Athenion from Cilicia, who was known for his bravery as well as his ability to predict the future.[38] Thus, we have one more prophet and charismatic religious man emerging as the leader of this new uprising. The difference is that, unlike Salvius, Athenion knew how to predict the future not by reading animals' entrails, but by reading the stars. Moreover, he had already developed advanced managerial skills, as his job as a slave involved being the administrator for a sector of his masters' – two wealthy brothers – businesses.

The masters' domains were obviously vast, and they were among the big landowners of the time, since Athenion directed some 200 slaves. Those were the first bulk of the new uprising. Athenion convinced the slaves he directed to follow him in a revolt, and then he began to incite slaves from the other estates in the area to join them. His actions had enormous success, as, according to Diodorus, within only five days, the number of slaves that had joined Athenion already reached 1,000. Then, following the known modus operandi of the Sicilian servile rebellions perpetrated by slaves originating from the Hellenistic East, Athenion was proclaimed king, and he also made sure to put a diadem on his head.

The new slave king also introduced a new policy paradigm, however. Instead of amassing as many slaves as possible for his army, he was very selective in his choices. He chose only the stronger and more capable to become good fighters, and told the others who were joining him in growing numbers to stay in their estates and continue working in agriculture, in order to provide his army with enough supplies. His claims were also indicative of his innovative political strategy. He claimed to have been informed by the gods through the stars that he would become the king of Sicily, so the farms and estates, with all the animals and plants, should be preserved and taken care of, since they would be part of his kingdom. This information demonstrates a conscious effort to establish a sustainable political entity, rather than engaging in continuous raids that plunder the countryside.

Athenion's rebellion continued to grow stronger, and soon he had a force of 10,000 men in arms, which led him to believe he could have a chance to conquer the city of Lilybaeum, thereby decisively upgrading the rebellion's level and his status as self-proclaimed slave king. However, the task was proven to be out of their reach for now, and Athenion had to withdraw his men back to the countryside. His political and religious acumen ensured that this unsuccessful attempt would not harm his charismatic image. He claimed that he withdrew not because his army could not capture the city, but because the gods had given him the order to do so. He added that if he hadn't withdrawn his men, the gods told him bad things were about to happen to the rebels.

Paradoxically, that failure and an additional misfortune worked in Athenion's favour and further enhanced his movement's momentum. After he began to retreat his forces from Lilybaeum, several auxiliary troops, made up of Mauritanians, arrived at Lilybaeum from North Africa. Diodorus does not explain whether that force was dispatched by the central Roman authorities in Sicily or by those of the city itself, given its North African Carthaginian origins. The fact is that the Mauritanian troops, led by a man named Gomon, launched a surprise night attack and inflicted considerable casualties on the rebels as they were retreating from Lilybaeum. After that surprise attack, the Mauritanian auxiliary forces returned to the city. Even though the operation had, in fact, failed and resulted in the loss of more men, it increased Athenion's credibility and charisma: the rebels and many other slaves in the region considered the event as further proof that he was a real oracle.

The siege had indeed brought misfortune to the insurgents, and thankfully, prompted by the stars, Athenion had managed to pull them out quickly.[39]

Diodorus concludes the first version of his account for the Second Servile War, pointing out the enormous scale of disaster brought to Sicily by the slave rebellions that erupted in that period.[40] The two massive uprisings of Salvius and Athenion were accompanied by a large number of other groups that committed brigandage and raids, and the frenzy was such that not only slaves participated in them but also freedmen. Murders of both slaves and free, robberies, and generalised lawlessness and violence reigned supreme in Sicily. Many people suffered throughout the large Mediterranean island, and the urban populations reached the point of considering their properties in the countryside totally lost, as they remained closed behind the cities' walls to avoid being attacked. Diodorus depicts a very negative image of the insurgents at this point, saying that they killed everyone they met during their criminal activities, to leave no witnesses for their other crimes.[41]

After the siege of Morgantina, Salvius plundered the countryside up to the area of the city of Leontini. There, he gathered his forces, and what was formed was an army of over 30,000 armed men. With his full troops around him, Salvius made a sacrifice to the Palici, dedicating one of his royal robes. It was then that he was proclaimed King Tryphon by the rebel slaves.[42] Tryphon's next goal was the conquest of the city of Triokala. Diodorus writes that the king of the slaves sent a letter to Athenion and summoned him as a king would have summoned his general. People then thought that the leader of the second slaves' uprising would have reacted by declaring his independence and sovereignty, and that a conflict would have erupted between the two slave armies.

However, that didn't happen. Athenion accepted the leadership of Tryphon and met him at Triokala with 3,000 men of his own, where Tryphon had marched with his entire army. Athenion behaved towards Tryphon as if the latter were a true king, while the rest of his forces were looting and devastating the countryside, recruiting in parallel as many more slaves as they could for the rebels' army.

Yet, the doubters perhaps weren't so mistaken after all. Or at least, Tryphon thought this way. Suspecting that Athenion appeared loyal while in reality he was plotting to overthrow him after some time and put himself in charge of the slave kingdom, Tryphon had Athenion arrested and placed in custody.

Meanwhile, he made improvements to the Triokala fortress and had stately buildings such as a palace erected inside the city to serve as the residence of King Tryphon, making the city more elegant and suitable for a kingdom capital. He also built an agora (market and public gathering place) that could accommodate a large number of people.

The name Triokala means 'Three Goods' in Greek, and Diodorus explains that people thought that the name came from three good things the location and the city had: one, springs of excellent sweet water; two, fertile fields around it, with vineyards and olive groves; three, high rocky terrain, which provided formidable natural fortifications, making it a powerful defensive position. Tryphon added a perimeter wall that was 8 stadia in length (around 1.5 kilometres), with a long, deep ditch. The city was secure and prosperous, with a wide variety of goods. Tryphon acted and also dressed up like a real king. He worked wearing a toga and a large chiton, and appointed advisers who formed a royal council under him. Moreover, he had lictors with rods and axes walking ahead of him when he went out in public, similarly to the Roman consuls and praetors.[43]

The Romans reacted to these developments by sending a powerful army of 17,000 men to Sicily, led by the praetor Lucius Licinius Lucullus (father of his famous namesake), who was appointed as the new prefect of Sicily in place of Nerva in 103 BCE.[44] We have a detailed account of these forces, and it's helpful to mention the list of the people involved. As mentioned by Diodorus, Lucullus' army consisted of 14,000 Romans and Italians, 800 Bithynians, Thessalians and Acarnanians, 600 Lucanians, and 600 from various other places. The first thing one can notice is that there is a mistake in the numbers, as the list adds up to 16,000, not 17,000, which is the total number Diodorus refers to. Therefore, either the total number is incorrect, or one or more numbers in the detailed list is wrong. But that's a secondary detail.

What's more interesting in this list is the ethnicities mentioned, as we can see that there were soldiers from Asia Minor, the Greek peninsula and the Italian peninsula. Even more intriguing, Diodorus mentions 'Lucanians' as if they were something different from 'Italians'. Naturally, it could be a typo in the version that came to us, like the one concerning the numbers, or a simplistic description, where the author mentions numbers and ethnicities without specifying that he is referring to different military units composed of soldiers of the mentioned tribes or ethnicities. Possibly one of the units was formed exclusively by Lucanians, while the other 'Italians', could be made of Italian Greeks, Samnites, Peucetians and other peoples of Italy. The Greeks from Thessaly and Acarnania, along with the Bithynians, evidently formed a single international unit. However, this presentation poses again the question I've briefly revisited earlier, about the terminology used by Diodorus and other ancient historians of a very different world than those familiar to us, dominated by what we call Hellenistic culture, i.e. the Greek culture combined with almost everything else in the Eastern Mediterranean and Western Asia, during the early phases of Roman political dominance. Indeed, Diodorus does not write 'Greeks' but 'Thessalians', 'Acarnanians' and 'Bithynians', and throughout his books, he insists on mentioning the precise local origin, or, as we'd call it, the nationality, of the various Hellenic and Hellenistic peoples he mentions, including the Greeks of Italy and Sicily.

The Lucanians were led by Cleptius, whom Diodorus praises as an expert general who was known for his valour. On the other side, Tryphon apparently started feeling the absence of Athenion's military skills. When the army of Lucullus entered Sicily, understanding that there was a big threat, much greater than the previous ones or the one posed by the supposed plot against him, Tryphon finally released Athenion. The slave king sought Athenion's advice on how to address the situation with the impending Roman intervention. Moreover, hearing him, Tryphon even changed his opinion on what to do. Initially, his view was that they should stay fortified inside Triokala and there expect the Roman army. On the contrary, Athenion thought that the rebels should campaign and engage the Romans in open field, fighting them in a pitched battle, instead of permitting them to trap and block them in a siege. Tryphon accepted Athenion's advice and the slave army, which now numbered at least 40,000 men, marched towards the Roman camp. When they reached the location called Scirthaea, which was 12 stadia from the Roman camp, the rebels encamped.

For a few days, the two armies engaged in light skirmishes. Eventually, they fought a massive battle, where they employed their full potential, and the Roman forces achieved a great victory. Athenion fought valiantly alongside 200 horsemen, covering the ground with dead enemies, as Diodorus writes. However, he was wounded in both his knees, and then got another wound, ending up nearly killed. He had to lie on the ground like he was dead until night came, before he could finally escape the battlefield and return to Triokala. Many other rebels were not so fortunate. The slave army broke down into pieces and fled to Triokala, but roughly half of them, around 20,000, never made it there. Tryphon and the remaining rebel slaves were in great part saved by the night, even though Lucullus could have easily eliminated them, too, if he had pushed the pursuit with insistence, says Diodorus.

Following the heavy defeat of the rebels at Scirthaea, the mood in the slave army darkened. Many of the insurgent slaves, frightened by the magnitude of the Roman assault and the heavy losses they had suffered, began to think about surrendering. Diodorus mentions that there was even an open proposal among the rebels to lay down their arms and submit entirely to their former masters to save their lives. Yet, the majority decided to keep fighting and defend themselves, as surrendering would have meant facing the vengeance of their enemies. Whether out of pride, desperation or belief in their cause, the rebellious slaves resolved to continue to fight. Right after that, they probably began an intense effort to further fortify Triokala as they understood that the Romans would have turned their gaze towards that central city of the rebellion after their victory in open battle.

Lucullus, confident after his victory, indeed marched his troops towards Triokala and attempted to capture the mountainous city before the rebels could regroup and strengthen their defences. However, the slave army, despite its losses, had regrouped behind formidable walls and took advantage of Triokala's exceptional natural defences. Salvius had transformed the city into a functioning capital of his slave Hellenistic kingdom, which included a palace, an agora and trenchworks.

Lucullus arrived with his forces in front of Triokala and laid siege to the fortress city nine days later. However, he soon found that the means at his disposal were not sufficient to reduce it. Diodorus does not list any substantial actions taken during this phase, but he does write that both sides had considerable casualties. So, Lucullus lifted the siege and retreated.

The slaves' spirit was rejuvenated. On the contrary, back in Rome they thought Lucullus' failure to end the war unjustifiable, and when he returned to the city, they put him on trial. Diodorus states that Lucullus neglected his duty either due to laziness and negligence or because he accepted bribes.[45] We can imagine that to his contemporary fellow citizens, that choice of Lucullus was nothing short of scandalous. A Roman general, fresh from a major victory and in command of a powerful expeditionary force, had failed to capitalise on his advantage while fighting against slaves. He instead abandoned the campaign without capturing a rebel leader or conquering the enemy's key stronghold.

The Rise of Athenion and the Roman Demise

In 102 BCE, Salvius died and was succeeded as king by Athenion.[46] The death of Salvius marked a turning point in the leadership of the rebellion. In a similar movement, born out of desperation and resentment rather than a vision and a plan, the demise of a charismatic founder can trigger infighting, fragmentation or dissolution. However, in this case, Salvius' death seems to have cleared the path for the rise of a more forceful and ruthless figure, who created further problems for the Romans and the Sicilians. Once crowned as the new king, Athenion, the astrologer and slave administrator from Cilicia, who had already proven his battlefield prowess and prophetic authority, took on the war and also expanded the slave kingdom.

Florus mentions that Athenion was a herdsman who had murdered his master and freed the other slaves his master owned in his barracks. The Roman historian adds that Athenion organised them in military units, which implies that he had served in an army or had military knowledge. Then, Athenion adopted all the royal symbols he could, just like Salvius before him, wearing a purple robe, putting a crown on his head, and even holding a silver sceptre.

Florus also states that the army that Athenion had at his disposal was as large as the previous one held by Salvius, but his approach as a commander was more savage. He conducted the operations with more aggression, and Florus underlines that Athenion applied more violence and released rage against loyal slaves even more than he did against their masters. In his view, the slaves who didn't join the rebellion but remained faithful to their households and cities were traitors.[47]

On the other side, Gaius Servilius was appointed as governor of Sicily by the Romans. However, he brought even worse results than Lucullus had, as he failed to strike any substantial blow against the slave forces, which continued to control the interior of the island.

He could have claimed that his predecessor was a significant factor in his failure, even though his fellow citizens did not seem to accept similar excuses. Yet, it was true that if the failure to take Triokala had tarnished Lucullus' record as a commander, what followed offered a very negative image of him in a moral sense. We can say that it also reveals just how somewhat fractured, petty and self-serving the Roman response to the slave war was up until that point.

Indeed, when the Senate finally recalled Lucullus and appointed Gaius Servilius as the new governor of Sicily to continue the war against the rebellious slaves, it is reasonable to assume that the natural expectation was that the transition would be smooth. However, Lucullus not only did not help his replacement, but he also intentionally did everything he could to make his work more difficult. Either out of resentment or a cynical calculation to see his successor fail in order not to appear as the failed one, or probably both, Lucullus, according to Diodorus, dismantled the entire military apparatus he had built in Sicily, making sure that Servilius would find nothing of it.[48] Lucullus disbanded his forces, burned the palisades and siegeworks that had surrounded Triokala, and destroyed supply caches, fortifications and tools of war, ensuring that nothing of value would be left for Servilius to inherit. We could accurately say that he sabotaged the Roman war effort and delivered a gift to the rebels, who now had respite from renewed pressure and time to regroup.

This act of political spite prompts us to reflect on how deeply the rot had set in among segments of the Roman elite during that period for a senator and commander of a Roman army to prioritise personal vengeance over public duty. Hoping to show that any failure in Sicily was not his fault, but rather that of his successor and the Senate for removing him, he didn't hesitate to gamble with the lives of thousands of citizens and allies, and to prolong a war that perhaps could have ended sooner.

Lucullus' treacherous actions were successful, as Servilius accomplished nothing of note and was soon recalled to Rome. However, Lucullus ended up gaining nothing, except for damaging Servilius' career as well, as both of them were equally prosecuted for incompetence, and banished from Roman politics and history. Without resources and the groundwork laid by his predecessor, Servilius was thrust into a hostile countryside ravaged by rebels and bandits and controlled by the capable leadership of Athenion. Not only did the Romans fail to put the situation under control, but, on the contrary, Athenion expanded his domination over more areas of Sicily, devastating the countryside and putting pressure on cities, even making a daring attack against Messene, and it was not long before he captured it. According to Cassius Dio, the people of Messene did not expect to be the target of an attack. However, Athenion and his bandits, learning that a large public festival would be held in a suburb and the Messenians would be unprepared for battle, launched a surprise assault and killed many of them as they fled back to the city. Athenion and his men couldn't conquer the city itself, but they fortified Makella, a strong position, and using it as their fortress, they plundered Messene's countryside in the following period, using a lot of violence.[49]

The episode is helpful to modern historians, not just as a footnote, but as a good example of the broader decadence of later Republican politics in Roman history. It seems that by that point, the Republic could raise armies and provincial governors, but it could not guarantee loyalty to the cause. A magistrate could see a war like the one going on in Sicily not primarily as a Roman war, but as a field for their rivalries and ambitions.

On the other hand, one could object that that had always been the case and always is, under every possible political structure, as personal success and failure is paramount for every person, and being the loser in a winning side sometimes could even be worse for your personal survival and well-being than being the loser in a losing side, let alone being a winner. Yet, the institutions exist to channel normal emotions of competition, resentment and vengeance into something positive, or at least not destructive for the community. In this sense, Lucullus' behaviour towards Servilius and Rome is an example for the demise of the Republic's functionality. Apart from personal ambitions and competition, similar events demonstrate the central problem of institutions created to serve a very different and much more limited reality than the one that existed during the second century BCE. Institutions formed to administer the city-state of Rome found themselves in the position of governing an empire with vast geographical dimensions and cultural diversity. While a praetor used to act within range of the direct gaze and surveillance of other officials and citizens, now the governors and generals were sent to distant regions where the influence of the Roman community was weaker, and self-interest could perhaps be the only factor in decision-making. In this sense, it was not just the slaves of Sicily who had risen against the Roman order. The Roman elite, too, had begun to undermine itself from within, as the Republic's institutions were no longer always suitable for channelling personal considerations into actions that would benefit the state as a whole. That's the elemental prism, in my view, through which we should study the century of the crisis of the Republic, and the rise of the imperial structure behind Julius Caesar and Augustus to respond to the new conditions.

Roman Victory, Yet Again

By the end of the year, the Roman leadership was furious with Servilius, who attempted to justify himself by blaming the failure on his predecessor and the situation he had inherited. However, as mentioned, the excuses did not save Servilius, who, in turn, ended up in exile, paying for his inability to put down the rebellion. After the failures of the provincial governors, the Senate decided to entrust the conduct of the war in Sicily to the consul Manius Aquilius.[50]

Meanwhile, despite the failure to put down the rebellion in Sicily, the year we call 102 BCE had not gone poorly for Rome. On the central war front of the moment, that of the north, Marius had scored a major victory over the Teutons in the Aquae Sextiae (Aix-en-Provence) in what is now southern France, eliminating the threat they posed to Italy. Then, in the summer of 101 BCE, Marius' legions also annihilated the Cimbrians at Vercello (modern-day Vercelli in Piedmont).

Freed from the needs of the war against the barbarians of the north, the Romans were now at liberty to move powerful and elite forces to Sicily to fight against the rebellious slaves, probably putting them at the disposal of the governor Aquilius. A short time later, the Roman troops achieved two crushing victories over the slave army. According to Florus, Manius Aquilius[51] followed a clever strategy of blockage and cutting off the rebel army's supplies, weakening them and bringing them close to starvation. Athenion had forced Roman forces led by praetors to retreat and captured the camps of Lucullus and Servilius, but he had no answer for the advanced strategy and manoeuvres. After that, destroying the slave army was much easier for the Romans. Florus mentions that in adopting this strategy, Aquilius had followed the successful example of a certain Perperna.[52]

Athenion, apparently in desperation, according to Diodorus challenged Aquilius to a duel. Aquilius, although in a highly advantageous tactical position, accepted the challenge to a duel and prevailed over his opponent, fighting like a hero, as Diodorus writes, killing Athenion. Aquilius was wounded, too, on the head, but he survived the blow and recovered.[53]

The story of the duel seems way too Homeric not to raise some doubts about its historical accuracy. Nevertheless, what's certain is that Aquilius and his troops won the war against Athenion, and after that, they marched to engage with the last remaining rebels, who by then were 10,000 men. Understanding that the rebellion had been substantially crushed and that they were in a desperate position, the rebel slaves retreated and avoided another pitched battle against the Romans. However, they couldn't go far enough. In the following year, the Roman forces in Sicily pursued and exterminated the remnants of the slave army, which had sought refuge in mountainous and fortified locations. We can imagine that rebel strongholds were dismantled, their forces broken, their commanders either dead or in flight. In the final months of the war, scattered groups of surviving rebels were hunted through the hills, forced from caves and cliffs, dragged from remote valleys where they had taken refuge.

In the end, about 1,000 rebels were left under the leadership of Satyrus, which seems a very suitable name for a mountain rebel, and I assume it is a nickname rather than his real name.[54] Aquilius blocked and surrounded them with his troops, and then he proposed to surrender instead of insisting on fighting, as they were doomed. Satyrus and the rebels agreed to surrender, and Aquilius did not execute them but instead transported them as prisoners to Rome. However, if they had thought that by surrendering they would have a chance to survive by becoming slaves again, they soon found out that the Romans had different plans for people like them, i.e. criminals who had defied the Roman order. They put them in the arena to fight with wild animals and die there for the entertainment of the spectators. Diodorus praises the fact that, reportedly, they refused to participate in the show and, with nobleness of mind and gallantry, preferred to kill each other. Satyrus remained the last standing, and he too took his own life, with a heroic spirit, as Diodorus sees it.[55]

On the other hand, one could argue that the spectators might have been satisfied anyway, as the prisoners' actions could have made for an even more noteworthy show due to their unconventionality. Indeed, in the end, Rome and the Roman order had prevailed once more, and the criminals had been justly punished. That could be the way a Roman citizen would understand the event, as will become more evident in the following chapter.

On his part, Florus concludes his account of the Second Servile War giving a different version, according to which the slaves did not surrender because they knew what awaited them, and they preferred to kill themselves. The only one who fell into the hands of the Romans alive was, according to Florus, the leader of the slaves, whom he doesn't name at this point, making it dubious whether he meant Athenion, Satyrus or someone else. However, whoever he was, he was not executed formally either. Instead, the crowd tore him apart after his arrest.[56]

On the other side, Cicero records that the Romans rewarded Aquilius for his service and bravery, which ended victoriously the war against the slaves in Sicily, by absolving him of a previous conviction for several extortion cases.[57]

Legacy

Diodorus mentions that during the Second Slave War, not only slaves but also free men who did not own properties in the countryside were affected.[58] Watching the riots and looting going on in many places, these free men followed the example of the insurgent slaves and began robbing and ravaging the countryside. They stole herds of cattle, corn and crops, plundering estates and livestock in many towns and villages of Sicily. They were ruthless and without mercy, killing anyone who was in their way, to leave no witnesses to their previous crimes.

Anarchy reigned supreme in Sicily, as the lack of law and order imposed by Roman magistrates allowed a dramatic situation full of crime, impunity and violence. The most prominent and wealthy citizens especially fell victim to atrocious actions, robbery and abuse by slaves and freedmen bandits alike. Properties outside the cities were considered lost by their owners, and insecurity and fear prevailed even within the cities. The rebels controlled the countryside and thus the roads, making the situation challenging for the cities and their inhabitants. The slaves were prompted by profound hatred and rage for their masters, and Diodorus adds that they were not content with what they had unexpectedly achieved; they wanted more. Fear and terror had set in throughout Sicily, as even inside big fortified cities, people were uncertain about their slaves' intentions.[59]

Athenaeus mentions that, according to Posidonius, a slave revolt also occurred in Athens during the time of the Second Slave War in Sicily. Some slaves murdered the guards at the mines of Laurion, occupied the citadel at Sounion, where the large temple of Poseidon still stands today, and from there, they made raids in the countryside of Attica for some time afterwards. Athenaeus adds that there were also other slave revolts in that period, and that the total number of killed rebel slaves was in the hundreds of myriads, that is, more than a million, since 'myriad' stood for 10,000. Another piece of information provided by Athenaeus is that many Romans owned vast numbers of slaves, and often used their slaves to accompany them in order to demonstrate prestige. On the contrary, Athenaeus says that in Athens, slaves worked mainly in the mines, and there were myriads of them as well.[60] Moreover, Athenaeus cites a book now lost that narrated the complete history of the slave wars, written by Caecilius, an orator from the city of Kale Akte ('Good Coast' in Greek) or Kalakta (modern-day Caronia), in north-eastern Sicily.

Cicero mentions that, in reality, the king of the slaves during those years was not Athenion, but a certain Timarchides, who was a freedman of Verres, the Roman governor of Sicily. Athenion didn't manage to conquer a single town, claims Cicero, while Timarchides reigned supreme in all of them around Sicily.[61] Cicero claimed the above during the trial of Verres where he was the accuser lawyer, and likely tried to add to the accusations that even the slave revolt and the related havoc and destruction were related to Verres and his people, instead of the weak slaves. That becomes clearer in another part of this speech, where Cicero claims that the treatment Verres as governor gave to Sicily was worse than anything Athenion and his rebels could have done had they won the war.[62] The famous Roman lawyer and politician repeats similar accusations later in this speech, stating that nobody, neither Hasdrubal during the Punic Wars nor Athenion during the slave war, provoked the irreparable damage to the peasant farmers of Sicily that Verres caused during his tenure as governor.[63] On his part, Florus claims that Sicily was more devastated during the slave wars than during the Punic wars.[64]

In another speech, Cicero mentions that during the Second Servile War, Manius Aquilius made loans of cereal grain to Sicilian cities.[65] This meant that, due to the destruction caused by the war, Sicily needed aid from Rome, whereas it usually was Rome and Italy's biggest grain provider.

Nevertheless, the Second Servile War would be the last event of massive violence in Sicily for centuries. In the following decades the battleground would be mainland Italy, where first the Social War (90–87 BCE), the conflict between Sulla and Marius with his collaborators, and then the Third Servile War (73–71 BCE) would complete what I classified as the first part of the transformation century for Rome, before the major civil wars. On the contrary, Sicily would be prosperous and peaceful, having finally overcome the intense imbalances that had led to the two great slave wars. Cicero reports that during the Social War in Italy, Sicily was instead perfectly peaceful, because the measures taken and the organisation that followed the slave wars made the province much more functional and prosperous. Roman entrepreneurs were closely linked to the Sicilians, as they had common interests and collaborated on deals and plans. The Sicilians, on the other hand, were delighted with Roman rule, as they were protected from another slave war. The Roman governors' administration and the discipline imposed by the masters upon the slaves ensured that no more turmoil and disasters could erupt in Sicily.[66] Finally, again in the speech against Verres, Cicero reports that after the Second Servile War, all governors, including Aquilius, forbade the possession of weapons by slaves.[67] The surprising information for us from this excerpt is not that the slaves were banished from possessing weapons after the slave wars, but that they weren't in the first place.

Archaeological Evidence

A list of slingshot bullets discovered in Sicily dating from the Second Slave War provides us with fascinating evidence. The bullets were found in both the eastern and western parts of Sicily, around Enna and Panormus (modern-day Palermo). Moreover, they are from the sides of both the rebels and the Romans. The important fact is that the bullets have texts engraved on them, from which we can glean significant information. The texts are all in Greek. The bullets of the slaves mention either the commander or a god who is considered to have led the unit to victory. Those of the Roman troops name the tribe, the phatria, and the commander. What emerges is that the Roman troops were ethnically Greek, at least in the greater part. The slaves' bullets mention twice Athenion, one a certain 'Sos', who could be Salvius, and one mention of Tryphon, while the rest of them attribute the victories to Zeus Keraunos ('Thunder' in Greek), Heracles, and the goddesses Athena, Artemis, Kore (Persephone) and the 'Mother' or 'Mothers', i.e. Demetra, or Demetra and Persephone.

As for the Roman troops' bullets, they are a typical example of the formal classification of the Greek city-states. They mention the tribe, the phratria, and the name of the unit's commander. For instance, on the bullet number 2407.11 is written, 'Second Tribe. Phatria Altri. Philonas son of Eupolemos', and the unit was from the city of Catana. The decoration of the bullet depicts a man on bended knee, who has a helmet on his left and a shield on his right. On another bullet, number 2407.13, is written, 'Second Tribe. Patria Lakyn. Agelaos son of Pyrrhia', from the city of Bronte, in the north-east of Enna.[68]

The salient point is that not only were Roman units composed of ethnic Sicilian Greeks, but also that their organisation and identifying references were precisely the same as those of the Greek states before the rise of Roman rule. This is another piece of evidence to support what I mentioned in Chapter 1: that behind terms such as 'Italians', 'Sicilians', 'Syrians' or even 'Romans', we often have Greek, Hellenistic or Hellenised peoples. That's a crucial aspect of the Hellenistic and Roman era, which modern historians sometimes neglect to explain to their readers – or they perhaps don't understand it themselves.

Another interesting archaeological discovery is a coin that commemorates the victory of Manius Aquilius in the Second Slave War. The coin was issued many decades later, in 18 BCE, and portrays Aquilius, armed, supporting a female figure representing Sicily, after he had saved her from the savage slaves. The woman is on her knees, and Aquilius grabs her left arm, holding her from collapsing and trying to elevate her. On the other side, there is an image of Emperor Augustus, known as 'Caesar Augustus'. The coin was issued by moneyer Lucius Aquilius Florus, descendant of Manius Aquilius. However, it's not just to honour a glorious ancestor; it's instead a political statement: Lucius Aquilius Florus had sided with Antonius during the last civil war and with that coin, celebrating Emperor Augustus and reminding his glorious ancestry, he hoped to restore his status among the Roman elite, after being in an obviously marginal position after his party defeat thirteen years before at the Battle of Actium.[69]

Chapter 3

The Social War and Its Era

Less than a decade after the end of the Second Servile War in Sicily, a new major war was about to erupt, this time even closer to Rome, in mainland Italy. The Social War (90–87 BCE) was not a slave revolt but I chose to include a concise account of it in this book because it happened right between the end of the Second and the beginning of the Third Servile Wars, and, most importantly, because it reveals with particular clarity the fundamental issues of that era. Consisting of a massive rebellion of most of the Italian peoples, not against the dominion of Rome, but its negligence to accept them as citizens of the Roman Republic, the Social War reflects the big structural question posed by the expansion of Roman dominance. This intense contradiction between the new dimensions of Roman dominance and the old institutions of the Roman Republic is the profound underlying cause of the slave wars, which cannot be understood without broader historical context.

The Big Contradiction

At the beginning of the first century BCE, the international and interstate relations network under Roman rule was highly complex. Rome was the centre of a heterogeneous and shifting web, consisting of provinces and cities that Rome had conquered, others that had entered the Roman Federation voluntarily or by force to accept its rule, as well as 'client' states, formally independent but within the Roman sphere of influence. Apart from the official provinces, the territories belonging to the Federation could be legally designated as allies, colonies or municipalities (*municipia*).

On the Italian peninsula, each city was part of one of the three legal categories mentioned above. The rights of their citizens recognised by the Roman state varied from constitutions regarding Roman citizenship to vassals without political rights. The same was true of their political institutions. In many cases, they retained full autonomy, continuing their previous social and political institutions and government methods within the Roman authority framework. In other cases, there was stricter supervision of political processes and functions with the direct presence of Roman representatives, and there were cases where internal public administration was carried out primarily directly by Roman officials.[1]

However, the Italian allies of Rome felt resentment for having contributed enormously to the rise of Roman power, through their massive participation in the Roman army with the *alae sociorum*,[2] yet were progressively marginalised instead of being accepted as equal citizens of the Republic. Velleius Paterculus admits that the Italians were perfectly right to feel rage, as they had contributed more soldiers than the Romans had for every Roman war, yet they were not accepted as citizens.[3]

The aristocracies of the respective Italian tribes and cities were exerting increasing pressure on the Roman leaders, wishing to share in the power of what they now perceived as a single political entity. Several members of the Italian aristocracies, especially Etruscans and Umbrians, were perfectly integrated on an economic level with the Roman landowners and the latifundium economy, and they enjoyed an indirect political influence, since their financial power and contacts with Roman aristocrats allowed their voices to be heard. However, they wanted their participation to become direct and official. At the same time, the people wanted to acquire Roman citizenship so that they could have access to the associated privileges. By the beginning of the first century BCE, the demands of the Italians had become imperative.[4]

In the ranks of the Roman elite, strong inclinations had long been flourishing that viewed positively such an opening to the Italians, including the granting of Roman citizenship to them, and therefore the right to participate actively in the political life of Rome. On the other hand, equally strong sections of the Senate were against that prospect.

The Attempted Reform of Drusus

On 10 December 92 BCE, a wealthy aristocrat, Marcus Livius Drusus, took office as tribune of the plebeian council.[5] Young and enthusiastic, he soon put forward an ambitious reform plan, which envisaged changes in many areas, intending to revitalise Roman society and the political system.

First, he prepared a restructuring of the judiciary, intending to curb the prefects' economic arbitrariness and predatory practices, which endangered the cohesion of the Roman Federation. Drusus' plan also provided for new land distributions and increased benefits for the poorer citizens.[6]

Drusus had the support of the people, similarly to what had happened with the Gracchi a few decades earlier. Moreover, a large part of the Roman aristocracy, of which Drusus was a prominent member, supported his plan. Some of them had realised that the Roman political and social system needed reform if it was to remain prosperous rather than fall into crisis and decline, as the expansion of the Roman state's dominance was so significant that the old traditional institutions were no longer sufficient. For others, reducing the judicial power of the knights was already enough reason to support Drusus' plan.

However, other parts of the Roman aristocracy firmly opposed the reform, as they had done with the Gracchi, rejecting every notion of land redistribution. Most importantly, the knights, the equestrian class, were largely against him. Drusus had attempted to make the reform appealing to them by proposing that the Senate be expanded and that knights be accepted for the first time. Yet, the majority of them preferred to maintain the judicial power rather than have the chance to become senators. Even though they would have been given direct access to the Senate for the first time, most of them opposed the reforms because this would have deprived them of exclusive judicial control, which for them was an essential source of wealth, as the knights used to exploit the provinces in collaboration with the governors they were supposed to control.[7]

Drusus' initial support, which relied on the backing of the Senate and the people, began to fade away. As he developed the plan for reform, more landowners turned against him. This included not only the wealthy Roman senators but also the large landowners of the Italian tribes, especially Etruscans and Umbrians,[8] who further obstructed his efforts using their indirect political power. Seeing his coalition unravel, Drusus decided to play the citizenship card, hoping that the powerful Italian landowners would support him and pressure their Roman contacts in the Senate.

However, he hadn't anticipated that his choice would further damage his grasp on coalition back in Rome. The prospect of granting citizenship to Italians was met with considerable resistance from Rome's lower social classes, who viewed Roman citizenship as a privilege granted exclusively by the state to them, not to other Italian peoples and tribes. The dispute had a precise economic dimension. Already in the previous century, the Roman state provided the free distribution of wheat and allocation of land for cultivation to the poorer Roman citizens. The eventual granting of citizenship to the other Italians would have included the poorer classes of their own among the beneficiaries of these privileges, reducing the quantities and the land allocated to the poorer Roman classes, something that the latter could not accept.

Thus, in trying to gain the support of the Italians, Drusus ended up alienating much of the Roman populace.[9] His position grew weaker as his proposals provoked intense opposition across all social strata, threatening entrenched interests. On the other side, his plan gave incentives to citizens of all classes, creating two rival coalitions that were not class-based, as he had supporters and opponents in all of them. It's an interesting and useful case in political history, as it presents clearly two crucial points: first, that political struggles tend to be between coalitions that cut vertically the social classes and not between allegedly homogenous and compact classes, and second, people are inclined to care more about maintaining their position and privileges than be open to new possibilities that include uncertainty and risk.

Drusus won a significant victory, finding a way to pass the laws for agrarian and judicial reform, and began promoting the next reform, which was about giving Roman citizenship to the Italians. With the majority of the poor populace against him, he faced the attack of the consul Lucius Marcius Philippus. The consul presented as a threat the forthcoming proposed law granting Roman citizenship to the Italians, implying a conspiracy by the tribune with powerful Italian actors to undermine the Roman constitutional order. He further argued that the laws Drusus had managed to pass should also be declared illegal by the Senate as violating Roman law and, therefore, invalid. On top of that, Drusus was very unfortunate, as one of his major allies, the great orator Lucius Licinius Crassus, suddenly died of natural causes in September 91 BCE.

The unstinting support of the Italians and the discontent of the majority of the Roman people towards Drusus enabled his opponents to question his patriotism, accusing him of not serving the interests of Rome; thus, after fierce clashes in the Senate, his position was weakened.

Eventually, in an erratic and intensely divisive atmosphere, with incidents between supporters of the two factions, Drusus was murdered. His assassin was never arrested, nor were the masterminds of the murder ever known, although suspicion long weighed on Lucius Marcius Philippus and other politicians extremely opposed to Drusus' plans.[10]

Acting with tremendous vigour, the anti-reform party had won this round. They had made clear that the radical changes that many in Roman politics and society sought would hardly be achieved without bloodshed.

Outbreak of the War

The death of Drusus in 91 BCE and the cancellation of his reforms was the final straw for the Italians, who were convinced that there was no chance of Rome accepting their request, and they began to prepare for war and to coordinate their efforts.[11]

The Senate sent ambassadors to various cities to ascertain their intentions and appease their spirits. The praetor Quintus Servilius, accompanied by his legate Phontius, was sent to Asculum (modern-day Ascoli Piceno). The Roman envoy perceived the hostile dispositions and preparations of the Italians, whom the citizens of Asculum and other Picentes were leading, and used harsh language in addressing the people, warning and threatening them. The crowd was enraged and murdered the Roman ambassador. Then occurred an indiscriminate massacre of all Roman citizens who happened to be in the area.[12] This horrible bloodbath was essentially the first act of a war that had for months already been decided and prepared.

Roman diplomatic missions to seven other Italian tribes also received hostile treatment. The Marsi, the Vestini, the Paeligni and the Marrucini in central Italy, and further south, the Samnites, the Hirpini and the Frentani were determined to join the war against Rome. Some non-Greek populations of Campania and Apulia did likewise shortly afterwards, and those of Lucania were generally in favour of rebellion. The Umbri and the Etruscans remained ambivalent, while the Italian Greeks, who enjoyed a generally very favourable treatment by Rome, remained indifferent towards the rebellion and stood with Rome.

The camp of the rebellious tribes stretched from the borders of Latium and Campania to the Adriatic, but it was not entirely compact. Settled geographically between the Picentes and the rest of the rebels, the Praetutii tribe, with their capital at Interamnia (modern-day Teramo), refused to participate in the war as they already had Roman citizenship, as did many Latin colonies and Latinised cities in the interior of the rebellious regions. There were also other cities and people of the rebellious tribes that preferred to abstain or even join Rome, such as Venafro and other cities of the Samnites, Pinna of the Vestini, and a few Hirpini.

Politically, the situation had now entered a new phase, as the assassination of Drusus and the failure of his successors to promote reforms radicalised the attitude and demands of the Italians. The latter were no longer demanding only to be accepted as equal Roman citizens but formally aimed to establish a new pan-Italian state, which would establish Rome as just a city among the rest. At the same time, extreme anti-Roman positions gained in popularity within the rebels' ranks. Consequently, the agreements between the Italian tribes were not limited to establishing a military and political alliance. On the contrary, they proceeded to establish a genuine confederation with a joint government, army and currency.

Due to its central geographical location, the newly formed Italian Confederation designated as its capital a hitherto unheralded city of the Paeligni, Corfinium, renaming it Italica, which would be the name of the new common currency too.[13] They chose this city also because of its small size and importance, as well as the fact that it did not belong to either of the two most powerful tribes (Samnites and Marsi), which ensured that it would be the seat of the Italian government without any possibility of becoming a hegemonic city.

Institutionally, the federation imitated the Roman political system, stipulating that the head of government would be determined by annual elections in which all citizens would participate and would consist of two subordinate heads of twelve praetors. At the same time, a central council of 500 members, equivalent to the Senate, would be formed. The difference was that there would be no popular assemblies with legislative power as in

Rome. In contrast, as the sole legislative body, the Italian Senate would be composed of elected representatives, not dignitaries who had served as high officials as in the Roman Senate.[14]

The Marsi Quintus Poppaedius Silo and the Samnite Gaius Papius Mutilus were elected as the first two supreme leaders of the newly founded federation. The Italians sent ambassadors to Rome, protesting that Rome refused to accept them as Roman citizens even though they had been instrumental in establishing its hegemony through their service in the Roman army, effectively trying to shift the responsibility for the outbreak of violence and war to the Roman leadership. The Senate responded that it would not accept any further dialogue and negotiation unless there was first a cessation of the rebellions and payment of compensation for what the Italians had committed against Roman citizens.[15] Then they announced the military recruitment. The two consuls, Publius Rutilius Lupus and Lucius Julius Caesar (a member of the famous house from which would descend Gaius Julius Caesar), were appointed as general commanders of the Roman armies on the northern and southern fronts of the war, respectively, each flanked by five commanders chosen from among the best officers of the Roman army.

Meanwhile, the internal political conflict in Rome continued unabated. Amid a climate of war, the tribune Quintus Varius Severus proposed the establishment of a special tribunal to hear cases of Romans who had encouraged the Italians to revolt and had collaborated with them. That was undoubtedly a blow against the majority of the senatorial aristocracy, which supported and promoted reformist ideas by the conservative senators and equestrians. The latter exploited the masses' anger, led and fomented by the skilled demagogue and populist Varius. On the other hand, some tribunes were allies of the senatorial aristocracy and were in favour of the reforms, which made the final decision and attitude of the plebeian council uncertain. For this reason, many armed equestrians surrounded the assembly on the day of the vote, effectively forcing the people to vote in favour of Varius' proposal, which they did.

The Senate remained calm and refrained from responding to this coup d'état with the *senatus consultum ultimum* (the ultimate decree of the Roman Senate), by which someone was declared an enemy of the constitution and the state.[16] They acted like this because many considered that a civil conflict would have significantly impaired the position of Rome at a time when it was on the brink of war and also because the coup plotters did not actually have the basis and power to hit the Senate.

Italian Rise: The First Phase of the War

The restraint of the Senate in the face of the challenge was justified since the war was predestined and, as it turned out, indeed one of the most difficult the Roman army had ever been called upon to fight. The opponents came largely from its innards, possessing and using the same equipment, organisation, and strategic and tactical knowledge, as thousands of soldiers and many officers of the Italian allied army had served in the Roman legions. Moreover, the numbers of the insurgent army were not at all inconsiderable. At the beginning of the conflict, the Italians assembled a force that reportedly totalled 121,000 men, with 110,000 infantry and 11,000 horsemen. The troops that the Romans opposed were of a similar number, except that they could count on hundreds of thousands of men who could be recruited very fast if the need arose, since, according to the surviving enumeration lists, the total Roman force on the eve of the Social War was 400,000 soldiers. The Roman side also had a unified and experienced leadership, more significant financial clout, and vast territories throughout the Mediterranean under its control, from which it could draw inexhaustible resources and military reinforcements.[17] These facts demonstrated Rome's clear long-term structural superiority, even if they did not guarantee immediate battlefield dominance.

The balance of power made it necessary for the Italian Confederation to conduct the war as quickly as possible if it wanted a realistic chance of victory. Therefore, the Italians' strategic objective was to achieve tangible and decisive results quickly before the giant Roman machine had time to mobilise a significant part of the resources and forces at its disposal, thanks to its vast provinces. For this reason, they decided to exert pressure directly against Rome. At the same time, they would attempt to seize its colonies and allied cities in the region of the Praetutii (Ager Praetutianus) and spread the insurrection to more parts of Italy.[18] The war began in the early months of 90 BCE.

The Romans, for their part, divided their troops into two sections. On the northern front, the consul Rutilius deployed his forces by blocking the road to Rome from the west at some point on the Valeria road, while in the south, the consul Lucian Julius Caesar deployed on the border between Samnium and Campania in defence of the allies and colonies loyal to him there.

Rutilius, while holding his defensive position, dispatched a portion of his forces under Gnaeus Pompeius Strabo (father of Pompey the Great) to march against Asculum, in which the flame of revolution had been kindled but was largely surrounded by lands loyal to Rome. After some initial Roman successes, the commander of the Italian troops in the area, Titus Lafrenius, attacked the Romans, forcing Pompeius to abandon the siege of Asculum and retreat northwards. The two armies clashed at the foot of Mount Falernus, near the banks of the river Tinna (modern-day Tenna). The negative outcome of the battle forced Pompeius to retreat even further north and fortify the Latin colony of Firmum Picenum, which Lafrenius and his forces besieged.

The success of Lafrenius resulted in the release of troops that had originally moved to reinforce the defence of Asculum, allowing them to move towards the Latin colony of Alba Fucens. Rutilius sent a force of 10,000 men to repel them near Lake Fucine. The Italians achieved a crushing victory, costing the Romans 4,000 men,[19] and began to lay siege to the city. Gaius Marius was sent to the area to regroup the remaining Roman forces. At the same time, Rutilius redeployed the bulk of the army, camping west of the Carseoli, in a strong position south of the river Tolenus (modern-day Turano), probably where the Via Valeria crossed it, about 60 kilometres from Rome.

Marius covered the northern flank while the Italian forces were wreaking havoc in the area and camped near him on the north bank of the Tolenus. The Roman general argued that his men should avoid reckless and hasty actions because the Italians soon would have had to retreat, as they had already advanced deep into enemy territory and were far from their supply centres. The consul Rutilius, however, had a different opinion and, wishing to crush the enemy forces immediately, ordered a surprise general attack, with the intention of moving his forces onto the opposite bank of the river during the night of 10/11 June 90 BCE. However, the commander of the confederate troops, Titus Vettius Scato, had been informed of his opponent's intentions in good time and had deployed his forces along the river bank at the point where the Romans were to cross. The Roman forces fell into the trap and suffered a heavy defeat, leaving behind them 8,000 dead, including many nobles and the consul Rutilius himself.[20]

Faced with the risk of being outflanked and suffering a similar blow to his forces, Marius ordered a hasty attack on the Italian camp, which was almost empty. He managed to take it by destroying the garrison. After this development, in the absence of supplies, Scato was forced to withdraw to the east, even being harassed by Roman units. However, Marius' success in rescuing the northern army from complete disintegration did not diminish the significance of the defeats of that first war period. The gruesome sight of the thousands of corpses of soldiers, officers and the subaltern himself caused so much sensation and alarm in Rome that the Senate ordered the dead be buried on the spot on the respective battlefields and not be carried into the city.[21]

The command of the northern army was jointly entrusted to Marius and the praetor Quintus Servilius Caepio, but the latter was killed in an ambush shortly afterwards. Marius in the west was blocking the road to Rome on the Via Valeria, while Pompeius was resisting the besieged Firmum Picenum. At the same time, on the southern front, the consul Caesar was blocking the Via Appia (Appian Way) in northern Campania and attempting to defend the Latin colony of Aesernia (modern-day Isernia), a Roman outpost in Samnite country, with some 26,000 soldiers at his disposal. Nevertheless, he was defeated by the forces of Vettius Scato in a battle in which the Romans lost 2,000 men. He was attacked by another Italian army from the west, under the Samnite Marius Egnatius, and suffered another major defeat near the river Volturnus (modern-day Volturno), with 8,000 Romans killed. The consul, who was also ill, retreated and fortified himself at Teano on the Via Latina (Latin Way), where, receiving reinforcements from Rome, he began to resist with determination.[22]

In the meantime, however, Aesernia was surrounded and, despite the brave resistance of its commander, Marcus Claudius Marcellus, shortly afterwards it surrendered for lack of food. Its conquest was essential for the rebellious Italians because of its strong fortification. Further south, Gaius Vidacilius had moved towards Apulia, capturing the Roman-allied city of Kanysion (modern-day Canosa) and the Latin colony of Venusia (modern-day Venosa), taking many Apulians with him. Also, Marcus Lamponius prevailed over the consul Publius Licinius Crassus in Lucania, even setting fire to the Roman camp. At the same time, the Italian consul Gaius Papius Mutilus stormed into southern Campania and conquered Nola, Stabiae, Surrentum (modern-day Sorrento), and Salernum (modern-day Salerno), joining the Samnite territories with those of Lucania. After these successes, he was repulsed by the Roman troops at Nuceria but then secured control of Pompeii and Heraclea and laid siege to Acerra, near Naples. Then the consul Caesar, reinforced with Gaul and Numidian horsemen, moved to help the besieged Acerra and prevailed over Papius Mutilus in a battle in which the confederate army lost 6,000 men.[23]

The city remained locked in a siege, so the victory of Caesar's Roman forces was not particularly significant. However, it gave the besieged a respite and, more importantly, provided a morale boost to Rome and the Roman army after the fear caused by the initial phase of the conflict.

Servius Sulpicius Galba, a former praetor, won a battle against the Marrucini and rushed to Firmum Picenum to reinforce Pompeius. The latter continued to resist the siege, having expanded his forces by recruiting local inhabitants. The two Roman armies attacked the besiegers in concert, crushing them and destroying their camp, in a conflict in which the Italian general Lafrenius died. The remnants of the confederate army fled to Asculum, which Pompeius again laid siege to.

These developments pleased the Roman Senate, which resumed its regular work. Marius, in coordinated action with Lucius Cornelius Sulla, then Caesar's second-in-command, defeated the Marrucini praetor of the Italians, Herius Asinius, in the mountainous region between Marsi and Samnite country, in a battle that left 6,000 Italians dead.[24] After that, and until the end of 90 BCE, the siege of Asculum intensified, while in the north, Marius was pushing an Italian army under Quintus Poppaedius Silo from Roman territory. At the same time, the army of the south was again pushing against the Samnites besieging Acerra.[25]

Lex Iulia

The war was beginning to take its toll on Italy. Both sides had suffered heavy blows and thousands of casualties, including political and military leaders. Thus, discussions started between the two sides, as in the case of a meeting between Marius and Poppaedius. Meanwhile, the internal political situation in Rome remained extremely tense and dramatic. The senatorial aristocracy had endured for some months the attacks launched by reactionaries and equestrians through the special court set up by Varius, with accusations and trials against several of its members, who were often sentenced to exile. However, gradually, the climate began to change. The recent successes on the war fronts and the partial restoration of order and normality had strengthened the authority of the Senate.

In contrast, certain excesses of Varius and his associates had put them at a disadvantage. Soon, the Senate would carry out its great counterattack, politically dismantling the faction of reactionaries and coup plotters, with Varius and other of its protagonists condemned and exiled. The forces of reform had finally prevailed, with the two newly elected subordinates siding with the aristocratic faction that Drusus had represented.

During the same period, Caesar, despite initial failures, returned to Rome victorious from the front and, convinced that the time had come for significant changes, submitted the historic law *Lex Iulia de Civitate Latinis Dunda*. It granted Roman citizenship to all communities in Italy that would apply for it and declare their loyalty to Rome, even if they had previously participated in the war against it.[26]

The reasons why the Romans finally decided to give citizenship to the Italians at that particular point are not clear. The ancient sources are ambivalent on the matter, with Appian being the only one who categorically states that the Roman Republic conceded to the Italians' request because it was in huge danger and almost panicked due to the military defeats. In his view, Rome conceded to save itself from the dangerous possibility of all of Italy uniting against it and perhaps leading it to complete defeat. From other ancient sources, such as Livy, Velleius Paterculus, Cicero, Plutarch and Diodorus, it is not clear what was the rationale behind *lex Iulia*. Among modern historians, Gaetano De Sanctis considers that the latest Roman victories before the law are the key to explaining this choice, as they restored the sense of control for Rome and especially the reformist wing of the Senate, which had been majoritarian since the beginning. Now, being again victorious and politically dominant at home and abroad, the reformist wing of the aristocracy had freedom of movement and a solid popular base to advance its plans. On the other side, Philip Matyszak doubles down on Appian's interpretation, claiming that the Romans were terrorised by the course of the war and the Italians' tenacity, and they substantially succumbed to their demand to avoid the worst. Moreover, by the spring of 89 BCE, the Etruscans and the Umbrians were close to joining the rebels, and offering them citizenship was an effective way to prevent such a crucial and dangerous development.[27]

What's certain is that the Roman Republic accepted the Italians' request, then demand, only after they revolted and also gained big military successes that caused fear amongst the Romans. Before that point, albeit a significant part of the Roman aristocracy, probably the majority, stood in favour of granting the Italians Roman citizenship, the opposition remained overwhelmingly prevalent in the Roman society, as we have seen. Thus, there is no doubt that the Italians earned the right to become Roman citizens on the battlefield, regardless of what the emotions and incentives were at the exact point of the vote for *lex Iulia*. Reform came not through the smooth adaptation of Roman institutions to expanding power, but only after violent crisis exposed the inadequacy of the old framework.

The new situation that emerged indeed decisively affected the course of the war, as not only did tribes and cities that were on the verge of joining the rebellion change their plans, but also many who had previously joined it abandoned the confederation and opted for the opportunity to obtain Roman citizenship. Most of the Italians felt that they had achieved their goal and that it had ceased to be a cause of war. Now, the desperate struggle against Rome was continued by those who had always been radically anti-Roman and those who had been radicalised in the previous period to the point where their acceptance by the Roman state as Roman citizens was no longer sufficient.

The Conclusion of the War

At the beginning of the second year of the war, Rome now had the initiative. Thanks to its vast resources, having constantly increased its forces since the beginning of the war, it now had a clear numerical superiority. The

Roman leadership decided that the time had come to strike a decisive blow. Therefore, they planned a major double attack on the northern front under the command of both subordinates. The southern forces were to hold the Roman positions and advance if given the opportunity. By attacking the north, the Romans intended to suppress Corfinium, since that location was the administrative centre of the confederacy, and to cut off the Sabellian tribes (Marsi, Marrucini and Vestini) from Asculum and the Samnites from central and northern Italy, ensuring that the rebellion would not spread to those regions.

In the winter of 90/89 BCE, Pompeius, with an army of perhaps 75,000 men, moved against Asculum. Vettius Scato confronted him with 60,000 men, reinforced by a body of Picentes who were defending the city. This great and decisive battle turned out to be a triumph for the Romans, who crushed the Italian army (18,000 dead on the field plus 4,000 from wounds, cold and hunger, and 3,000 prisoners).[28] Pompeius' legions then broke up another Italian corps of 15,000 soldiers in the area, supporting the besieged and trying to escape. Pompeius also attacked the Vestini tribe, recapturing Pinna and eventually forcing the Vestini to surrender for good. After these developments, the grip on Asculum, the city that had been the spark of the revolution, became tight.

On the other side of the Apennines, as the spring of 89 BCE approached, the consul Lucius Porcius Cato fought several battles with the Marsi forces, mainly near the northern shore of Lake Fucine, managing to advance the Roman positions but losing his life during an attack on a fortress. Except for this unfortunate loss, it was an exceptional period for Rome, as troops commanded by Pompeius subdued the mountain tribes of the Marrucini and Paeligni tribes and eventually captured Corfinium, the capital of the confederation. This event forced the Italians to move their capital to Bovianum (modern-day Bojano) in Samnium.[29]

Developments were not only positive in the north for the Romans but also in the south. There, the Roman legions under Sulla, Titus Didius and Gaius Cosconius, supported by a fleet from the sea, had recaptured Heraclea and Pompeii by May and had also destroyed Stabiae. On 11 June 89 BCE, the Roman army from the south clashed at the foot of Mount Vesuvius with the Samnite forces, whom Gallic mercenaries had reinforced. Initially, the Romans under Sulla drove the Samnites back – indeed, legate Titus Didius was killed in the battle. The Samnites redeployed at Nola, regrouped and fought back, but the new battle turned out disastrously for them. The Samnite troops were disbanded with 18,000 dead, including their commander, Lucius Cluentius,[30] and the Romans captured the Samnite camp and their permanent military base in the area.[31]

Sulla then placed Nola under siege and moved towards Samnium, the centre of the rebellion. The Roman leader invaded the land of the Hirpini and captured Aeclanum, Compsa and other cities, forcing the Hirpini to surrender. The blow had already been a great one to the confederation, but Sulla continued invading Samnium too, where he crushed the forces of General Papius Mutilus. The latter fled wounded with a few men to Aesernia, which was used as the new capital of the federation, as Sulla's legions marched unmolested towards Bovianum. The Samnites resisted stubbornly, but eventually, Bovianum fell. After that, Sulla preferred to consolidate and fortify his positions and return to Rome at the end of the autumn.[32]

General Cosconius also achieved significant successes for the Roman arms during the same period, always on the southern front. He captured the regions of the Frentani and invaded Apulia, where he destroyed crops and towns, before taking Cannae and establishing his forces there. Then, refuelling from the port of Brundisium, he moved against Canusium. This vital city would have given him control of a large part of Apulia, but he was forced to retreat after a fierce battle with a Samnite army, with many casualties on both sides. Eventually, Cosconius' forces prevailed over the Samnite army near the river Aufidus (modern-day Ofanto), inflicting losses of 15,000 men. The few surviving Samnites fled with their general, Trebatius, to Canusium. At the same time, the Roman forces under Aulus Gabinius were having success in Lucania, capturing towns and forts. However, even more important were the victories achieved by the Roman legions in the north, where the generals Lucius Cornelius Cinna and Quintus Caecilius Metellus Pius broke the Marsic resistance, forcing the rebellious tribe to surrender.[33]

The development of the war on the southern front also played a catalytic role in the outcome of the siege of Asculum, as there were not enough forces to send to reinforce the besieged. The Romans repulsed a desperate attempt by the Italians to send reinforcements, and eventually, the exhausted city surrendered. Rome made an example of those who had first dared to challenge its dominion, razing the city to the ground. They rebuilt it later as a Roman municipality. The victor Pompeius had his triumph in Rome on 25 December 89 BCE.[34]

At the beginning of the following year, in the south, Cosconius was replaced by Metellus Pius, who, in the following months, would continue to occupy the rest of Apulia. He achieved a series of victories for the Roman arms and eventually recaptured the important Latin colony of Venusia, restoring peace to the region. In the north, winter halted hostilities, and the Samnites were preparing for the last stand centred on the new capital of the confederation, Aesernia. The army was led by the Marsi general Poppaedius Silo, who had fled when his fellow citizens succumbed to the Romans. Poppaedius managed to assemble an army of reportedly 50,000 men, 20,000 of whom were slaves, and continued the war. At the same time, the Italians appealed for help to the king of Pontus, Mithridates VI Eupator, who had conquered Asia Minor, driving out the Romans. Mithridates replied that he had to first secure control of his new possessions before sending troops to Italy. In the end, of course, what was to happen was that very soon, Rome would almost simultaneously crush both of its adversaries, consolidating its dominance across the Mediterranean.

Poppaedius, with the new confederate army, achieved some successes and even recaptured Bovianum. Soon, however, even this desperate effort by the Samnites and Italians was suppressed by Roman power, as a Roman army, probably under the command of Sulpicius Galba, crushed the confederate forces inside Samnium, probably near the river Trinio (modern-day Trigno), in a battle in which Poppaedius himself died, as did another Italian leader, Obsidius. After these evolutions, the war was finally decided. The last resistance of the Samnites in Aesernia and Nola, under the suffocating siege of Sulla, would soon be broken, with Rome confirming its unchallenged and absolute domination of Italy.[35]

In 87 BCE, along with the conclusion of the Social War, the reform effort that had begun a few years earlier was completed in a way, with the Roman state granting citizenship also to the inhabitants of Cisalpine Gaul and the monopoly of the equestrians in the judiciary coming to an end. After that, the judiciary would also be able to include senators and plebeians.[36]

The Social War (or Italian/Marsic/Allies War) and the internal political conflict associated with it are often overshadowed by the subsequent civil wars that shook the world of that historical era. However, the Social War's importance is fundamental because it was the first time that a city with democratic and oligarchic political institutions moved from hegemony to the establishment of a political organisation that incorporated and acclaimed as equal citizens huge populations who previously were merely vassals.

What was required was tighter control over the governors of the provinces so that they would not completely plunder the latter for their own benefit. Instead, the governors would treat provinces as parts of the Roman territory, securing a tolerable standard of living for the people so that social peace and order would not be disturbed, as well as encouraging the integration of more populations into the Roman political entity. The extent of the Roman possessions was such that there could no longer be a monopoly of a minority in the political life of the dominant and central pole of this construction. Italy's inhabitants finally had to obtain the right to participate in a common identity if the construction was to become more solid and develop relations of legitimacy and identification with its components. The Social War was a crucial step towards this, even though the following years and decades would prove that the process was still far from complete.

The Rise of Sulla

At the end of the Social War, the Romans had prevailed but also finally acceded to give Roman citizenship to the Italian allies, both because much of the aristocracy had long supported such a position and because a major offensive by the king of Pontus, Mithridates, against the Roman provinces in Asia Minor and the Aegean had taken place at the same time.[37]

During the war in Italy, Gaius Marius had not shown the same dynamism and efficiency that had characterised him in the past, and he remained sluggish and indecisive. The result was to diminish his prestige while increasing that of Sulla, who was the main protagonist of the war. Capitalising on his success, Sulla was elected consul for the year 88 BCE.[38] However, ambition and the thirst for power had not left Marius, although he was now also facing health problems. In the war for the recovery of the eastern provinces that was about

Relief depicting a Roman harvesting tool, found in Trieste, Italy.

Monument to Eunus at the Castello di Lombardia, in Enna, Sicily.

Roman lighthouse known as the 'Tower of Hercules', located in Galicia, Spain.

Roman coin minted in 109–108 BCE, displayed at Palazzo Blu, Pisa.

Coin issued by the Italian Confederation during the Social War, in which the Samnites played a leading role.

One of the best-preserved Roman temples, located in Nîmes, France.

Roman pool. Similar structures were found in aristocratic villas throughout the Roman world.

Detail from a Roman mosaic showing a master about to strike his slave with a rod. From the Villa del Casale, Sicily.

Slaves working in a mine. Corinth, fifth century BCE.

Roman mosaic from the second century CE depicting rural life. Discovered in Saint-Romain-en-Gal, France.

Roman mosaic from the second century CE illustrating scenes of rural life. Found in Saint-Romain-en-Gal, France.

Mosaic from the fifth century CE, discovered in the Great Palace of Constantinople, depicting two gladiators fighting a tiger.

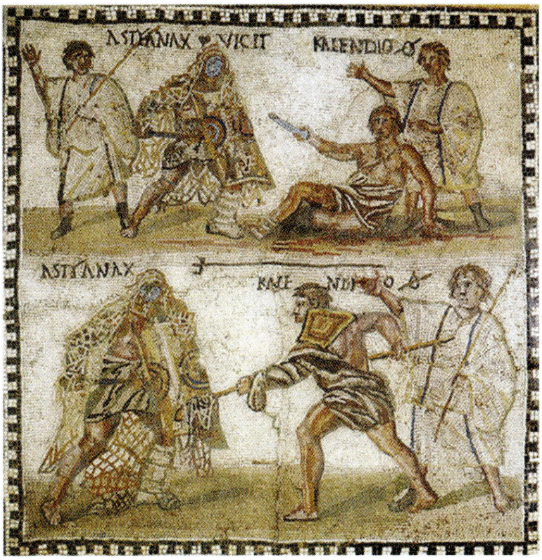

Roman mosaic depicting two scenes of a gladiatorial fight, under the gaze of the judges. On display at the Archaeological Museum of Madrid.

Mural showing a fight between gladiators. From Villa Nennig, Germany.

Fresco from Pompeii depicting the famous riot that occurred in the city's amphitheatre and surrounding streets during Nero's reign, involving fans from Pompeii and Nuceria.

The ancient amphitheatre of Capua.

Street in ancient Pompeii, preserved as it appears today.

Mosaic from the third century CE, found in a private house in Curium, Cyprus, depicting two gladiators and a referee, with their names inscribed in Greek.

Statue of Spartacus at the Louvre, created by French sculptor Denis Foyatier in 1830.

Ancient Roman temple dedicated to Bacchus in Baalbek, Lebanon. Dionysian worship remained relatively distinct from the official religion of Rome and the Greek cities.

Detail from the 'Mosaic of the Gladiator' (*c.* 320 CE), Villa Borghese, Rome.

Relief depicting Roman legionaries from the time of Emperor Trajan.

The impressive Roman aqueduct Pont du Gard, spanning the Gardon River in southern France. One of the best-preserved Roman aqueducts.

The Roman bridge over the Tagus River at Alcántara, Spain – an enduring example of Roman engineering and provincial development.

to begin, the 70-year-old leader saw an opportunity to restore his reputation and regain control of the political situation. But in the office of the consul was Sulla, and so he assumed the leadership of the campaign in Asia Minor.

The marginalised Marius, seeking an ally to help him return to the limelight, allied himself with the tribune Sulpicius.[39] The latter was trying to emerge as a spokesman and defender of the Italians to strengthen his political position,[40] and was supported by many Roman horsemen, who were the second upper class of Roman society after the aristocrats. He had also assembled a corps of 3,000 armed men, who used intimidation and violence to his advantage, as mentioned by Plutarch, while Livy, Appian and Dio Cassius mention the extended violence that characterised Sulpicius' tribunate.[41]

Sulla was preparing to depart for the East, but Sulpicius proposed that the chieftaincy of the war be put to a vote, arguing that the position should be given to Marius.[42] Sulla returned to Rome to respond to the machinations of Sulpicius and Marius, but the former mobilised the underground network of armed men he had created, resulting in great unrest and violence. Faced with this situation, the Senate lost patience, and Sulla hurriedly returned to his troops. Understanding that the climate in Rome no longer favoured politicians who were not accompanied by a sufficient number of armed men, he marched with a portion of his forces towards the capital.[43] This was an unprecedented coup d'état in the annals of Roman politics, but an equally unprecedented terrorism had been Sulpicius' previous attitude.

Marius fled Rome and later ended up in Africa. At the same time, Sulpicius was arrested and executed by Sulla's forces. The preceding clashes caused many deaths and destruction in the city.[44] Sulla then repealed all the laws passed by Sulpicius and departed for Asia Minor with his entire army, just as planned before the intervening riots. However, it was certain that on his departure, his political rivals would seize power in Rome. He did so because his soldiers had supported him precisely on the condition that they would go off and fight against Mithridates, winning spoils and lots of land after victory. Additionally, the reconquest of Asia Minor and the Greek cities that had sided with Mithridates would bring him glory, wealth and prestige, thereby strengthening his position in the Roman political scene.

After Sulla's departure, Marius returned to Italy and allied himself with the aristocrat Cinna, who had also distinguished himself as a general during the Social War. They marched in turn with military forces to Rome.[45] After seizing power, they carried out persecutions and executions against Sulla's supporters, including senators.[46] Quintus and Marius then held elections, in which they were, of course, elected consuls for 86 BCE. However, Marius died a month after assuming the seventh consulship of his career.[47]

In the following years, Sulla conducted the difficult war against Mithridates, while Cinna, despite his efforts, failed to consolidate his power in Rome, as he was stopped by soldiers and executed in 84 BCE.[48] It is noteworthy that Cinna had tried to mobilise slaves in his favour, but they remained indifferent.[49] Essentially, the same had previously happened to Marius, when he tried to mobilise slaves during the clashes against Sulla's supporters, but only three of them joined him.[50] In 82 BCE, having reconquered the eastern provinces, Sulla decided to land in Italy and march his troops back to Rome, where political forces hostile to him continued to rule.[51]

The two new consuls, Marius' son Gaius Marius the Younger, and Gnaeus Papirius Carbonus, tried to intercept him with troops largely composed of Samnites and Lucanians, but Sulla prevailed overwhelmingly and entered Rome. Mass persecution of opponents followed, and an even greater massacre than that previously committed by Marius and Cinna. Sulla carried out the infamous 'proscriptions', during which a total of 4,700 citizens, the majority of them wealthy, including dozens of senators, were executed.[52] Sulla then revived an antiquated institution, that of the dictator, which had formerly been provided for in very special cases of danger.[53] The dictator had extraordinary powers at his disposal, but his term of office was limited to six months. Sulla circumvented the latter provision, giving himself unlimited time to overcome the crisis. However, in the end, he did not stay in the position of dictator for long. After he ruled from that position for a year, he retired from politics and occupied his private estates in Campania.[54]

The fact that Sulla voluntarily left office when he was in complete control of the situation proves that his dictatorship was not aimed at perpetuating his own power but rather that he considered it necessary to normalise political life and carry out the reforms he believed were necessary. The latter were essentially an attempt to return to the older, classical Roman political system, with a stronger role for the Senate and a drastic weakening of the role of the tribunes.[55] It also weakened the role of the equestrian class, but doubled the number of senators, from 300 to 600, with new members coming from the equestrian class.

Apart from institutional reforms, Sulla carried out actions aimed at strengthening his political influence. First of all, he kept his promises. He offered his soldiers substantial tracts of land, distributing to them the estates of his executed political opponents, as well as lands belonging to Italian cities. A large number of veterans, probably numbering more than 100,000, received land lots from Sulla,[56] who, in this way, carried out, in a sense, by force what the *populares* had failed to achieve politically – namely, a redistribution of land. In addition, he freed 10,000 slaves, who belonged to people who had been prescripted, and named them Cornelius, after his family name.[57] Thus, this further increased the number of his followers as the freedmen received Roman citizenship.

However, Sulla's reform failed to consolidate, and by 77 BCE, the year he died, it had already become clear, following new armed conflicts in Italy, that the bloody political instability would not end. Also in the same year, the prefect of Spain, Quintus Sertorius, rebelled against the aristocratic government of Rome, with almost all the local Iberian element on his side.[58] Sertorius was a former officer of Sulla but a member of the lay party and a follower of Marius.[59] The Senate then sent more troops to Spain, with the 29-year-old Gnaeus Pompey as general,[60] who thus made his entrance into the historical limelight. The war against Sertorius proved complex and lengthy, and it would not end until 71 BCE.

It was in this historical context that the third great slave revolt in Roman history, led by the Thracian gladiator Spartacus, broke out in 73 BCE.

Chapter 4

The Third Servile War and Its Era

The revolt of Spartacus was to go down in history as the most famous of the three major slave revolts of Roman history. As will become clear in the following pages, this was not because the events that accompanied it were greater in absolute magnitude than those of the previous ones; it was quite the opposite. The first two slave wars attempted to create new states in Sicily, whereas the third did not even come close to being a similar scenario, remaining primarily a violent uprising marked by looting, plundering and disorder rather than by sustained state-building.

If we want to indentify an objective reason for which, nonetheless, this particular revolt ended up being more famous than the others, it would be that it took place not in Sicily, but in mainland Italy. The first two slave wars were rebellions that took place in a province, and the insurgents lacked the means to threaten the Roman heartland directly, as they had no fleet and Sicily remained at a considerable distance from Rome anyway. In contrast, the Spartacus rebellion originated in Capua, located near the border between Campania and Latium.

Besides this, the very lack of a broader political plan and aspiration makes the Spartacus revolt very comfortable for whatever ideological and propagandistic use one wants to assign to it, while that's not the case with the Hellenistic-style kingdoms that the two great Sicilian slave revolts attempted to establish.

Spartacus and the Rebellion

According to Appian, Spartacus had served in support units of the Roman army,[1] among those formed by the allies and vassals, acting in support of the legions. His later actions suggest that he was probably more than a simple auxiliary soldier, perhaps even a man of command experience, and certainly an accomplished warrior.[2] The fact that the rebellion that he led was to break out in 73 BCE makes it possible that he had served in one of the corps composing Sulla's troops a decade earlier, when he was fighting in the East against Mithridates. Sulla had subdued the Thracian tribe of the Maedi, among other tribes and cities that had aligned themselves with the king of Pontus, and had also recruited forces from local allies or vassals. It is therefore plausible that the Thracian gladiator had served in one of these units.

The Thracians were a group of tribes that were always on the periphery of the Greek world, both politically and culturally. After the annexation of Macedonia and the rest of Greece to Roman territory in the previous century, they had been involved in constant wars with the Roman forces stationed in the region. One of these wars between Romans and Thracians was raging at the time of the Spartacus rebellion in Italy, with Marcus Terentius Varro Lucullus, consul in 73 BCE and brother of the more famous Lucius Licinius Lucullus. The latter had been consul a year earlier and was at that time fighting against the Pontic king Mithridates VI in Asia Minor.

Thrace, for the most part, had undergone less urban development than neighbouring Macedonia, remaining more similar to Illyria. In the early first century BCE, it remained a region known primarily for its skilled hunters and hardy warriors. The Thracians, similar to the Celtic and Germanic tribes, enjoyed hand-to-hand combat, hunting and drinking, and were known for raiding and pillaging. They were excellent as horsemen and light infantrymen, and were also very proficient in guerrilla warfare.[3] They constructed effective traps and ambushes, carried out surprise attacks that perplexed heavy infantry, and knew how to reinforce their lines to withstand cavalry charges.

Thracian tribes known for their tough and warlike nature included the Maedi, who lived in the present-day south-western Bulgarian mountains, the Bessi, the Getae and the Odrysi, who lived between the Aegean coast and the Rhodope Mountains. Several of them had fought either for or against Rome.

Spartacus may well have come from a noble or otherwise prominent family of Thrace.[4] The same is true of some of his comrades in the uprising. This particular possibility is reinforced by the fact that the rebellion had a significant appeal to several slaves in Italy, similar to what had happened earlier in Sicily, where, again, the leaders of the rebellions were of aristocratic and priestly origin rather than mere slaves. Also, Plutarch, wishing to emphasise the personal merit of Spartacus, notes that he was the 'most Greek' of his race,[5] a designation that in antiquity was given as a title of honour, and in this particular case indicates that Spartacus was of noble birth and a similar ethos, or that in any case he was accepted as a man who possessed some of the high and refined qualities that characterised the most civilised and advanced parts of the world. The same is not, however, true of the rebellion that he led.

Spartacus eventually deserted and was declared an outlaw by the Roman authorities, as he likely engaged in criminal activities, including robbery, pillage and guerrilla warfare against the Roman military forces. It is unknown whether Spartacus' actions were politically motivated, whether they were merely criminal, or whether they combined both elements to some degree. What is certain is that he was captured as an outlaw, enslaved, taken to Italy and, because of his strength and military experience, bought to be a gladiator.[6]

He was acquired by one of the most famous and great gladiatorial schools of the time. The school was located in Capua and belonged to Lentulus Batiatus, who was reportedly a former slave. After being freed by his owner, Batiatus pursued a career as an entrepreneur in the field of gladiatorial fights and shows.[7]

The Beginning of the Insurrection

Capua was an ancient Etruscan city situated at the foot of the Apennines; its climate was extremely sunny, and on its southern side lay a vast plain, part of the particularly fertile lands of Campania, one of the wealthiest regions of the ancient world. Capua, in 216 BCE, had broken away from its alliance with Rome, allying itself with Hannibal and Carthage. However, the Romans soon recaptured the city as early as 211 BCE, even though Hannibal was still in Italy, and punished it for the treachery, as they would subsequently do with all the other Italian cities and regions that had turned their backs on them during that perilous time. The autonomy of Capua was abolished, and it became henceforth a city without a civil life of its own, the government of which was directly exercised by a Roman governor.[8] This happened only on special occasions. As a rule, within the Roman Federation and later empire, the various cities, including Rome itself, continued to have their own political institutions and to regulate their internal affairs under autonomy.

However, although Capua had lost all political significance, from an economic perspective, it experienced significant development in the second century BCE, becoming once again one of the richest cities in Italy and the Roman territory as a whole. The city was the main meat market for Rome and an important producer of wheat, as well as a centre for metallurgy and textiles. But in addition to these, Capua was also known for the gladiatorial schools it hosted.

The latter fact was also due to the Romans' preference for keeping the gladiators and the relevant schools at some distance from Rome, even though it was there that the most mass spectacles were organised. Capua, located at a considerable distance from Rome, close to 200 kilometres, but directly connected to it by the famous Via Appia and another essential road of the time, the Via Latina, was the most ideal place to become a centre for the training and residence of gladiators.

In the school of Gnaeus Lentulus Batiatus, hundreds of inmates were trained to become gladiators, with the majority being Gauls and Thracians. There were probably also Germans and Italians, and even Romans who had voluntarily become gladiators. It is noteworthy that, in general, towards slaves, and especially in the case of gladiators, the Romans were careful to create and maintain multi-ethnic groups,[9] as this made it much more difficult for them to achieve understanding and unanimity; it therefore became easier for the owners to control them. This was essential in the case of gladiators, as they were slaves who had access to weapons and military-type training, and consequently dangerous.

The gladiatorial trainees lived under very stringent restrictions in the school of Capua, as was usually the case in similar establishments at that time. Spartacus, having been at large until recently, urged the other gladiators to rebel and escape. As Appian writes, the Thracian gladiator told them that it was better to risk their lives for freedom than to entertain the spectators of the duels, and eventually, about 200 were persuaded and began to plan their escape.[10]

The rebellion probably began in the spring of 73 BCE. The gladiators of Batiatus had probably started to prepare at that time for the great games held annually in Rome. The games included various spectacles, such as duels, and took place over two weeks from 5 to 19 September. The gladiators attacked the training school guards, and several of them managed to escape, taking with them as many weapons as they could, especially knives and spears. The exact number of those who finally managed to escape varies in the ancient sources between thirty and eighty-four.[11] What is certain is that after they had left the training school, the escapees attacked wagons carrying weapons for gladiators to another city and also attacked pedestrians passing by, and in this way armed themselves with gladiatorial weapons, knives and clubs. They then fled to nearby Vesuvius,[12] where they occupied the highest and most inaccessible part of the mountain.

The insurgents raised three leaders, the first being Spartacus. The other two gladiators who emerged in leadership roles were Oenomaus and Crixus, both Gauls.[13] It is often assumed that Spartacus was the undisputed leader of the rebellion from the beginning. However, there is also a version, probably adopted by Titus Livy, that Spartacus was initially equal to Crixus in leadership of the rebellion.[14] Oenomaus is not mentioned at all by Livy, or by other writers, as he was killed in one of the early conflicts following the escape from Capua, and was not connected with the later, more important events. The version of parity between the leaders of the rebellion at its beginning is very likely. As will be analysed, the insurgents were not a solid and indivisible group; instead, there were differences between them that eventually led to their splitting into two distinct bodies, one led by Spartacus and the other led by Crixus, and they followed independent paths.

These differences were very likely rooted to a significant extent in ethnic and cultural distinctions since, although internationalist thinkers who interpret society only in terms of class stratification have assured to the contrary, ethnic, religious and cultural differences have, over time, had a crucial influence on the choices of human groups. This is something that has more recently been demonstrated in a deafening and undeniable way by the developments recorded in the latter part of the twentieth century in the socialist countries themselves, which predominantly adopted class and internationalist doctrines as their official ideology.

Also, ancient societies were structured and hierarchical in a clear and relatively rigid way, in which descent played a crucial role, and there was no notion of independent and equal individuals. The latter concept coincided historically with the emergence of industrial mass production and was impossible in earlier societies, as will be discussed further in Chapter 5.

Therefore, if, for example, the Thracians and the gladiators and slaves of Eastern origin were willing to follow a gladiator of aristocratic origin, who was experienced in the military and capable, and who was also presented as a favourite of the god Dionysus, this was not necessarily the case for gladiators of Celtic and Germanic origin. They would have recognised a different hierarchy, in which they could only be headed by one of their own kindred, probably also of aristocratic origin and regarded as a favourite of their own gods.

In the ancient world, broader supra-local identities certainly existed, especially within large empires, but they rested on the dominance of particular peoples and political orders without the pretext of anything resembling a modern internationalist or class-based universalism. At the time of the Spartacus revolt, no such framework existed that could allegedly dissolve ethnic and cultural distinctions inside the rebel camp – one could add that something like that did not happen even in the modern era despite the existence of similar frameworks.

However, after the escape from the school of Batiatus and possibly the predominance of the insurgents over a city militia corps or mercenaries of the school owner, the rebellion consolidated its presence at Vesuvius and began to spread.[15] Several slaves from the nearby fields, who had previously escaped from their owners' farms, also rushed to join them, learning that escaped gladiators had barricaded themselves on the mountain. Some desperate poor people of the surrounding countryside, outlaws and thugs, may have done the same.

The crowd of insurgents then began to plunder the farms and houses in the nearby areas, attracting more and more slaves to the ranks of the rebellion. These slaves, who were being freed, hoped that they too would benefit from the looting, theft and plundering. In this way, the rebellion began to acquire mass characteristics, a fact that was reinforced by the leadership of Spartacus, who took care to keep all his men satisfied by dividing the spoils equally.[16]

A central role in the life of Spartacus, and to some extent in the course of the revolt, was probably played by a woman from Thrace, who was a priestess of Dionysus and a seer,[17] and was the mistress or wife of her gladiator compatriot. Marriage and cohabitation were the same for gladiators as for slaves, i.e. there was no specific legal regulation, but it was up to the owner whether or not he would allow them to marry and form steady relationships. It seems that Batiatus allowed his gladiators to have relations with women, which for the owners was often legitimate since it made the gladiators' lives more pleasant and tied them more to the school and the place. The priestess lived with Spartacus in Capua and left the school of Batiatus with him during his escape.

According to tradition, Spartacus once recounted that he woke up with a snake wrapped around his head or that he had seen the event in his sleep. Then, his priestly companion explained the oracle, claiming that it meant that Spartacus was to be surrounded by great and terrible power, just as the snake had wrapped itself around his head. It is not known whether the oracle was given before or after the escape from Capua and the explosion of the rebellion. The critical point in any case is that through Spartacus' companion, divine favour and divination played a prominent role in the third slave revolt in Roman history, just as they did in the two previous ones, where the leaders were themselves priests and seers.

Religious sentiment and the belief that the leader possesses or is surrounded by supernatural or special powers, along with a glorious destiny, have been essential elements in politics throughout time. Charismatic leaders, whom the masses follow with greater enthusiasm and conviction, are often distinguished by similar characteristics. It is likely that Spartacus' companion was highly evocative and used her skills to create and promote the sense that there was a legendary aura around the Thracian gladiator, which further made him attractive and persuasive to the masses of desperate and outraged people, mostly slaves, who followed him.

First Military Conflicts

In the initial phase of the rebellion, the Romans did not consider themselves to be dealing with something significant that required special attention. They believed that what had happened did not yet constitute an insurrection, let alone a war, but a simple disturbance taking place in the countryside, something like a temporary upsurge in the activity of criminal gangs committing robberies and other crimes.[18] Consequently, initially, no regular troops were sent against Spartacus and the crowd of gladiators, slaves and outcasts who followed him; instead, 3,000 soldiers were dispatched and recruited on a makeshift basis. At the head of this essentially police and not military force, which was to be the first to confront the rebellious gladiators and slaves of Spartacus, was, as Titus Livy and Appian report, the praetor Gaius Claudius Glaber.[19]

Glaber was not a member of the well-known house of Claudius – perhaps he was just a distant relation – and he was of plebeian origin. In the absence of any particular details and references about his person, all the evidence suggests that he was, therefore, a praetor of little political influence and importance who could hardly hope for a future election to the consulship. The choice of the Senate to entrust to an official of not very high standing the handling of the rebellion is evidence of the little importance that the Roman leadership attached to it, and of the fact that it caused them no particular concern. It was, after all, standard Roman practice to gradually escalate the intensity of their response to external threats, trying to eliminate them with the least possible use of force and to mobilise powerful troops only when an enemy had proved impossible to neutralise with limited forces. This practice also favoured the emergence of talented young men, who were thus allowed to demonstrate their worth and gain fame, thereby gaining momentum for their political careers.

Additionally, at this particular juncture, the best units of the Roman army were, in any case, far from Italy, engaged in fighting in the West and East. It is also unlikely that Sulla's veterans, many of whom had settled in areas near Pompeii and Capua, would have been eager to serve under a commander like Glaber in what seemed at first to be a mere police operation. For the veteran legionaries, putting down a rebellion of gladiators and slaves was a police, not a military, operation, so it was of no interest, especially since the head of the troops would be an unknown official with no credentials. Consequently, the forces that Glaber assembled to attack the position of the insurgents at Vesuvius were unarmed and constituted more of a militia corps than a regular army.

When Glaber approached the position of the rebels at Vesuvius, he found that there was only one road leading to the summit where Spartacus and his men were, and it was narrow and rough. Consequently, a straight attack would be difficult, and the defenders would have the advantage. The Roman praetor, therefore, decided not to attack but to hem in the insurgents on the high ground, which they had occupied and roughly fortified, blocking with his forces the only road leading to their position in order to starve them out. All around were precipices, and the escape of the trapped men seemed impossible.

However, the men of Spartacus made use of a large and wild vine that had grown on top of the fortified area, and with the branches, they wove long stairs. After constructing them, they hung them up, and thus, they safely descended the cliff.[20] The Romans did not understand what was happening, and while they thought the slaves were blocked at the top, they were suddenly attacked from many different directions in the rear. The surprise attack by the slaves created a disturbance, and the Roman soldiers fled, resulting in the gladiators taking over and looting the Roman camp.[21]

The insurgents then raided the areas around Vesuvius in order to secure the necessary supplies. Also, after these developments, the number of insurgents continued to grow, adding significant numbers, soon reaching perhaps as many as 10,000.[22] It should be noted, however, that no one can know with certainty the exact dimensions of the slave army at any stage of the story, as it is also impossible to calculate to what extent the numbers reported by the sources were of fighting men, and to what extent women, children and old men followed the rebellion at any given time.

After this failure for the Roman side, which allowed the rebels to carry out new raids and plunder in various parts of Campania against the inhabitants, committing murders, arson, robberies and rapes without any discrimination, the suppression of the rebellion and the elimination of the growing army of slaves was entrusted in the autumn of 73 BCE to the praetor Publius Varinius. Varinius was required to recruit forces en route from Rome to Capua and Vesuvius. At the same time, or shortly afterwards, the Senate also sent the praetor Leucius Cossinius to the region with the mission of gathering other forces to support Varinius.

When the Roman forces finally approached Capua and Vesuvius, Varinius immediately moved against the slave army with approximately 2,000 soldiers, led by his second-in-command, the legate Furius, while Cossinius and his forces were moving against Spartacus. Legate Furius was suddenly attacked by the rebels, probably in some part of Campania, and after a skirmish, was forced to retreat. Meanwhile, Spartacus led his forces against the other part of the Roman army, which Cossinius commanded. The raid was made again by surprise while Cossinius was taking his bath in the salt marshes of a villa situated on the outskirts of Pompeii, and his soldiers were scattered and wholly unprepared for battle. The result was that the Roman officer at first narrowly escaped capture by hastily abandoning his baggage, and his camp was taken. The Romans fled, and Spartacus' forces pursued them and killed several of them, among whom was eventually Cossinius himself.

The incident is indicative of the disparaging way in which the rebellion was treated by the Roman commanders and legionaries who undertook to suppress it in its initial phase. Although they were inexperienced and had no involvement in large-scale conflicts, they despised Spartacus' men because they were not real soldiers. They were gladiators, slaves and outcasts,[23] and they were considered unworthy opponents for the glorious Roman army that had subdued the entire Mediterranean. Yet this underestimation, and the consequent negligence, proved fatal to the Roman troops on several occasions, as Spartacus and his forces proved far more capable than expected from a military standpoint. Instead, aware of his limited capabilities, Spartacus used guerrilla warfare tactics and tried to take the Romans by surprise.

As far as the events that immediately followed this point of the uprising are concerned, modern historical research has at its disposal the few surviving details from the historian Gaius Sallustius Crispus' text on the Third Servile War. Sallust's complete account was more extensive and detailed than those that have reached modern times; however, it is unfortunately included in the portions of his larger work that have survived only in fragments.

According to Sallust, the slaves were attempting to improve their equipment, including using fire to heat their spears and make them stronger,[24] as they did not yet have many regular weapons at their disposal. On the opposite side, several Roman soldiers had fallen ill due to the harsh autumn climate. Furthermore, the corps that had suffered the previous defeat had not returned to their base, ignoring Varinius' order calling for them to join the rest of his forces.[25] The situation was by no means favourable to the Roman commander since even among the soldiers who remained in their posts and were fighting, many were failing to perform their military duties with due devotion. The praetor, therefore, sent his quaestor, Gaius Toranius, to Rome to report to the Senate exactly what was happening with regard to the slave rebellion and, in particular, the cases of indiscipline and disintegration that were appearing within the Roman troops that had been sent to suppress the rebellion.

Varinius eventually led 4,000 soldiers willing to follow him and approached the slave camp, setting up camp close by themselves. The Romans then constructed fairly strong fortifications, with bastions and a moat around their site. Sensing the presence of Roman forces nearby, the rebels realised that their situation could become complicated if they remained in the same place. The fortifications that the Romans were constructing were mighty, given the capabilities of the slaves. On the other hand, the slaves would have found it very difficult to cope with a Roman attack at this stage, even though Spartacus and Crixus had managed to organise the camp to the usual military standards.

Wanting to avoid a confrontation or the possibility of being blockaded and imprisoned by the Romans, the rebels planned and succeeded in escaping from the camp during one of the following nights, without the Romans realising anything was happening. The slaves managed to mislead their opponents by pinning corpses adorned with clothes and weapons on beams in various parts of the camp so that, from a distance, they would give the impression of living sentries. At the same time, they lit several fires to create the impression that the camp was busy and that everyone remained inside. In this way, the Romans did not notice anything remarkable during the night, as the slave camp looked seemingly the same as on previous nights.

However, in reality, Spartacus and his men had escaped and fled in total silence during the night. Varinius realised what had happened when in the morning he found that there was no noise or movement in the slave camp, and no stones or profanity being hurled towards his men, unlike what had been happening in the previous days. He then sent his horsemen to search for the insurgents' traces and discover their location and direction of travel.

At the same time, although he was sure that the slaves had fled as far away as possible, he and the rest of the force redeployed to a more secure area to exclude any possibility of surprise, in case of any infinitesimal possibility that the movement of the slaves was part of a deceptive plan of aggression.

Discord and Disasters

A few days later, after the new location of the slaves had been identified, the morale of the Roman army had improved considerably, and the soldiers were eager to face the enemy forces. Meanwhile, the negative mood had shifted to the slave side. Varinius led his men against the new enemy camp, where dissension prevailed and quarrels were taking place. Crixus, together with the Gauls and Germans he commanded, wished to march directly against the approaching Roman army and engage with it in a general battle of array.[26]

Spartacus, on the other hand, argued that such an action should be avoided for the time being, as the existing forces were insufficient and not ready for a proper battle. The Thracian gladiator advocated a tactic of delay and guerrilla warfare, which would allow his forces to grow and strengthen before directly clashing with those of Varinius. The disagreement, as is evidenced by the course of events that followed, concerned not only the given situation but also the broader, general aspirations and intentions of the two leaders of the rebellion. Crixus sought to expand the war in Italy, continuing to plunder, seek revenge, and acquire wealth and power. Spartacus, however, understood that, sooner or later, a crushing was likely and believed that the rebels' only valid pursuit was escape from Italy. In Crixus' attitude, one can see the passion and vigour of the warlike barbarian tribes such as the Gauls and the Germans, while in that of Spartacus, his similar Thracian temperament was counterbalanced by the rational, practical spirit, which his service in the Roman army, and the contact with Greek education he might have had, had instilled in him.

In particular, Spartacus suggested that it would be better for the rebels to move to some larger nearby plains, where there were many herds of cattle, as well as villages and towns from which men could be recruited. In this way, the rebels would have the opportunity to strengthen themselves before Varinius arrived with his forces and engaged in battle against them.

However, as reported, only a few people who had some culture and noble origins supported Spartacus, while the majority of the rebels sided with Crixus' perspective. The recent successes had led the slaves to believe that they could stand up to the Romans and continue their plundering at the expense of the Italian countryside.[27]

There was, however, a sound strategic rationale for Crixus' view of attacking Varinius and staying in Italy, as Barry Strauss notes.[28] If the rebels followed Spartacus' suggestion and attempted an immediate flight from the peninsula, Varinius would have been left in their rear, and retreat would have become dangerous. Also, autumn and the coming winter were not suitable seasons for an attempt to cross the Alps, and it would be better for the slaves to establish themselves for the time being in the south and move northwards from the following spring. Furthermore, the Roman army remained committed to the great wars being fought in parallel in Spain and Asia Minor, and it would not divert its forces from these theatres to deal with a slave revolt that posed no significant threat to Rome.

Spartacus accepted the decision but persuaded the rebels to avoid the Romans and move to the southern pastures, where they could find supplies and recruit new men. This time, the rebellious gladiators and slaves were convinced by the arguments of their Thracian leader. In the autumn of 73 BCE, the slave army moved south, probably through mountainous, rough terrain, rather than the Roman roads, to avoid encounters with Roman military forces. An organised army, such as the Roman army, with heavy armament and transport vehicles, would have difficulty passing through such terrain. In contrast, the lightly armed slave army would not. The slaves also made sure to use as guides inhabitants of local areas who had been captured as prisoners.

After escaping from Varinius, the slaves marched to the road that led to Nola. There, in previous years Sulla had acquired a villa and had distributed land to his supporters and legionaries, which he had expropriated from his political opponents. After looting in Nola, the rebels moved on to Terina (a colony of Croton, now Nocera). The city was located to the south-east of Vesuvius and was built on the hills rising above the plain of the river Sarnus (modern-day Sarno), on the road from Nola to Salernum (modern-day Salerno). It was a prosperous community of mainly farmers and merchants, against which the rebels carried out extensive looting, causing great destruction.

After leaving Terina, the slaves moved inland and passed through Abella, a small town north-east of Nola, at the foot of the wooded present-day Mount Parthenio, where the valley of the river Clanio lies. Spartacus and his men then moved towards the mountains of Picinis, which formed the natural border between this region and Lucania and were almost 50 kilometres away.

Spartacus aimed to cross the mountain ranges, enter Lucania and attack the town of Forum Annii, which was located in the foothills, without his forces and their movement being noticed by the farmers of the surrounding countryside. Indeed, the slaves crossed the narrow mountain pass of Nares in Lucania, cloaked behind the hills, and made a surprise surge against the town, where Romans and local Lucanians lived.[29]

The rebellious slaves then engaged in looting and destruction, as well as raping girls and women and indiscriminately slaughtering the inhabitants. Those men who resisted were exterminated in the worst way, as the slaves often did not limit themselves to killing them but also subjected them to horrible torture, as mentioned by Sallust.[30] Indeed, in some cases, they would mercilessly mutilate people. However, they would not finish them off, leaving them half-dead to die in horrible agony. 'Nothing was sacred or inviolable to these men, who had the savagery of barbarians and the temperament of slaves,' Sallust declares.[31]

The Roman historian, however, notes that Spartacus himself was not directly responsible for the actions of his men, as he had given them contrary orders and had tried to restrain them from committing such brutalities and atrocities against civilians.[32] The Thracian gladiator understood that such behaviour would create revulsion and rage against the rebellion, but would also provoke more forceful reactions on the part of the Romans. However, since he failed to prevent this development, he begged his men to avoid, at all costs, the spread of information about what they had committed, which obviously meant that they had to leave no one alive.

However, this proved impossible, as some survivors quickly escaped to nearby villages and informed the residents of what had happened, urging them to take what belongings they could and move their families away to safer places. Thus, when Spartacus and his men halted their march the next day in a spacious plain where there were several houses, they found that no one was there. Although the slaves had started at first light, a few hours later, all the inhabitants had already moved away to spare their lives and as much of their property as possible.

Nevertheless, the rebellious slaves looted numerous arable and livestock farms in the region, primarily fields of cereals, as well as sheep and goats, thereby obtaining a substantial supply of goods. They also recruited several young men, thanks to whom they increased their overall strength by a considerable extent, as slaves from the region chose to join them, finding the opportunity to participate in the looting and violence, even betraying in some cases the hiding places where their masters had tried to preserve money and valuables, or even themselves.

The surviving passage from Sallust stops at this point, and the other sources do not recount the events with similar detail and accuracy. What is certain is that Spartacus and the rebels prevailed after clashes with Varinius' forces.[33] Indeed, the Roman commander was in danger of being killed or taken prisoner, and his horse and his lictors were captured.

The lictors were men who marched in front of a Roman official, six in the case of the praetor, twelve in that of the consul, carrying the fasces, i.e. bundles of rods tied tightly with ribbons, which symbolised the authority of the official. When the consul or praetor was outside the limits of the city of Rome, in the middle of the fasces was an axe, symbolising that there he had the authority to execute people if he so decided. However, he did not have this authority over Roman citizens, as no one could execute a Roman citizen without a proper trial.

The men of Spartacus did, however, secure other spoils thanks to this success, among which were several weapons of the Roman army. This event particularly pleased the rebellious slaves, as the weapons they acquired enabled them to significantly improve their equipment and fighting ability. In the victory over Varinius, which was achieved through guerrilla warfare methods, the rebels also seized the banners of Roman centurions, in addition to Varinius' lictors and his horse.[34] The value of these symbols was immense, and the possession of Roman army insignia gave even greater fame to Spartacus and the rebellion.

The news that the rebellious gladiators and slaves had prevailed over Roman military units created a great sensation, as it indicated that the rebels were not mere escaped slaves, bandits and looters but a group led by competent and experienced military men who had organisation and dynamism. Also, this second victory and the consequent further strengthening, as well as, of course, the spoils, prompted many of the shepherds of the surrounding area to join the army that was now being formed under the leadership of Spartacus.[35] These were wild men who lived in the countryside and mountains and had no military training or experience, but were hardy, fast and pro-war. As Spartacus was probably aware, similar shepherds had participated in the two slave rebellions in Sicily and in the resistance of Iberian tribes against Rome, managing to trouble the Romans with their unconventional guerrilla warfare methods. The gladiators recruited some of them to serve as lightly armed vanguards while others were fully armed.

The Peak of the Uprising

The victories and the increase in the number of available men strengthened the position and dynamism of Spartacus' army. With their new extent, the rebels expanded their operations to more southern territories, committing massive looting and destruction in the countryside of Calabria, in an attempt to further strengthen their army. The area was rich, surrounded by hills and dense forests in which slaves could take refuge if needed. It was also home to many slaves, as well as pirates, other outlaws and outcasts in the ports, who could join Spartacus' forces. The rebels freed the slaves and thugs and used the furnaces on the farms and in the villas to turn chains, cell doors and other metals into swords and spears.

Having established themselves in their new base, the slaves escalated their activity with new attacks and raids around towns such as Thurii, Terina and Metapontion (or Metapontium in the Latin version), as if they were not satisfied with the robberies and raids on houses and villages in the countryside, as Lucius Annaeus Florus criticises.[36] The behaviour of the insurgents and what was suffered by the inhabitants of the areas where the raids and looting took place, who probably were primarily Greeks since all the aforementioned cities were Greek colonies, led the Roman historian to call Spartacus and his men 'predatory monsters'.[37] The information is confirmed by Paulus Orosius, who states that after the military victories, the rebels plundered the areas around the cities of Metapontion and Concentia (modern-day Cosenza), located 80 kilometres south of Thurii on the Via Annia (Annia Way), committing murder, arson, robbery and rape without discrimination, while at the same time quickly gathering a large army.[38]

These developments enabled Spartacus to strengthen his position dramatically. More and more slaves escaped from their owners and joined the army of the insurgents, and the latter became increasingly serious. According to Florus, new slaves were arriving daily and joining the forces of the rebellion, increasing their numbers to the scale of a regular army.[39] According to Orosius, by then, Spartacus commanded a force of 30,000, and Crixus commanded one of 10,000. The third initial leader of the uprising, Oenomaus, had already been killed in one of the early clashes, when the size of the rebellion had not yet reached those numbers.[40] According to Appian, the resulting flow of slaves dramatically strengthened the forces of the rebels, which in the spring of 72 BCE amounted to 70,000.[41] It is more likely, however, that this figure refers to the total number of people following the rebellion. In contrast, according to modern estimates, the combatants probably totalled 40,000 men at this stage. Of these, 10,000 were under the control of Crixus, who had compromised with Spartacus the previous autumn but retained some autonomy and continued to reject escape from Italy as the ultimate goal.[42]

The insurgents controlled territories and infrastructure of considerable size, which allowed them to be better supplied than before, build more weapons and gain increasing military power. They also stole enough herds of horses to create cavalry forces.

However, Spartacus remained grounded and prudent, knowing that although his forces had grown dramatically in numbers and improved their equipment, they were no match for the professional and well-equipped Roman army, which also had an inexhaustible supply of recruits. Further, the insurgents were severely lacking in training and cohesion, and Spartacus had considerable difficulty enforcing discipline. The Thracian gladiator made efforts to assemble his forces as much as possible along the lines of a regular army, and he used the rods and emblems he had snatched from

Roman officials as symbols of authority to increase the awe he inspired and enhance his charisma. However, these characteristics were insufficient to create a disciplined and organised army capable of responding to any situation and achieving great victories.

Moreover, the slaves' equipment may have been improved, but it remained weak compared to that of a regular army. The insurgents made their shields using basketry techniques, braiding branches covered with animal skins, and often their spears were made of wood. Even their metal swords and weapons were improvised constructions of molten iron, formed from prison cell doors and chains taken from plundered areas, thereby freeing and recruiting imprisoned criminals and slaves.[43] In contrast, on the opposing side were solid iron-barred troops, equipped with heavy metal shields, armour, sharp swords and sharpened iron spears. Spartacus, therefore, knew that if war became generalised and Rome mobilised its powerful forces, there was no chance of survival for his army, but its fate would likely be annihilation. Thus, the Thracian leader of the rebellion set his sights on fleeing the Italian peninsula.

Spartacus planned to take his army across the Alps to Gaul, and then each man would return home along the road. Up to this point, he had a good chance of success, as the Romans had not given primary importance to the slave revolt. They still regarded it as a temporary disturbance, a seasonal upsurge in the activity of criminal bands of bandits who operated in the countryside, looting farms and settlements and attacking travellers and traders on the major roads of the territory. It was by no means perceived as a movement that posed any significant threat to the Roman state. The attention of the Senate was always turned to the West, where the war in Spain was going on between Pompey's legions and the troops of Sertorius and his local Iberian allies,[44] and at the same time to the East, where the legions of Lucius Licinius Lucullus were fighting with the troops of the Pontic king, Mithridates,[45] while the forces of his younger brother, Marcus Terentius Varro Lucullus, were facing the fighters of the Thracian tribe of Bessi.[46] On these three fronts were about 150,000 Roman legionaries, i.e. the bulk of the experienced and ready-to-fight forces of the Roman army. It is therefore obvious and plausible that Spartacus and his forces were greatly favoured by the fact that Rome was waging two large-scale wars simultaneously in those years, in Spain and Asia Minor, plus a third in Thrace. Otherwise, the rebellion would never have assumed the proportions it did, and it may be safely assumed that it would have been suppressed at its birth.

However, it seems that the sudden and incredible sense of power experienced by the slave rabble made many of them greedy and arrogant. Contrary to Spartacus' exhortations to escape through the Alps from Italy, most continued to desire to remain on the peninsula so that they could continue to plunder its wealth and farms. The facts suggest that it is most likely that Spartacus did not fully control the motley crowd that made up his army, and certainly, most of the insurgents did not have the same understanding of the situation as their leader. The position of power that they unexpectedly found themselves in, having been in the hands of slaves, marginal individuals and adventurers, made them arrogant. Meanwhile, the constant plundering and theft committed against the people and farms of the Italian countryside created expectations of even greater loot and enrichment. It is also clear from the facts that, at the same time, there were internal divisions and conflicts between groups of different ethnic origins in the slave army. As a consequence, the section of the forces that consisted mainly of Gauls and German slaves, commanded by Crixus, was completely cut off from the forces controlled by Spartacus, disagreeing with the Thracian gladiator's proposals. Personal ambitions and rivalries likely also contributed to the division of the slave army. However, Spartacus and Crixus did not become enemies, as each understood it was in the other's interest to keep the other strong, thereby creating as much trouble as possible for the Romans and distracting them from their cause.

Escalation of the War

However, the growth of the slave army and the increasing violence and destruction it caused in the Italian countryside finally brought about what Spartacus had feared and had tried to avoid. The growing looting of farms, as well as the constant reports of murders, rapes, robberies and violence committed by the insurgents against the inhabitants of the country, alarmed the Roman leadership and led them to change their attitude and treat the situation as a regular war.

In the spring of 72 BCE, the Romans decided to react more forcefully, aiming to exterminate the slave army to protect and pacify the Italian countryside without, however, resorting to mass conscription or mobilising large forces. The two consuls undertook the operation, each with two legions under their direct command.[47] While they were preparing to intervene, they learned that the slave army was divided into separate sections. Crixus, with the Gauls and Germans, had remained in the south and were heading for Apulia, a rich agricultural region, while Spartacus had moved northwards, following his plan to escape from Italy through the Alps.

The consul Lucius Gellius Poplicola attacked Crixus' forces, which, according to Appian, were at that time up to 30,000 strong and were on Mount Garganus (modern Gargano).[48] The consul Gnaeus Cornelius Lentulus Clodianus moved against the part of the slave army still under Spartacus' control. The latter, after the split of the army, was trying to cross the Apennine Mountains and then approach the Alps, hoping that he could reach an understanding with the Gauls who lived to the north-west of the mountain range and be accepted into their territory in the first instance.[49] The fact that the two leaders of the rebellion and their followers took a quite different and opposite course further demonstrates that the idea according to which the army was divided into two parts for tactical reasons on account of its size is unfounded, and those opinions that speak of dissension and division are correct, even if it did not lead to relations of enmity between the rebel leaders.

On Mount Garganus, the consul Gellius and his two legions easily crushed the corps of Crixus' Gauls and Germans, annihilating two-thirds of his force.[50] Feeling great confidence after the victory over Crixus, Gellius marched from Apulia northwards to move against Spartacus.

At the same time, utilising a very good intelligence network, the consul Lentulus moved quickly with his troops and managed to block the road to Spartacus before he reached the Apennines.[51] Then, he attempted to block and surround the forces of the leader of the rebellion, even though his forces were vastly outnumbered. Spartacus, faced with the danger of being surrounded and knowing that the other two consular legions were approaching from the south, reacted with determination and coolness. Instead of trying to fortify and defend himself, he realised that he had to break the threatening cordon before it was too late so that he could free himself and escape at speed towards the Alps. Possessing an army of perhaps as many as 40,000 men, he launched a vigorous and impetuous attack against Lentulus' two legions, probably at a pass of the Apennines north-west of the modern-day city of Florence.

Spartacus hoped to repel Lentulus and his forces, thereby gaining space and time to face the second consular army in a separate battle. A fierce conflict ensued, in which Spartacus and his men managed to prevail with difficulty.[52] The Roman troops retreated, having suffered several casualties, while Spartacus' men also managed to seize the baggage of some Roman officers.[53]

Plutarch recounts a slightly different version of events at this point, stating that Spartacus' march towards the Alps was halted by the proconsul Gaius Cassius, who was stationed with about 10,000 soldiers at the river Po or Padus, in Gaul, on the other side of the Alps, without a previous battle with the consul Lentulus before the crossing of the Apennines. Gaius Cassius, according to this version, moved south to stop the slave army and at some point met Spartacus with his forces. There, a battle ensued which Spartacus managed to win, inflicting heavy losses on the Roman army. Cassius was in danger of being captured and fled.

This victory of Spartacus and the slaves in a real battle, as well as those that followed, is undoubtedly a remarkable event. It must be considered certain, however, that even in the arrayed battles, Spartacus used unconventional tactics and methods, setting up ambushes and launching surprise attacks to disorientate the Roman troops as much as possible and create confusion in their ranks before and during the conflict.

For his part, Florus mentions that after the victory over Lentulus, the forces of Spartacus attacked and destroyed the camp of Gaius Cassius, which was located in the city of Mutina (modern-day Modena).[54] It is likely that Spartacus descended from the Apennines to the valley of the river Po after the victory over Lentulus, and continued to Cisalpine Gaul. His scouts informed him that about 15 kilometres to the north was Mutina, one of about ten Roman and Latin colonies in the area. There was the headquarters of Gaius Cassius Longinus, the governor of the province, who had two legions at his disposal. Gaius Cassius Longinus had been consul the previous year, and his then 15-year-old son with the same name was to be one of the conspirators who would assassinate Julius Caesar twenty-eight years later in 44 BCE. Probably at Mutina along with the proconsul Cassius was the propraetor Gnaeus Manlius.

It is, therefore, possible that Spartacus fought a second, separate battle after the victory over the forces of the consul Lentulus and the passage of the Apennines, in which he triumphed again, this time at the expense of the proconsul Cassius, whose camp he also occupied. Such a version is confirmed by Livy, who also refers to a separate battle of Spartacus against the former consul Cassius. Livy relates that Crixus and his forces were defeated and decimated on Mount Garganus by the troops of the praetor Quintus Arrius, who seems to have been in command of the legions of the consul Lucius Gellius as his second-in-command, and that Spartacus prevailed over the consul Gneaus Lentulus, and then defeated the consul Lucius Gellius and the praetor Quintus Arrius. Furthermore, Livy also mentions the involvement of the proconsul Gaius Cassius, who in turn is said to have been defeated in battle against Spartacus, as does Orosius, who, however, dates the battle with Cassius to a later time.

The exact sequence and development of events cannot be attributed with absolute certainty, based on the sources available in our time, but what is certain is that in this phase of the war, one or two clashes of greater magnitude than the previous ones took place between Roman troops of subaltern rank and the forces of Spartacus, which resulted in a new success for the Thracian gladiator and the revolt. It is also certain that after they failed to neutralise Spartacus separately, the two consuls retreated in different directions and then converged, deciding to face the slave army together.

Spartacus' new victories provided significant spoils for the rebels. Not only were the weapons useful, but various camp materials were also essential for the survival and functioning of the slave army. Also, the fact that this time, they had been achieved at the expense of Rome's vassals and regular legions caused great excitement and had further strengthened the flow of slaves joining Spartacus' army wherever it passed. This flow had not ceased since the beginning of the rebellion and, after the latest events, had further increased the insurgents' numbers, which, according to Appian, had now reached 120,000,[55] as it is probable that the surviving men of Crixus' section were reunited with Spartacus. However, as before, it is unclear whether this number refers to combatants or includes children, women and old men. The latter is undoubtedly more likely, as Eutropius, closer to modern estimates, suggests that Spartacus' army at its peak consisted of 60,000 fighting men.[56]

After the double victory, Spartacus, according to Appian, ritually executed 300 Roman prisoners in honour of Crixus,[57] thus performing a kind of mass human sacrifice. It is most likely that the ritual execution to which Appian refers consisted of forcing the captives to fight to the death, as this was a common practice of the slave army. According to several sources, including Florus, Spartacus honoured the warlords of his army who were killed in battle with ceremonies similar to those of the Roman generals. However, in addition, he ordered the captives to fight in front of the funeral pyre.[58] The Thracian leader of the rebellion acted as if he wanted to wash away the shame of having been a gladiator by becoming a gladiator himself, the Roman historian writes with scorn and irony.

The same information is conveyed by Orosius, according to whom Spartacus and his men organised duels among their captives. On one occasion, at the funeral of a noblewoman who committed suicide because she had been gang-raped by some of the rebellious gladiators and slaves, they staged a spectacle in which 400 captured men participated, slaughtering them all in the end. The leaders of the rebellion were acting like gladiators staging a spectacle rather than like military leaders, Orosius notes,[59] and just as they had previously been the objects of spectacles, they had now transformed themselves into spectators of the same spectacles.

On the other hand, the contemporary East German communist Rigobert Gunther maliciously points out how the roles had changed, concerning the forcing of Roman prisoners to fight to the death,[60] without drawing the obvious conclusion that follows from this behaviour of Spartacus and his men. That is, it is unfounded to morally blame the 'slave owners' for their actions and attitude towards gladiators and slaves since similar practices were not morally reprehensible for Spartacus and his men, although they had rebelled precisely to escape from them. The rebels not only did not oppose such duels and did not morally condemn them but were quick to adopt them as their primary form of entertainment as soon as they were freed, in an increasingly cruder form. The intellectual dishonesty displayed by this author is, of course, pervasive in any essentially ideological rather than scientific approach to history, politics and social phenomena. Gunther's book is an account of the Spartacus uprising and of that era in general, whose primary purpose is to promote and vindicate Marxist doctrines and only secondarily to examine and reveal the historical truth.

Change of Plans and Stay in Italy

The Thracian leader of the rebellion then ordered the indiscriminate slaughter of all prisoners, as well as the pack animals, and the burning of those supplies that were not necessary. Perhaps one of Spartacus' aims in slaughtering the prisoners was also to psychologically influence the Romans. However, fundamentally, these actions were aimed at facilitating the movement of his forces. It seems that the Thracian gladiator, radically changing his attitude, had now abandoned his earlier plan to flee Italy and had decided to march inland into the peninsula, perhaps even against Rome itself.[61]

In Appians' account, Spartacus is said to have decided on his own to make a drastic change of plan and course. At the same time, other sources claim that, instead, he was forced to return to the interior of the peninsula against his will because a significant part of the army did not want to leave Italy. This second version is adopted by Plutarch, who argues that, as mentioned earlier, the slaves had become arrogant after the victories and wished to remain in Italy to continue plundering. According to Florus, conceit and insolence took hold not only of the army but also of Spartacus himself, who, now overestimating his forces, began to plan an attack on Rome.[62]

According to Strauss, the main reason why Spartacus and his army remained in Italy was probably that many of his followers simply did not wish to leave the peninsula. This may have been especially true of those who had lived there for a long time and no longer had any practical connection with another land. He further hypothesises that Spartacus may have misled his men during the northward march, presenting it as a campaign of plunder in Italy in the hope of persuading them, once they approached the Alps, to leave the peninsula, but ultimately failed.[63] Perhaps even the victories on the way to the Alps made his attempt more difficult since they gave their men the feeling that they were strong and had nothing to fear from the Romans but could defeat them decisively. In reality, of course, they had not yet faced a vast Roman army, but scattered forces led by commanders who clearly did not understand the difficulty of the situation, and did not take care to coordinate their actions and cooperate sufficiently to form a strong army.

One may further hypothesise, however, that Spartacus himself realised that the crossing of the Alps was more difficult than he had expected and that he may even have received indications that the Gauls were not willing to admit such a large body of people, already hardened by pillage and violence in Italy, into their territory.

The choice of Spartacus was likely the result of a combination of some or all of the above factors to a greater or lesser extent. In any case, the choice to remain in Italy raises questions that are quite unresolvable since whatever the cause or combination of causes that prompted it, it remains unclear what exactly Spartacus and his associates hoped and aimed to achieve and what their plan for the future may have been at the time. However, the attitude that the Thracian leader of the slave army had maintained during the previous period, and that which he was to maintain later, demonstrates that he was a commander who was aware of the difficulties and possibilities, who had no illusions about the limits of his options, and who did not act with recklessness.

Therefore, even if his decision was influenced by overconfidence that came over him after his hopeless victories and the strengthening of his army, it is unlikely that Spartacus believed he could threaten Rome itself. The latter could call upon inexhaustible forces and, in addition, had impenetrable walls, which were very long, thick and high, and behind them there was a plethora of launching weapons. On the opposite side, Spartacus had no siege engines, nor did he have expert engineers who could design and build them.

Additionally, contemporary views that argue Spartacus' intention from the beginning of the revolt was to attack Rome to eliminate what they call the centre of 'slave society', commit a fundamental factual and methodological error. On the one hand, these views support a conclusion that does not reflect the facts. On the other, they interpret choices made in a completely different conceptual context, according to the ideological perspectives of their time rather than those of the protagonists. It is not even vaguely apparent from the evidence that Spartacus and his army may have been convinced that they were battling against a social system, let alone that they were claiming its overthrow and social transformation. Instead, they were fighting to improve their own particular conditions of life without conceiving of this improvement in terms of wider political and social change.

The actions of Spartacus and the slave army are typical of every uncivilised barbarian horde of antiquity and the Middle Ages, as well as of modern times, and have absolutely nothing to do with political revolution and proposals for social transformation in the context of an organised and developed society. Such actions, on the contrary, are fairly frequently observed in the history of Rome itself, as well as of the Greek city-states, and could have nothing to do with nomadic tribes or mobs of desperate people who destroyed and plundered established and advanced societies. Historical figures who can indeed be considered reformers and revolutionaries are people such as Tiberius Gracchus, Julius Caesar and Octavian Augustus, and not leaders of barbarian hordes or rebellious mobs like Spartacus, who put forward no suggestion of social organisation or development.

Spartacus' plan of action after deciding not to escape from the Italian peninsula but to turn again towards its interior could only involve some kind of settlement and consolidation in the Italian territories, which in turn would presuppose an alliance or understanding with some of the cities and peoples of the area. This conclusion is based on two pieces of information conveyed by Plutarch and Appian. According to the former, Spartacus tried to win over Italians and turn them against Roman rule, while according to the latter, Spartacus, at this stage of the revolt, refused to accept some autocrats into the ranks of his army.[64] Perhaps the leader of the rebellion feared the infiltration of spies and subversives into his already not particularly solid forces, or wanted to exclude opportunists, adventurers and rogue elements. Selectivity was necessary now that Spartacus was intent on being accepted as an interlocutor by organised political entities and stable societies. On the contrary, the image of an uncontrollable mob that ravaged everything it encountered in its path, such as the ongoing insurrection, left no hope for any conversation with the cities and inhabitants of the Italian peninsula.

At the same time, the two Roman consuls essentially merged their forces and moved in a combined effort against Spartacus and his army. They met him in the land of the Picenes,[65] where the greatest battle of the war up to that time was then fought. After the defeats that the two consuls had suffered separately, there now came to be another unexpected defeat, this time of both at the same time, which forced them to retreat. Spartacus, his gladiators and the army of slaves had now prevailed over a fairly strong Roman army, capturing much booty.

Orosius claims that after these events, the city of Rome was gripped by a fear similar to that of the time of the Carthaginian invasion.[66] Eutropius, on his part, claims something similar in his brief account about the Third Servile War, estimating that this war was no less severe for Rome than the one against Hannibal.[67]

In the case of Hannibal, after the Carthaginian army's victories against some border troops and the consular legions, there followed at Cannae, in 216 BCE, the crash of the largest army ever mobilised by Rome, where 8 Roman legions plus 8 allied wings were crushed, i.e. an army of about 90,000 men. In contrast, in the case of Spartacus, a Roman force equal to about half that number was sufficient, as described below, to annihilate the slave army, leaving virtually no survivors, with comparatively few casualties.

The wars against Carthage were the largest in Roman history, constituting a clash of the superpowers of the ancient world, with decisive historical results for the Mediterranean and Europe. Given the Romans did not panic after the debacle at Cannae, when they refrained from negotiating with Hannibal and continued the war until achieving a final victory, it is unlikely that there was any such great concern after the defeats of the consular legions since there had not even been any particular mobilisation and recruitment. Furthermore, the total forces that Rome could count on were many times greater than those that were available during the Punic Wars. Typical of the fact that the Roman leadership never felt that it was facing any kind of existential threat from Spartacus and the revolt of the gladiators and slaves is that after the defeats of the consuls, the Senate did not consider recalling Pompey or either of the two Luculli to Italy, but simply formed a new army.

What prevailed in Rome was indignation at the developments and anger at the two consuls who had proved unable to quell a slave revolt. Faced with the new circumstances, the Senate made the matter a priority and decided to confront the slave army with all its might. Somewhere between the late summer and early autumn of 72 BCE, the two consuls were ordered to give up command of the troops and take no initiative, confining themselves to presiding over the sessions of the Senate. It was then decided to raise a powerful army, which was to have the purpose of annihilating the slave army and completely crushing the rebellion.

The Sweeping Roman Counterattack

The new Roman army was to consist of six legions, and with it, the remnants of the four consular legions were to be merged[68] to create a force worthy of a real war. However, when the nominations for the chieftaincy were opened, there was hesitation in the ranks of the Roman aristocrats.[69] This was evidently because while Spartacus had proved a much more difficult opponent than expected, on the other hand, a victory over an army of slaves would nevertheless confer no special glory on the general who won it. The Roman aristocrats were, therefore, reluctant to take command of the army, for they knew that victory would likely do little to increase their prestige and influence, while a possible defeat, however unlikely, would bring complete disrepute and result in political and social marginalisation.

Crassus and Pompey

In this particular situation, the 44-year-old praetor Marcus Licinius Crassus, who saw an excellent opportunity to advance his political career during the war against Spartacus, took responsibility. Crassus was a member of an aristocratic family of plebeian origin.[70] At that time, he was one of the wealthiest men in Rome and Italy,[71] as well as a hero for a part of the citizenship. As a general, he was instrumental in the Battle of the Colline Gate in November 82 BCE, in which Sulla and his troops definitively defeated those of Cinna.

Also, his father, Publius Licinius Crassus, had been consul and censor, and he celebrated a triumph after defeating the Lusitanians as governor of Hispania Ulterior in the years 97–93 BCE.[72] It is notable that in Lusitania (roughly modern Portugal and western Spain), the Romans had faced extensive guerrilla warfare tactics similar to those used by Spartacus. Crassus, having possibly lived alongside his father during the war against the Lusitanians in his early twenties,[73] therefore either had some direct experience and knowledge of this mode of warfare, or at least it formed part of his familial and political background.

As a man, Crassus led a moderate and frugal lifestyle while simultaneously being very philanthropic. He was actively involved in the real estate and construction industries, amassing a substantial wealth. A typical business tactic of his was the purchase of problematic or demolished buildings and surrounding blocks and their subsequent development. Crassus had a large number of slave architects and builders in his employ, who ensured that whenever a house or building collapsed or was destroyed by fire, they would purchase it at a very low price. Crassus' people would then persuade the owners of nearby houses or plots of land to sell their properties to him, as their value would decrease after the catastrophic event. By buying properties at very low prices, Crassus ended up with a substantial real estate portfolio that he used in a variety of ways.[74]

He had also taken particular advantage of the opportunities offered during the Sulla dictatorship, significantly increasing his wealth. Sulla had confiscated the property of the wealthy who were hostile to him and had distributed some of it to his legionaries while he auctioned and sold the rest at low prices to his rich supporters. Crassus was one of the aristocrats and businessmen who had taken advantage with the greatest energy and without moral restraint of the opportunities that presented themselves to him at that time, increasing his fortune considerably.[75]

Apart from his wealth and lineage, the element that made Crassus popular was his kind and cheerful demeanor. He chatted willingly with anyone and returned the greetings of poor citizens by calling them by name.[76] He knew how to please both the social elite and the masses, whom he gratified by organising large public dinners, shows and charitable activities. He treated equally well his many slaves, who covered a wide range of professions and specialties. Among Crassus' slaves, in addition to those skilled in the field of construction, there were copyists, readers, coin identification specialists, bankers, janitors and many others, and he worked directly with them and advised them.[77]

The Roman aristocrat was very methodical and diligent, and his friendly disposition was accompanied by great severity. Thus, for example, while he lent money to his acquaintances interest-free when they asked him for financial help, he required them to repay him promptly. As a politician, Crassus was successful due to his rhetorical skills, which he cultivated through perseverance and effort in his studies of the art of rhetoric, becoming one of the best speakers in Roman politics despite not possessing superior natural talent to others. He also read many history books and possessed some philosophical knowledge, particularly of Aristotle's philosophy, which he had studied under the tutelage of the philosopher Alexander,[78] who was probably a native of Miletus or Myndos, on the coast of Caria in Asia Minor. The Greek philosopher was a good friend of the Roman aristocrat and even accompanied him on his travels.

Crassus had lost his father and brother when Cinna and Marius seized power and carried out persecutions and massacres against the aristocrats. At the same time, he fled to Spain to friends from his youth.[79] Crassus afterwards succeeded in rallying around him a relatively large number of aristocrats in Iberia. He joined Sulla's party with great ardour and loyalty when Sulla returned from the East to Italy to seize power in Rome and restore what he regarded as the constitutional order.

In those years, Crassus stood out and emerged as a protagonist of Roman politics, but at the same time, his rivalry with Pompey grew. Pompey had already begun to be surrounded by a glamour that did not accompany Crassus, even though he was ten years younger. Sulla himself showed a special sympathy for Pompey, and the charismatic young general earned, somewhat prematurely, it is true, the nickname of 'Magnus'.[80] The enthusiasm that pervaded both the elite and the popular masses of Roman society for Pompey annoyed Crassus, but he was not jealous and did not treat him badly.[81]

The two rising leaders of Rome had radically different characters, attitudes and styles. Crassus based his image on his wealth and the ease with which he could establish social connections. In contrast, Pompey based his influence on his distinctive grandeur and the admiration he garnered through his achievements at a young age.[82] Crassus was familiar and engendered sympathy, whereas Pompey was inaccessible and awe-inspiring. Their attraction was, therefore, based partly on their different communicative characteristics and also on their mutual rhetorical skills, as well as on their firm powers of persuasion over their listeners and interlocutors.

However, the two Roman leaders do not appear to have had a deeper understanding, or at least have focused on the historical problems facing the Roman political and social structure at the time, unlike the Gracchi,

Sulla and, later, Julius Caesar and Octavian Augustus. Their rivalry lacked the ideological characteristics of the earlier political conflicts, instead being more personality-centred.

Many prominent Roman aristocrats who had friendly relations with Crassus, as well as ambitious young men attracted by his fame, were happy to join his army and participate in the campaign. Also, as an old general of Sulla, and a victorious one at that, as well as a renowned wealthy aristocrat, Crassus was sure to attract to the ranks of the army veterans of Sulla and other experienced legionaries, with the result that his forces were much more ready for war than those that had been used up to that time in the war against the slaves. Crassus' six legions would then be joined by the remaining sections of the troops already engaged in the war, with the result that the size of the army would eventually be between 45,000 and 50,000 men.

Persecution and Retreat

Spartacus, for his part, knew that despite the victories he had won, he still had no way of having the strength to threaten Rome and face the mighty armies Rome could raise or transport from other geographical points of the vast Roman territory. He had hoped to provoke a general uprising of various Italian populations against Rome, but his expectations had proved to be utterly unrealistic. Only outcasts and slaves approached his army and joined the rebellion, but no city or tribe in Italy supported him or even recognised him as an interlocutor.[83]

Perhaps in earlier times, a similar attempt would have had some chance of success, even if limited. However, after the developments of the previous decades, and especially after the granting of Roman citizenship to all the inhabitants of Italy we've seen in the previous chapter, the latter had become wholly identified with the Roman state. What they sought from Rome was to be entirely accepted as Roman citizens and to participate more in the political institutions and the exercise of power, i.e. the opposite of turning against it. Opposition to Roman rule was an attitude of the past for the Italian people. Italy was now overwhelmingly integrated into the Roman state, and the older anti-Roman forces that had once represented a genuinely alternative Italy had been decisively weakened.

Appian reports that this fact caused Spartacus to change his mind and abandon any thought of marching against Rome, as he realised that he could not face a strong Roman army in a major battle.[84] The historian does not clarify, however, whether Crassus' troops had already been assembled and were marching towards Spartacus' position when he made this decision. Indeed, in his account, Crassus' election follows Spartacus' decision to retreat south and turn against the city of Thurii. There, according to Appian, the forces of Spartacus first occupied the high ground near the city and, having gained control of the area, then launched an attack on it, and succeeded in taking it.

Plutarch, for his part, does not mention the capture of Thurii or any other city by Spartacus. He claims that Crassus, after assuming control of the Roman army, headed for the region of Picenum, where he camped, waiting for the army of slaves.[85] As mentioned, the battle in which the two consuls had been defeated had previously taken place in this area. Therefore, when Crassus and his legions left Rome, Spartacus and the slave army were probably still in close proximity to the site of the battle. This possibility is supported and confirmed by the account, which states that Spartacus after he defeated the consuls considered marching on Rome and attempted to recruit Italian cities and tribes to his side. It would, therefore, be natural that in the next period, he should not make any considerable movement of his forces but should settle in the region, examining the possibilities he had and endeavouring to strengthen his position. At the same time, in Rome, political proceedings took place, which resulted in Crassus being appointed the general commander of the war against the rebellious slaves.

Naturally, the Roman general's primary concern in the circumstances was to eliminate any possibility of a direct threat to Rome from Spartacus and his forces. It is therefore highly likely that Spartacus' retreat southwards was driven not simply by the realisation that he lacked both sufficient troops and a foothold in the region, but also by the fact that a particularly powerful Roman army had in the meantime been assembled under Crassus and was moving against him. This means that from the moment the Roman leadership decided to take the challenge seriously, the choice for Spartacus and his army was to retreat hastily, and at a fairly long distance, to boot.

This choice was quite natural, as the power differential between the two factions was heavily in favour of the Romans, despite the numbers of the slave army exceeding those of Crassus' forces. The position of great Roman superiority despite the numerical disadvantage should not be surprising, as the strength of the Roman army was based mainly on its organisation and equipment. For this reason, even though as early as the second century BCE the Romans had vast resources of troops, they considered it unnecessary, and perhaps also organisationally and economically detrimental, to assemble armies of huge numbers. A Roman army of the size commanded by Crassus could, thanks to its organisation, discipline and equipment, confront larger enemy forces without losing confidence in victory. Moreover, even if this were to happen, several other equivalent armies could be raised or mobilised by the Roman state.

The Roman military concept generally considered quality more important than quantity, focusing on perfect equipment, organisation and absolute discipline. The Romans typically fought with smaller numbers against barbarian tribes, believing that their military superiority would ensure victory, or at least, that was what they claimed. We should be cautious about enemy army numbers, as inflating the enemy's force and casualties is a very common practice in war historiography, from ancient times to the present. The largest armies the Romans assembled and sent into theatres of operation amounted to 40,000 to 50,000 men, and the only time these numbers were exceeded was in the Battle of Cannae against Hannibal.

By retreating southwards, Spartacus was opening up the possibility of his army escaping by sea, which was the best possible option at that moment since his original plan of escaping overland through the Alps could no longer be implemented. In addition, he tried to secure a base for his forces, which, according to Appian, was achieved by the capture of Thurii, which may have taken place after the victory over another Roman army in the area led by the propraetor Manlius, thanks to which Spartacus and his men also secured useful booty and equipment.

After breaking the resistance of the city and dispossessing it, Spartacus banned the entry of merchants carrying gold and silver and forbade his men to acquire these precious metals. He allowed only the entry and trade of iron and copper, which his men even bought at normal market prices, that is, quite expensive, and without financially damaging the merchants by imposing lower prices on them.[86] Spartacus' prohibition against gold and silver, and his preference for iron and copper, was a natural attitude given the circumstances, as the primary need of the army at that stage was the supply of materials suitable for the manufacture of weapons. The available resources had to be utilised for this purpose rather than in terms of economic investment. Furthermore, gold and silver could perhaps create the temptation for many to seek wealth and abandon the rebellion, pursuing their fortunes individually based on the financial comfort they would acquire.

At the same time, Crassus and his legions marched south. They camped at Emburum (modern-day Empoli), on the Via Annia, from where they could control the plain of the river Silarus and the passages from Picenum to Campania and Lucania. The location was also particularly fertile and provided the necessary supplies for the Roman army. Spartacus, for his part, had probably in the meantime shifted further north, moving from Thurii to north-western Lucania, perhaps returning to the fertile plain of the region, which he and his forces had plundered the previous year.

Decimation and the First Victory of Crassus

Crassus advanced his forces to the south and sent two corps from the legions of his subordinates to advance under the command of Mommius, with orders to observe and supervise the enemy's movements while avoiding any engagement or skirmishing. The two corps were probably to follow a route that crossed the Via Annia. Then they marched on well-trodden and relatively flat paths, moving north across the plain and then east to finally approach the territory of the town of Volcei (modern-day Buccino), moving south without encountering Spartacus.

However, when Mommius arrived in the area, disobeying Crassus, he did not execute the planned manoeuvre. He was instead directly involved in a battle with Spartacus' forces, resulting in a heavy defeat and the loss of many of his soldiers. The rest fled in disorderly fashion, and some 500 of them even threw down their weapons to escape.[87]

After scolding Mommius and bringing him into disrepute, Crassus decided to take a very stern and harsh action. He used an old military tradition, that of decimation, in which a body of soldiers who were thought to have dishonoured the arms of Rome were divided into decades, and then by lot, one soldier from each group of ten was condemned to death and executed on the spot. The execution was carried out by the nine remaining soldiers who had just escaped, as cruelly and painfully possible, namely by beating their fellow soldier to death, knowing that they were not in his place simply because they had been more fortunate and not because they had been acquitted.[88] It is evident that this was a terrible punishment that caused great shock amongst the troops, as it not only led to the death of those condemned but also scarred for life those who remained alive, sending the most chilling and horrific message to all the rest. Also, thereafter, at least for a time, Crassus forbade the survivors of the decimation from residing inside the camp, forcing them to camp separately, and stipulated that they would not be fed with regular food but with that intended for the troops' animals.

In this particular case, according to other sources, as Appian mentions, not only were the 500 soldiers who threw down their weapons and turned their backs on the enemy decimated, but so too were other troops whom the slave army had defeated. The total number of executed soldiers would be 4,000.[89] However, the number reported by the unknown sources has to be an exaggeration. The execution of fifty men by decimation already constituted an unsurpassed shocking event. It indeed far exceeded the magnitude of the practice, even in the times when it was more often in use. Previous to this, no more than ten to twenty soldiers at most had been executed in similar decimations, so the number of fifty was already enormous, and one can assume that Crassus' decision tested the limits of tolerance of Roman leadership and society.

By decimation, the Roman aristocrat wanted to put a definitive end to the laxity and irresponsibility with which many Roman officers and legionaries had treated the war against Spartacus up to that time, the latest instance being Mommius' action of engaging in battle in disregard of his commander's orders, and the dishonourable abandonment of their weapons by some soldiers.

As mentioned earlier, for the Roman military, the slave army was not a serious opponent, and they laughed at it.[90] Nevertheless, the fact that they underestimated it led to an attitude characterised by carelessness, unpreparedness and ignorance of danger. Florus writes about this attitude of the Roman army and Roman society in general. The Roman historian considers it a disgrace to call the gladiators and slaves who made up Spartacus' army 'enemies', since, as he writes, the former were men of the worst kind and the latter of the most humble kind, and were therefore totally unworthy to be considered respected opponents of Rome.[91] Mommius' action proved that this attitude prevailed within the army as it had at the beginning of the war, even though the Senate and Crassus himself treated the war with due seriousness, regarding Spartacus as a real and feared enemy.

As Appian puts it, the terrible punishment of Crassus convinced everyone in the Roman army that even if they continued to ignore Spartacus and his army, they had every reason to fear their own general[92] if they did not perform their duties with discipline, professionalism and responsibility. After the decimation and other punishments, which created a new climate in the ranks of the Roman troops, characterised by absolute discipline, Crassus finally rearmed the soldiers who had lost their weapons and mobilised his forces to attack Spartacus.[93]

The latter knew that he had no chance against the mighty Roman army marching against him if he faced it on the plain of Picenum, and he retreated through the lands of Lucania, again displaying awareness and prudence as a commander. In this way, the leader of the slaves aimed to approach the sea, while he knew that the mountains of Lucania were a preferable place to confront the forces of Crassus if he had to engage in battle.

Spartacus' general attitude and the realism with which he attempted to lead the rebellion demonstrate a man with awareness and virtues that could not be present in people who were uncultured and inexperienced in command and military tactics, as also proved by the inappropriate behaviour of most of the slaves during the rebellion itself. Therefore, and based on the analysis of the facts, it is indeed possible that Spartacus was descended from an aristocratic family of Thrace, as Plutarch and other ancient sources convey. If this is the case, then the third great slave revolt in ancient history was led by a man who was not only born free but also descended from the upper social strata, similar to what is observed in several other cases in history.

According to Appian and other sources, a part of the slave army had been cut off from the main body and camped in a remote area for reasons that were unclear. Perhaps this particular corps was cut off from the rest of the army to follow the retreating Romans after the victory over Mommius, or to seek supplies. However, there is also the possibility that a new split among the slaves had occurred, as many of them would undoubtedly have resented and disagreed with Spartacus' attitude, who was continuing his retreat after the new victory.

Crassus realised that he had the opportunity to easily eliminate this isolated body, whose strength was reported to amount to 10,000 men, and he attacked immediately, indeed succeeding in annihilating most of the enemy force. Appian says that the Romans killed two-thirds of that slave force, and Orosius claims explicitly that the number of slaves who died in this battle was 6,000,[94] while many others were taken prisoner by the Romans.[95]

Having broken up the isolated corps, Crassus moved his forces against the main body of the enemy, and the two armies met in northern Lucania. Then, according to Appian, a great conflict ensued in which the entire opposing army participated, and the Romans prevailed, driving their opponents into flight.[96] However, other sources do not mention such an extensive battle at this point in the war. No major battle is likely to have taken place. Instead, skirmishes, which Appian also mentions as occurring after the larger battle, may have confused the timeline.

Those skirmishes and the conduct of this new Roman army were enough for Spartacus to realise that he now had a powerful force and a capable commander against him, whom he could not mislead, trap or surprise as in previous instances, and so he continued his retreat. Perhaps the Thracian gladiator had momentarily halted his retreat precisely to ascertain the degree of readiness and strength of the new and larger Roman army moving against him. It is also possible that he had yielded to the pressure of his men, who did not understand the advisability of retreating after the successive victories they had achieved, the latest being the recent one against the forces of Mommius. Pretending that he had decided to stand and confront Crassus and his legions directly, perhaps Spartacus wanted to give his men a chance to understand for themselves the danger they were in.

The experience of the Thracian gladiator in the Roman army helped him understand the level of preparedness and cohesion of the Roman troops he faced at any given moment. And this time, he realised that he was no longer facing inexperienced soldiers who would lose their formation and flee with an unexpected attack or ambush, but instead, he was up against fully disciplined legionaries. Aside from their reaction during skirmishes and sudden mock attacks used in guerrilla warfare to test the opponents' limits of cohesion, one of the characteristics that someone familiar with the way legions operated would notice was whether the forces he was facing tended to behave in a dishevelled and undisciplined manner. The Romans directly associated delinquent and careless behaviour with indiscipline. For this, they punished it severely, knowing that a body of soldiers left to behave uncontrollably could not possibly maintain its cohesion and organisation at a critical time by faithfully following the orders of its commanders.

Seeing that the conduct of the legionaries he now encountered, as well as their military function, resembled that of the expert units he had known in the past and not those that had hitherto been sent against him, Spartacus became still more convinced that he should draw them deeper into the heights of Lucania, rather than risk a general battle in more open country. At the end of 72 BCE, he accordingly moved southwards, probably along the Via Annia, towards the city of Rhegio, at the southern end of the Italian peninsula, hoping to cross the strait and escape into Sicily.

It is more likely that he hoped to find on the large Mediterranean island the footholds he had not managed to acquire in mainland Italy so that he could continue the war with new and larger forces, forts at his disposal and cities to support him. Perhaps he was also simply trying to avoid a general conflict with Crassus and his legions, hoping that in the future, he would be able to secure a fleet with which to escape to the Mediterranean. In any case, the fact is that he contacted pirates from Cilicia, who agreed to put about 2,000 of his elite men on board their ships to go to Sicily.[97] According to the plan, this corps would try to establish the necessary bases and conditions to enable the whole army to be transported to the large Mediterranean island, while the rest would remain waiting in the hills of Calabria. The possibility that Spartacus might have agreed with the Cilician pirates to transfer the whole of his forces immediately is unlikely, as it was not possible to have a pirate fleet of such a large size as to be capable of carrying tens of thousands of men at once. It would also have been too risky to transfer the entire army to the coast and take it gradually by the limited ships available. In any case, after the payment, the pirates deceived Spartacus. They left without putting their ships at Spartacus' disposal,[98] perhaps because they did not want to risk a Roman pursuit and, from a wider perspective, did not want to be more strongly targeted by Rome, or simply because their intention from the beginning was to deceive and rob Spartacus and the slave army, as would be typical of pirates. In any case, if they hoped that they would escape Rome's attention and persecution, it did not come to pass, as only four years later, the Romans decided to completely rid the Eastern Mediterranean and international trade of the phenomenon of piracy, placing a powerful fleet under the command of Pompey, who swept the pirates off the coast of Asia Minor and the Aegean.[99]

Blockade

After the deception and the flight of the Cilician pirates, Plutarch and Florus mention that the slaves attempted to build themselves some boats using materials collected from the surrounding area to escape from mainland Italy. However, they failed.[100] Consequently, Spartacus, having no other choice, was forced to move his forces and return to the interior of Italy, where Crassus was waiting, preparing and perfecting his war machine. Spartacus encamped relatively close to the town of Rhegio. Crassus approached with his troops in position but refrained from attacking directly; instead, he tried to exploit his vantage point methodically. Thus, in the following period, the Romans, following Crassus' orders, took care to block the enemies at the southern end of the Italian peninsula and cut off their supplies while wearing down their forces with limited-range attacks.

Spartacus moved away from the coast and towards a street located in the centre of Calabria, between the Tyrrhenian and Ionian coasts. At the south of the former was the fertile plain of the city of Metauros, which was known for its olive trees and vineyards, and at the south of the latter was the city of Locri. Control of this main road ensured general control of the road networks in the south of Italy. Crassus, on the other hand, occupied and blocked every route from the southern end of Italy to the north, at the geographical height where the shortest distance separates the Tyrrhenian and Ionian seas, i.e. at the geographical height of about 80 kilometres north-east of Rhegio. At that altitude, the distance between the Tyrrhenian and Ionian coasts of Italy is approximately 55 kilometres, most of which is impassable because it consists of rocky outcrops and deep gorges. It was possible to cross the strait either by walking along the coast or by taking the main road leading to the north, which was less than a kilometre wide. Therefore, by blocking the coastal and main roads, Crassus could be sure that he had blocked Spartacus and the slave army at the southern end of the peninsula. The Romans were indeed imposing their control over the region, sealing off any possible route for Spartacus to the north. To achieve this, they built a moat wall on the main road.[101] Some ancient historians exaggerate that this wall covered the entire distance of 55 kilometres, meaning that the passage to Spartacus and his men had been blocked, but this, it has been explained, did not require the construction of a wall along the entire distance, even in the unlikely event that such a colossal construction would have been possible.

However, in this case, one of the elements of Roman power, namely the ability the Romans developed to carry out large construction projects in a short time, is impressively demonstrated. The progress made by the Romans in the fields of engineering and construction, which aligned perfectly with their practical and technocratic spirit, gave them a significant advantage on various levels. The vast Roman aqueducts, the unprecedentedly large roads and bridges that crossed the territory, and the possibility of constructing works for military use gave them tremendous advantages in the interconnection of cities and, therefore, in their internal activity, as well as in the operation of the Roman military machine, which was able to move massed troops at high speed. It is also significant that the work involved was carried out by army engineers and by the legionaries themselves, without the use of labourers or slaves, since working on public schemes was one of the legionaries' duties, which also shows that the Romans understood the activity of the army as being integrated into the wider state function.

Crassus and his fortifications cut Spartacus off from the plain of Calabria and prevented any transport, depriving him of the possibility of obtaining supplies. To the south of the Roman line of defence, Spartacus controlled an area extending to the tip of the peninsula, and measuring more than 2,500 square kilometres. However, it was arid and mountainous, and the season was not a harvest period. When Spartacus learned, while already marching north, that the Romans had begun working to block his way to the plain by fortifying the only passage through the mountains, he initially scorned and underestimated their ability to actually stop him. He considered that he and his army were decisively superior to the heavy Roman infantry in mountainous, unconventional operations and that, consequently, a wall at that point could not drastically affect the tactical situation to his disadvantage. Subsequently, however, he found that the earlier spoils were dwindling, and the land he controlled was insufficient to support his troops, as the available resources were limited. Spartacus and the slaves tried to obstruct the works of the Romans and awaited the arrival of the horsemen that they had sent to roam the countryside in search of food and recruits.[102]

Finally, the Romans successfully completed the construction of the wall, contrary to what Spartacus had initially believed, which managed to block the slave army and cause great difficulties in supplying it. Spartacus' men resented this. Since the autumn, when Crassus had entered the war scene, they had been constantly in a problematic position, whereas until the previous summer, they had felt powerful and triumphant after the victories over the consuls. They had also hoped until a short time ago that they would at least manage to escape to Sicily. The earlier euphoria had given way to disappointment, accompanied by protests, tensions and disintegrative phenomena, which probably included tendencies towards surrender and defections. Spartacus, seeing that his forces were gradually moving towards despair, panic and disintegration, crucified or hanged a Roman prisoner in the middle of the distance between his camp and the enemy's position,[103] wishing to unsettle his men by showing them the fate that could await them if they lost the war, or if they faltered and gave up the effort in the hope that by surrendering, they would win the pity and favour of the Romans.

The Triumph and the Via Appia

At the beginning of 71 BCE, the situation was even worse for Spartacus and his forces than they knew, as Pompey had finally completed the war in Spain and was already marching towards Italy with his legions. At this point, Crassus sent a letter to the Senate, requesting that they instruct Pompey and Marcus Lucullus to move their armies towards the southern extremity of Italy,[104] thereby strengthening his efforts and ensuring the complete annihilation of Spartacus and the slave army.

This particular action of Crassus is strange and very interesting from the point of view of political tactics, since with this letter, he gave Pompey, his great political rival, the opportunity to appear as the catalyst that led to the suppression of the slave rebellion, while Crassus, by his strategy and victory in the war against the slaves, was aiming to raise his own position in Roman politics. If Pompey had intervened and actively contributed to the victory over Spartacus, he would have gained further political influence with minimal effort, thereby securing a significant advantage over Crassus. Especially since, thanks to his victory in Spain, he was already the face of the day for Roman society and would soon have a triumph.

Also, Crassus' request could easily be used against him as a sign of weakness, cowardice or inability to complete the war on his own. Indeed, it is reported that Crassus' letter created discontent in the Senate, which, like the people, was beginning to resent the fact that the disbanding of the slave army was not yet complete. And certainly, many opponents of Crassus and supporters of Pompey would have used the opportunity to damage the prestige of the former and promote the latter as the only great leader for the future.

However, the fact that Crassus was a highly experienced businessman and politician known for his methodical and careful approach to issues makes it doubtful whether he made this choice due to a momentary mistake or misjudgment of the situation. Barry Strauss develops an interesting and very possible hypothesis that Pompey's entry into the war had, in fact, already been decided by the people of Rome and Italy before Crassus sent the letter, as it is clear that there was resentment at Crassus' slow approach and the fact that the crushing of the slave rebellion was being delayed. The prevailing mood of public opinion was, on the contrary, extremely favourable to the triumphant Pompey, and the popular assembly was sure to vote in favour of his intervention in the South to bring the war to an immediate end.

Therefore, having learned from his people in Rome the intention of the popular assembly, Crassus probably hastened to send the letter, wanting to prevent the vote, to pretend that he had directed the events and requested Pompey's intervention, and that it had not taken place against his will, and indeed because of the people's discontent with him. In calling for the intervention of Marcus Lucullus at the same time, Crassus underestimated Pompey's importance, implying that the latter represented neither something special nor the catalyst for victory but merely one of the generals who were to assist in ensuring victory with the least possible loss to the Roman army.

I think that another possibility could be that Crassus sent the letter to 'annoy' Pompey politically, preventing his immediate triumphant return to Rome after the victory in Iberia. If Pompey entered Rome and triumphed immediately, all eyes would be turned away from Crassus, once the glorious victor of Spain returned to Rome. This was not going to change after Crassus' humble victory over Spartacus and the slaves, which everyone took for granted. Perhaps Crassus was aiming to move Pompey and his legions southwards and, in any case, away from Rome, hoping that he would eventually be able to complete the suppression of the rebellion before Pompey could get involved in the war himself. Thus, Crassus could hope to keep his attention focused on himself by completing the war against the slaves while Pompey was marching aimlessly through the countryside and also reaching Rome before Pompey triumphed and established himself in the city.

Finally, the Senate granted the people's and Crassus' request, ordering Pompey, who was approaching northern Italy, not to approach Rome but to head for the southern end of the peninsula to help disband the slave army. He also instructed Marcus Lucullus to move his troops to the eastern coast of the Adriatic and then board a fleet that would take him to the south-eastern coast of the Italian peninsula, specifically to Brundisium (modern-day Brindisi).

Crassus, having realised his political mistake or trying to carry out his conscious plan, asked a little later for the cancellation of the request he had made to emphasise that Pompey's intervention was unnecessary, but the order of the Senate had already been given, and Pompey was moving his legions to the south. Crassus, therefore, sought to end the war immediately, before Pompey and Marcus Lucullus arrived in the region, so that he might win the glory alone.

Spartacus' Escape Attempt

At the same time, on the other hand, Spartacus was now in a desperate situation, stranded and almost out of supplies. The morale of the slave army plummeted even lower when news arrived that Pompey's troops were also approaching the area. Appian reports that Spartacus became very worried on hearing the news of Pompey's arrival and sent Crassus a proposal of capitulation.[105] Spartacus' proposal, which shows that the slave leader had political flexibility, was apparently to become a 'client' of Rome and especially of Crassus himself, since when a general accepted such a surrender, he regarded the 'client' as his protégé and follower. Spartacus based his hopes for a positive response on the fact that Crassus would want to avoid Pompey's involvement. However, his proposal was unlikely to be accepted, as listing a warlord who for two years had been murdering, raping and robbing the peoples of the Italian peninsula as a 'client' of Rome would mean, first and foremost, the recognition of him as the legitimate ruler of the land he was at that time in control of. This was, of course, politically and morally unthinkable for the Romans, but also strategically useless, since the military situation was highly favourable to them. Therefore, as was to be expected, Crassus rejected with contempt Spartacus' proposal and ruled out any discussion.[106]

Spartacus knew that the dramatic situation in which he and his forces found themselves would inevitably culminate in utter defeat should Pompey's army enter the war while he remained blockaded. He therefore decided to mobilise the whole of his forces and proceed to the only option left to him: trying to break through the wall and smash the blockade. The operation took place shortly after the cavalry finally returned, in February 71 BCE.

According to Plutarch, the forces of Spartacus crossed the moat and penetrated the wall, taking advantage of the severe weather conditions that prevailed during a specific night. It was snowing and there was a strong wind.[107] To cross the moat, they filled a small section with earth, tree branches and other pieces of wood that they had collected. Meanwhile, the Romans had a reduced ability to see what was happening due to the weather conditions. According to Frontinus, Spartacus and his men cut the trench in the middle of the night, having previously piled into it the bodies of prisoners and oxen they had killed.[108]

It is reported that initially, only a third of Spartacus' forces managed to penetrate the wall before some Roman forces arrived and closed the wall again, but eventually, the massive and impetuous movement of the slave army managed to break the blockade once and for all. Spartacus and his men moved swiftly to reach Brundisium before Crassus had time to draw up his forces and engage them in battle, aiming to seek escape again by sea or, failing that, to consolidate and plunder the fertile and rich Apulia, also hoping to find new slave recruits. Little did they know, however, that another Roman army would soon be landing in the area.

When Crassus realised that the slave army was penetrating the wall, he was concerned, according to Plutarch, that Spartacus might intend to march on Rome.[109] The Roman general reacted immediately, gathering his troops, and began to pursue Spartacus' forces, while at the same time, Marcus Lucullus landed at Brundisium and Pompey was approaching from the north. Thus, the last vestige of hope for Spartacus and his men to escape from Italy was lost while the mighty Roman war machine closed an overwhelming grip around them.

Learning that he had found himself caught between three Roman armies, each of which was sufficient to defeat forces more powerful than those at his disposal, Spartacus tried to escape to Samnium.[110] The area was generally favourable to the rebels and posed perennial problems for the regular Roman army because of its mountainous topography. Additionally, the anti-Roman Samnite tradition may have given Spartacus hope that he could forge an alliance or recruit new troops. This, of course, was ruled out for reasons already mentioned, including the fact that the Samnites had been militarily decimated a decade earlier by Sulla.

Additionally, it is evident from the course of events that dissension and discord likely prevailed among the rebels once more, as the slave army was once again divided at this point. Considering that the strategy pursued by Spartacus had failed and led to a stalemate, the Gauls and Germans, led by Castus and Gannicus, separated from the rest of the forces and approached a lake, where they camped on a mountain called Camalatrum. It is not clear to which lake and mountain these ancient names correspond. It is believed that the lake was connected to the sea and was likely situated near the coast of Lucania, as its water was reported to be both fresh and salty at times. It is also possible that the lake mentioned in the sources was a marsh that existed between Poseidonia and the river Silaros, from antiquity until the twentieth century. As for the mountain named Camalatrum, it could be Mount Soprano, which rises above the modern-day town of Capaccio and is located almost 8 kilometres east of Poseidonia. At the foot of this mountain lies a fertile plain, close to which the ancient Via Annia ran, the road through which Crassus and his legions passed in pursuit of Spartacus and his army of slaves.

Roman Strategy Against the Gallic and Germanic Tribes

The Gauls and Germans probably intended to move against Rome or oppose Crassus' army directly, as their militant but uncultivated and unthinking spirit could not, for a long time, comply with what rational tactical considerations dictated, as had happened during the first period of the revolt. They were formidable warriors individually and treated war with pride and joy, as the activity par excellence that offered one the possibility of distinction and glory. They did not fear death on the battlefield. However, they lagged in organisation, tactics, discipline and collective functioning. Spartacus had certainly tried to train his forces as much as possible so that they could counter the mode of operation of the Roman army, but this was not so easy to achieve in the case of the Gauls and Germans. They probably viewed war as a series of duels and clashes between groups of warriors, reminiscent of the heroic Archaic era. In contrast, the Romans had developed elements such as organisation, coordination and discipline to the utmost extent.

The fact that on two different occasions, in particular, the Gauls and Germans not only maintained their distance from Spartacus but separated themselves from him altogether, following an independent course, proves that a radical ethnic division existed between the rebellious gladiators and slaves. One could say that the Spartacus rebellion consisted, at least to some extent, of two parallel, cooperating but separate rebellions with a common principle: one that always remained under the administration of Spartacus, consisting of slaves mostly from the eastern provinces of the Roman state, as well as desperate, impoverished people of Italy itself, and another composed of slaves from the Celtic tribes of the north-western provinces and frontiers.

Contemporary writers who have referred to the history of Spartacus do not focus their attention on this particular dimension of the subject, as they usually adopt narrowly class-based interpretations of society and history, analysing the uprising based on their own generally internationalist ideological convictions and overlooking the distinctly different perceptions and choices of its protagonists.

From a strategic point of view, the choice of the Gauls and Germans to separate from the rest of the slave army and adopt a more aggressive attitude towards the Roman troops was undoubtedly wrong and damning for them, as in these circumstances, their elimination would have been easier. Seeing that a portion of the enemy's forces was isolated and cut off from the rest, Crassus immediately deployed a body of troops against them to supervise their movements, position and size while considerably stronger troops followed. The Roman force occupied a hill in the vicinity and attempted to conceal their presence in order to prepare the ground for a surprise attack. However, fortune smiled momentarily upon the rebellious slaves. It so happened that two Celtic women who were following them were at that time performing a sacrifice at a point from which the Roman forces were visible. They therefore hastened to report what they had seen so that the Roman surprise was averted. It seems, however, that the Gauls and Germans eventually hesitated in the face of the possibility of clashing with Roman troops or felt that their position was not suitable for a large-scale battle and so chose to abandon Camalatrum and retreat.

The Romans pursued them, but before they could reach them and engage them in battle, Spartacus arrived with his forces and covered their retreat, giving them a chance to regroup. The Thracian gladiator had not moved far away after the dispersal of his army and the withdrawal of the Gauls and Germans, as the direction to Samnium was not separated from the Via Annia away from Poseidonia and the area in which, as it turns out, the above operations were conducted.

The attack of Crassus was finally to take place in the new position occupied by the Gauls and Germans on Mount Cadena, which is less than 5 kilometres south of modern-day Capaccio. Spartacus and his forces also remained close to the spot, but, as will be discussed, Crassus managed to pin him down away from the battle, thus confronting the Gauls and Germans alone, with most of his own forces.

The battle was extremely fierce, with several thousand fighters from both sides engaging in intense combat. At the end of it, the Romans were overwhelmingly victorious, as many thousands of slaves had been left dead on the field, and the corps of Gauls and Germans had been completely broken up, the survivors fleeing disorderly in different directions. On the Roman side, the losses were very few. According to Plutarch, the dead slaves numbered 12,300,[111] and it is probably to this battle that Appian refers when he claims that in Spartacus' attempt to flee to Samnium, his forces suffered a heavy defeat at the hands of Crassus' legions, and in two engagements fought on the same day they lost a total of about 12,000 men, while the Romans had only 3 dead and 7 wounded.[112]

Livy agrees that Crassus achieved a great victory over a part of the slave army that had been cut off from the rest of the forces, and claims that the number of dead was 35,000, as reported by Frontinus,[113] and that this body was composed of Gauls and Germans. Citing Livy, Frontinus gives a piece of information not found in the accounts of Appian and Plutarch, stating that the leaders of the Gauls and Germans were called Castus and Gannicus.[114] The crushing of a body of Gauls and Germans at this stage of the war, with over 30,000 dead, including their leaders, is further mentioned by Orosius, who adds that it took place while Spartacus was setting up his camp at the head of the river Silarus.[115]

The reliability of the above is confirmed by a relatively detailed account of Sextus Julius Frontinus. The latter must be considered accurate, not only because it is detailed but also because Frontinus' book constitutes one of the most important strategy manuals of antiquity, retaining its importance to this day. The author could, therefore, only cite examples that he was certain corresponded to real historical events. According to Frontinus, Crassus sent 12 cohorts (6,000–7,000 men) against the Gauls and Germans at Camalatrum, led by Quintus Marcio Rufo and Gaius Pomptinus, who were legion commanders.[116] The Roman cohorts moved, without being seen, by the rear of the mountain about the hill where the Gauls and Germans were and attacked by surprise with a gallop down the slope, with the result that the enemy were put to flight, without a general engagement and battle taking place at any point on the front. At the same time, Crassus had encamped at two different points to control both the forces of Castus and Gannicus and the main body of the enemy under the command of Spartacus. The two camps were placed at locations peripheral to Mount Cadena and were fortified with stockade fences.

Then, during the night, Crassus moved his troops but left his headquarters in the larger of the two camps, the one facing the forces of Spartacus, to mislead the enemy and prevent him from realising that most of the Roman troops had moved in the direction of the Gauls and Germans. The Roman general led his troops himself, and stationed himself at the foot of the mountain. He then divided his cavalry into two divisions. He ordered his second-in-command, Lucius Quintus, to move one division against Spartacus, causing skirmishes but not engaging in regular combat. At the same time, he unleashed the other against the Gauls and Germans of Castus and Gannicus.

He aimed to 'hook' Spartacus, making him think that the Roman troops were about to attack him while simultaneously enticing the Gauls and Germans to engage in battle. Afterwards, however, the cavalry that had charged against them would pretend to flee to draw them into pursuit, leading them upon the actual line of battle which Crassus had placed and which consisted of the greater part of his forces.

The barbarians indeed fell into Crassus' trap and pursued the Roman cavalry. The latter, executing its mission to perfection while galloping, eventually split in two, and suddenly, a strong and dense force of Roman infantry sprang up behind it. At the same time, the horsemen continued their gallop and drew up at either end. As soon as the cavalry opened, the Roman troops rushed swiftly with a war cry against the astonished and unsuspecting barbarians, who thought they had put the enemy to flight and were pursuing them. The conflict ended with the complete disintegration of the Gallic and Germanic slave armies, as, according to Frontinus, who cites Livy, 35,000 men were left dead, together with their leaders. In addition, five Roman legionary eagles and twenty-six standards held by the slaves from previous battles were recovered by the Roman army. Much booty was captured, and five praetorian sets of rods and axes were recovered.[117]

It is noteworthy from the point of view of strategic theory that the specific tactics that Frontinus attributes to Crassus are a precursor of the 'internal lines' theorised by Raymond Montecuccoli in the seventeenth century and used in many cases by Frederick the Great in the eighteenth century. 'Internal lines' refer to fronts that are not unified but where the opposing forces are deployed in at least two different places, split up. In this case, if one general places his troops at a shorter distance from each other than the enemy, he can move the bulk of them towards one part of the enemy forces, pinning down the other part by using a small portion of his own. He can thus deal with the two factions of the enemy's troops separately, employing almost the whole of his forces both against the one and against the other, provided, of course, that he succeeds in crushing or repelling the former rapidly, to be able to move the whole of his army against the latter. An example of an 'internal lines' operation is the triumph of Napoleon Bonaparte and the French at Austerlitz in 1805 against the overall more numerous forces of the Russian and Austrian Empires, as well as their near-victory at Waterloo, which turned into a debacle, against the British and Prussians ten years later.

Therefore, the work of Frontinus contains a description of a tactic that has been of key importance, even in modern strategic thinking and military history. This fact, like many others, demonstrates the extremely high level of strategic thinking among ancient Romans and highlights the great organisation and operation of the Roman army. Frontinus' account also reveals that Crassus possessed considerable strategic ability, although the end of his career, marked by his crushing defeat and death at Carrhae in 53 BCE, makes it problematic to include him among the great generals of antiquity.

As far as the Gauls and Germans were concerned, it is reported, however, that all but two of the dead slaves were found after the battle to have received a fatal blow to the front of the body. This fact demonstrates that all of them had been killed fighting in their positions and not fleeing, which is an indication of the determination and stubbornness that characterised the slave army at that time.

Having become desperate, knowing that if they were taken prisoner, their fate would be a miserable one, and having no other choice, escape was out of their thoughts, and they were determined to fight to the end in their position.

The Final Clash

Some of the Gauls and Germans may have become prisoners of the Romans, and the survivors who may have managed to escape can reasonably be assumed to have been reunited with Spartacus' forces. However, this crushing victory had already tipped the balance of power definitively in favour of Crassus and against Spartacus, demonstrating the vast difference in the capabilities of the two armies. Spartacus, understanding his predicament, tried to avoid further clashes with the Roman legions. The Thracian gladiator retreated again, apparently seeking a more suitable location to make a last desperate stand, and departed for the mountains of Petelia, as Plutarch calls them.[118]

It was a mountainous and rugged area with natural fortifications that would have enabled him to apply guerrilla warfare tactics, the only way to confront the sweeping Roman war machine with the forces at his disposal.

However, it is not entirely certain which mountains are named in this way by the ancient sources. It is likely that the hills of Picenum, particularly the area of modern-day Caposele, are more probable, as the mountains are surrounded by the plain of the river Silarus, next to which Spartacus was camped before the crushing of the Gauls and Germans, according to the account of Orosius. This point is approximately 70 kilometres from the area of Poseidonia, where the previous conflict likely took place, and is near Samnium; therefore, it is relatively safe to assume that this was the last position occupied by Spartacus and the slave army.

The retreating Spartacus was pursued by a corps sent by Crassus, led by his commanders, Lucius Quintus and Gnaeus Tremellius Scrofa. The former was the commander of the cavalry that had succeeded in the manoeuvre at Cadena, while Scrofa was the quaestor. However, they committed the mistake of advancing their not particularly strong forces up the hills without considering the possibility of a sudden attack. As part of his guerrilla tactics, Spartacus made a quick turn and attacked them by surprise, managing to put them to flight. In fact, during the attack, the quaestor, Scrofa, was wounded and eventually escaped from the retreating Roman soldiers.

However, this success ultimately did not benefit Spartacus, as it made his men feel, as they had in the past, more powerful than they were. Carried away by the excitement and the unfounded sense of omnipotence created by their limited victory over the small Roman body that had followed them, they demanded that they should at last stop retreating, avoiding a great general battle against the main body of the Roman army, and turn against it. On the other hand, it is common in military history for soldiers to resent their commanders when they choose to retreat after victories. Similarly, the stalemate and desperate situation in which Spartacus' men had long been trapped could justify their particular attitude. There were also among them men of warlike morals who would prefer a glorious death on the battlefield to the ignominy of cowardice, as they would see continued retreat.

Indeed, it is reported that in some cases, they went as far as disobeying their commanders and even forcing them to change course, sometimes using violence.[119] This fact, conveyed by Plutarch, shows again that the control Spartacus exercised over his forces was probably, at least relatively speaking, limited. The slave army was not a solid, organised and orderly whole but an aggregation of disparate groups and mobs with different origins and sometimes different aims, which was, of course, natural for such a revolt, which had not emerged and been founded as part of a social or national movement with a coherent and well-founded objective and broader theoretical foundation.

The attitude of the slaves was instrumental and beneficial to Crassus, who, as mentioned earlier, after asking the Senate to order Pompey's intervention in the war against the slaves, wanted to put down the rebellion as soon as possible, thus preventing, in practice, the involvement of the brilliant 34-year-old general. Thus, while Pompey was approaching the region with his legions, Crassus quickly moved his own forces against the slave army. It was probably April 71 BCE, and the slaves were marching south across the plain of the river Silarus while the Romans were approaching them and moving north. It is most likely that the two armies met at some point in the plain surrounding the river.

When the scouts located Spartacus' exact position, Crassus moved quickly against him and camped nearby, which drew some criticism. According to this criticism, his haste to win the war before Pompey's arrival led him to abandon the methodical approach and patience he had previously shown for an equally excessive risk-taking attitude. However, the criticisms are probably excessive, as, in fact, Crassus followed his usual tactics on this occasion, ordering his men to dig trenches and ditches to impede the movement of Spartacus' forces and to exclude sudden attacks, especially from cavalry charges.

However, the Roman works were never completed, as the slaves began to attack the legionaries, throwing bales of wood at them and lighting fires to obstruct the works and cause damage. Spartacus attempted to protect his forces by utilising natural fortifications and made sudden exits at various points, thereby harassing the Romans. At the same time, he was pinning his hopes on the somewhat unrealistic possibility of a new flow of slaves to his army so that it could be reinforced.[120]

The raids and attacks were aimed more at impressing, delaying and frightening the opponents than at securing any real results. However, at some point, the conflict began to escalate on one front, as many Romans rushed to reinforce their fellow warriors, while the slaves on the other side did the same. Thus, as time went on, more and more men from both armies gathered at this particular point, and the conflict grew. Seeing what was happening, Spartacus realised that the time had come for the final battle and mobilised all the forces at his disposal. Having no choice but to engage in a generalised battle of deployment, hoping for a martial miracle that would perhaps give him some chance of escaping from the suffocating Roman encirclement, he launched a desperate attack on Crassus with the whole of his army.

The battle was particularly fierce. One can imagine the slaves rushing in, shouting, and the Roman legionaries moving slowly and steadily, throwing their spears when the distance from the enemies would have been about 15 meters before the collision of the two factions took place. Spartacus' men fought with the vigour and stubbornness of men who knew that there was no future for them beyond death or enslavement in the event of defeat. At the same time, the Roman legionaries prepared to finish the war victoriously in the confidence and self-assurance of their superiority, freeing Italy from the scourge of the murderers, bandits and rapists they faced.

The clear superiority of the Roman army broke the resistance of the slaves, who, despite their large numbers and initial determination, were overcome by panic and fled in disorder as their lines were broken entirely. More and more slaves were left dead on the battlefield, and Spartacus himself was wounded in the thigh, according to Appian. The Thracian gladiator continued to fight covered behind his shield, but was eventually surrounded by his enemies and killed.[121]

Plutarch's description of the end of Spartacus aligns with modern cinematic extravaganzas. As the Greek author states, before entering the battle with sword in hand, Spartacus killed the horse they brought him to ride, in a not very rational and empathetic decision, saying that if he won, he would have many good horses at his disposal to take from his enemies, and if he lost, he would no longer need a horse.[122] He then rushed into the fray and began to fight. While the battle was underway and the situation looked increasingly dire, Spartacus made a desperate attempt to approach Crassus and kill him, trying to pass through the enemy lines, despite being wounded. He allegedly managed to kill two centurions, but his fellow warriors around him were being crushed and slaughtered en masse by the Romans, and in the end, he was left alone to fight numerous enemies. Having been surrounded, he eventually succumbed and was killed by the Roman soldiers.[123] Also, Florus mentions that Spartacus and his men fell fighting valiantly, meeting a death worthy of men.[124]

Regardless of whether Plutarch's romantic description – which is, anyway, distinguished for his highly literary and descriptive approach to the issues – is true or not, the fact is that Spartacus was killed in battle, as were all his men, since the crushing of the rebellion was total. At the end of the war, all those who had participated in it had been exterminated or captured. It is also a fact that Spartacus' body was never found, and therefore, probably no one could know exactly where, when and how he was killed during the battle to be certain of the details of his death.[125]

A few thousand slaves managed to escape to the mountains, but the Romans, although they had already won a crushing victory, were determined to eliminate any possibility of survival of cells and foci of new unrest and rebellions. They therefore pursued the retreating slaves persistently. The latter divided into four different corps and tried to resist, but Crassus' forces overpowered them and captured the 6,000 survivors. At the same time, Pompey and his legions, while marching south, encountered and exterminated some 5,000 slaves who were trying to flee north after their army was disbanded. Finally, a few hundred or a few thousand slaves who managed to escape to various parts of the territory were eliminated in the process by local Roman commanders and their forces.

According to Livy, the slave army left 60,000 dead on the battlefield,[126] and Orosius confirms, and adds that 3,000 Roman citizens were recovered.[127] Although the number of killed slaves reported by the two ancient chroniclers may be considered exaggerated by modern historians, it is certain that Spartacus' army was annihilated in this general conflict, while on the Roman side it is reported that there were about 1,000 dead.[128] The latter figure is not, however, negligible, and to some extent it does honour to Spartacus and his men for how they fought, as often the Roman war machine had recorded equally or even more crushing victories with similar or even smaller losses. For example, in the battle fought at Aquae Sextiae in 102 BCE, Gaius Marius' approximately 40,000 legionaries had annihilated an army three times their number of the Germans, inflicting 90,000 casualties and taking 20,000 prisoners, while their own losses were less than 1,000 men. Even if these numbers are inaccurate and inflated, they still tell us something about the Romans' perception of the enemies' ability to cause casualties. It is telling that Florus, though extremely caustic in his characterisations of the rebellious slaves, acknowledges that Spartacus and his men nevertheless died with honour, fighting to the end.

The great victory did not prevent what Crassus feared and had anxiously tried to avoid, namely Pompey's active involvement and his appearance as the victor of the war against the slaves, even if only to a minor extent in comparison with Crassus. This fact allowed the glorious Roman general to send a letter to the Senate, which, while it imperiously acknowledged that the victory belonged to Crassus and congratulated him, was careful to add that Pompey himself had crushed the rebellion completely and utterly, down to its roots.[129]

For his part, Crassus, knowing that there was no way he would be allowed to triumph in Rome, and wanting to impress and make a show of force, crucified the 6,000 slaves he had captured along the Via Appia, hanging one every 120 metres or so.[130] As mentioned, the Via Appia connected Rome to Capua and was one of the longest, busiest and best-known roads in Roman territory. Therefore, the sight of 6,000 crucified slaves sent an emphatic message in every direction that opposition and resistance against Rome was futile, and could only have a disastrous outcome for those who would choose it.

Spartacus and the slave army had been wiped out. Thereafter, Roman politics evolved around the basic antagonism between Pompey and Crassus, as was already the case during the last phase of the war. Pompey achieved a glorious triumph for his victory in Spain and the suppression of Sertorius' mutiny, and he also won credit for his contribution to the extermination of the slave army, so that the citizens of Rome were effectively celebrating both victories simultaneously. Consequently, the so-called pedestrian triumph (*ovatio*) that Crassus finally achieved was marked by even less enthusiasm and participation.[131]

Triumph on foot was reserved for smaller feats, and the suppression of a slave rebellion was not considered a feat worthy of a proper triumph. Indeed, in this particular case, the foot triumph of Crassus followed in time the complete triumph of Pompey, so that it became a completely minor event and was treated as almost incidental to Pompey's triumph. It is doubtful whether its performance benefited Crassus in any way or instead humiliated rather than exalted him, and it is possible that the Roman aristocrat would have helped his image and political prestige more if he had refused to perform it, contenting himself with the terrible spectacle of the Via Appia.

Writing almost five centuries after the events and using different criteria, Orosius argues that no one should underestimate this war, even though it was just a war against slaves, as it caused great destruction and fear in the territory. Even consular armies suffered defeats on the battlefields. Also, the number of aristocrats who died in this war was not negligible, while on the other hand, over 100,000 rebellious slaves were killed during the conflict.[132]

However, the Romans of the time viewed the suppression of a slave rebellion as a self-evident fulfillment of an obligation, rather than a victory that glorified Rome and increased its power and sovereignty. It is significant that, unlike Crassus, later in the same year Marcus Lucullus performed a regular triumph. Lucullus, after his small contribution to the suppression of the slave rebellion by his landing at Brundisium, had returned to Thrace, where he defeated and subdued the tribe of the Bessi. Moreover, he captured several cities belonging to the territory of Mithridates, achieving yet another blow at the expense of the king of Pontus, and further reducing his power and influence in the region. By these successes, Lucullus had assisted in his work his brother, Lucius Licinius Lucullus, who would finally and victoriously conclude the war against Mithridates a few years later.

The victory over a hostile tribe and the spread of Rome's dominion was in the perception of Roman society much more important than the suppression of any large-scale slave revolt, since the latter did not mark an expansion of Roman power, but merely imposed order in a region. Roman society reserved the greatest honour and glory only for those who grew and strengthened the limits of its dominion. An attitude reminiscent of and consistent with the coming-of-age oath of Athenian teenagers, who at the moment of acquiring the status of Athenian citizen promised to deliver their city greater and stronger than they received it.

Chapter 5

Ancient Slavery and Modern Misunderstandings

The importance of slavery was limited for Roman society until the expansion of the third century BCE, while it increased sharply during the second century BCE after the victory over Carthage in the Second Punic War.[1] The leading cause of this phenomenon, apart from the greater availability of slaves after the conquests, was, as mentioned in previous chapters, the creation of vast landed estates in place of traditional, autonomous agricultural production, as extensive arable land was accumulated in a few hands.

The wars brought about a depopulation of the countryside due to conscription and deaths, as most of the legions were manned by autonomous peasants. There were also shortages of technical equipment, which was generally weakened by destruction and abandonment. With the drastic reduction in the number of small farms and the resurgence of large landholdings,[2] the need arose to find many workers for the countryside. The latter was satisfied through the massive use of slaves. At the same time, an urban proletariat began to take shape, comprising former peasants who, due to their inability to produce adequately in the agricultural sector and having either sold or lost their estates, migrated to the cities in search of work.

These developments also caused a drastic change in the position of specific categories of slaves and the relations between them and their masters. In the earlier phases of Roman society, slaves had been regarded as members of the traditional patriarchal family. Their position was naturally inferior to that of free members of the household, but their relationship with the master and his relatives was direct and permanent, often resulting in relations of cooperation and friendship.[3]

With the development and spread of large-scale land ownership, this archaic model of the house was abandoned as production became increasingly mass-produced. In the second century BCE, the typical large landowner not only had no personal relationship with the slaves working on his estate but did not even know them. They numbered dozens, or in many cases, even hundreds of people who lived and worked exclusively in the fields, having no contact with the houses and activities of their owners. However, that was only true in cases of slaves working in agricultural mass production and did not apply to urban slaves or to categories of slaves who held administrative positions.

Therefore, the significant increase in slaves in Italy was associated with the phenomenon of the creation of large landed estates. In contrast, in earlier Greek history, the corresponding culmination of the importance of slaves for the economy and society, which occurred during the classical period, was primarily concerned with industrial sectors rather than agricultural production. The most extensive use of slaves in the Greek world was recorded in classical Athens, where slaves were used en masse in craft workshops, while the agricultural sector had remained essentially unchanged from the archaic past.[4] Subsequently, during the Hellenistic period, the number of slaves declined markedly, as they had less involvement in crafts, probably because the expansion of the Greek world ensured a great abundance of labourers.

Conversely, the importance of slavery to the Roman economy was significantly reduced during the imperial period compared to the last century of the Republic.

From a legal point of view, the slave was the property of his master. However, he was granted human status, so one could say that the legal status of the slave was something in between free man and inanimate property.[5] The fact that the slave was an asset of the owner provided him with legal protection against attacks from third parties in the context of defending private property from insults or harm. However, there were also restrictions on the owner's power, as the murder of a slave was punished with a specific penalty, initially much less than the murder of a free man; however, with time the murder of a free man and a slave became equal under legal terms.

In general, the limits of the owners' power over their slaves were gradually reduced, inversely with the recognition of the human status of slaves.[6] During the imperial period, in particular, the mistreatment of slaves was mitigated, but they were also allowed to lodge complaints without the mediation of a free citizen. This was not previously the case since the slave was not considered a fully legal person. For the same reason, a slave's testimony in court was equivalent to evidence only if it had been extracted after torture. Otherwise, it was a mere reminder that the judge was not obliged to take it into account, and was not testimony of binding value.

As far as personal and family life was concerned, it depended mainly on the owner's intentions. Slave families were certainly formed, but it is unclear whether there were any specific legal regulations. Perhaps the marriage of two slaves could not take place without the owner's permission.[7] However, it was, in any case, generally permitted since, in this way, the house acquired slaves by birth through the union of its slaves and needed to buy fewer or no slaves in the future.

The situation was similar for slaves regarding whether they could own property and whether they could engage in private occupation. Usually, owners allowed their slaves to own some limited property and to work for themselves in their spare time. It is noteworthy that slave ownership could include their own slaves, and in this case, the slave was both an asset of his master and a slave owner himself.

Social and Economic Position of the Slaves

The massification and intensification of agricultural production in the second century BCE, along with the new conditions created in the relationships between owners and rural slaves, led to a significant deterioration in the living conditions of the latter compared to the past. Many agricultural slaves lived in terrible conditions, often without any social and personal life, subject to severe restrictions and oppression.[8] Even worse off were the mine slaves, who were, more often than not, prisoners of war or slaves who had been sentenced to work in the mines as punishment for criminal or problematic behaviour. The worst working and living conditions existed in the mines, and the slaves had no human dignity, as their lives were essentially limited to hard and unhealthy work.

The extensive exploitation of slaves in the fields is one of the key elements of the fundamental issue in Roman politics during the latter part of the second century BCE, namely the issue of land distribution. It was in this historical, social and political context that the major conflicts and civil strife within the

Roman state erupted, part of which were the various slave revolts, including the three mass revolts that took place in 135 BCE, 104 BCE and 73 BCE – even the dates indicate the structural nature of the phenomenon in that period, as there is a perfect temporal sequence.

The revolts originated and were almost exclusively carried out by the two categories of slaves mentioned above, namely those of the extensive farms and the miners. These two categories are the only ones that correspond to the modern picture of slavery, which is, however, very far from the usual situation of slaves in antiquity and their way of life. Slavery in antiquity was an extraordinarily complex and distinct phenomenon from that in modern and contemporary history, to the extent that it becomes completely incomprehensible when viewed through modern categorisations and perspectives.

First of all, slaves in Greek and Roman antiquity were not a 'class' in the economic sense in which the term is used in modern times. Ancient slaves were not limited to specific sectors of production, unlike those of modern history, but were active in many different occupational sectors.[9] Their way of life, standard of living, and class in the modern economic sense were almost as varied as those of the free. Slaves in antiquity were, above all, a legal and political category and, to some extent, a social one, rather than an economic class in the modern sense.

Consequently, while modern class-based interpretations capture some valid elements, they often distort the reality of ancient society, such as, primarily, the Marxist image of slaves as the 'proletariat' or working class of antiquity. Marxist interpretations often project modern social categories onto the Greco-Roman context anachronistically, overlooking or misinterpreting key elements of social reality at the time, particularly the nature of slavery, which led to conclusions that fail to account for the specific historical context. This was mainly because while Marx's work is exhaustively analytical about the modern capitalist economy and the specific issues surrounding it – without this implying that his conclusions are correct – it nevertheless remained to the end highly oversimplified and abstract in terms of its basic premise and thesis, that of the historical evolution and alternation of socio-economic systems on which the fundamental Marxist and communist beliefs were based.

For Marxists, the economy of antiquity was underdeveloped and based on the exploitation of slaves. Although the Greek and Roman cultural achievements were indeed brilliant and fabulous, they primarily concerned a small minority of society at the time, while the vast majority lived in miserable conditions. The works of the economic historian Moses Finley on the ancient economy seemed to provide a more recent scientific cover for the speculative assumptions of Marx and his followers. The famous sociologist Max Weber's conception of the ancient economy and society coincided with similar positions.

According to Finley's theory, economic activity remained relatively underdeveloped throughout antiquity in terms of technological progress and productivity growth. International trade did not develop sufficiently to create a single market but instead remained fragmented and limited. The result allegedly was that there was never a significant increase in consumption for the majority of society.[10] Finley's picture contrasted with earlier positions on ancient social and economic history and, for quite some time, reversed them, at least to some extent, such as those of historians Edward Gibbon and Michael Rostovtzeff, who understood the ancient economy as much more developed and 'globalised'.

However, the findings of archaeological research, as well as the work of economic historians such as J.G. Manning, Ian Morris, Bryan Ward-Perkins, Philip Kay, Walter Scheidel, Sitta Von Reden, Filippo Carla, Arnaldo Marcone[11] and others have overturned the 'primitive' model of Marx, Weber and Finley. Thus, more recent archaeological and economic research has shown with much greater clarity that the structure and institutions of the Roman-era economy were more developed than the older 'primitive' model allowed, resembling those of the late Middle Ages, on the verge of the Renaissance and the emergence of the first forms of modern capitalism in northern Italy. Moreover, consumption in the ancient world was not limited to a small minority but rather concerned the entire society. The imperial era in Rome saw an increase in living standards that was only to be repeated in the modern industrial age.

Beyond these recent scientific works on the ancient economy and their conclusions, however, a careful study of Finley's work, as well as Marx's, shows that their conceptions of an underdeveloped economy with slave production in antiquity run up against the historical data already known from earlier times, concerning slavery and the social structure of the Greco-Roman world.

Finley and proponents of the 'slave-owning society' model for ancient Greece and Rome, on the one hand, overlook the fact that the condition that they set for this characterisation, namely that 20 per cent of the total population of society should consist of slaves, applies only to the classical period of Greek history and the century of crisis of the Roman Republic, while in all the others, the percentages were much lower. For example, as can be seen from the well-preserved Egyptian scrolls, the percentage of slaves in Roman Egypt during the period of the empire ranged from 7 to 11 per cent, while the percentage of slaves in the Hellenistic period was similar.[12]

It is also clear that the economy of antiquity, as in all the eras that followed until the Industrial Revolution, was essentially agricultural, with the majority of the population working in the fields. However, except for the particular historical period in which the slave revolts occurred, namely, the century in which the Republic declined and the transition to empire was prepared for Rome, the participation of slaves in agricultural production remained a minority. The norm in both Greece and Rome was small-scale autonomous agricultural activity, while the central importance of extensive farms with hundreds of slaves was only in this period.[13] In classical Greece, or more precisely, Athens, i.e. the earlier historical period in which slaves are estimated to have reached or exceeded 20 per cent of the total population, agricultural production was based on free, autonomous farmers, as large landed estates like those of second-century BCE Italy were never formed. Slaves mostly worked in the craft sectors, which continued to be the case in the Hellenistic period.[14]

Therefore, the only period of antiquity in which the agrarian base of the economy functioned primarily using slave labour was this particular turbulent century of Roman history.

The basic temporal structure of the Greek, Hellenistic, Roman and Italian economy was limited to autonomous land ownership. Slavery, for its part, was primarily for the wealthiest segment of the population,[15] but it was only during the century of the Roman Republic's crisis that it controlled most of the agricultural production. For this reason, it is inherently wrong and arbitrary to conceive of the ancient economy as slave economy as such, as is made clear by a wealth of other evidence as well. Significantly, even historians who accept the term 'slave society' for Greece and Rome are quick to point out that it is nonetheless untenable to refer to a 'slave economy', such as Jean Andreu and Raymond Descat.[16] The French writers make this distinction because while it can be argued that the institution of slavery had a significant impact on the lifestyle of the upper strata of Greek and Roman society, it is clear that it did not play an equally important role in their economic base.

Moreover, slavery as an institution was not decisive for the division of labour if one excluded work in the mines, where not free men but exclusively slaves worked. Beyond this case, however, the division of labour among slaves was as differentiated and complex as the division of labour among free men.[17] Slaves in antiquity were not confined to a few specific branches of production, even low-skill-intensive ones, as was the case in modern times; on the contrary, their presence was spread over almost all productive sectors and occupational branches, with the sole exception of the legal professions.[18] Also, slaves and free men who were not citizens could not, of course, participate in the political and legislative process. Yet, their position as assistants and sometimes close associates of politicians often ensured them a much more important substantive role in the political process than they formally had.

It is characteristic, for example, that in the republican period of Rome, there was no stable administrative organisation in the provinces manned by trained professional staff, and the administration was manned at the highest level by people of the prefects. The prefects, for the most part, placed in these positions slaves who were educated and capable and who were utterly loyal to them.[19] Also, the permanent, lower administrative staff of the provinces was composed throughout the republican period of state slaves. In contrast, the central administration exercised little or no control over the actions of the prefects. This mode of operation, along with other institutions of the republican period, favoured the promiscuity of the governors, who enriched themselves personally by arbitrary action at the expense of the provinces. Moreover, it is evident that for the free citizens of the provinces, even the rich ones, these particular state slaves of Rome were the direct face of conceit and exploitation and not, of course, oppressed people but oppressors.

It should be noted that this awful situation for the provinces was overcome only at the beginning of the imperial period, after the administrative reforms of Augustus, when, among other things, a stable professional administration of the provinces was established, independent of the political governance of the prefects, and in direct contact with the imperial centre.

Other cases of state slaves were the bodyguards provided by the state to Roman senators – various kinds of permanent assistants to officials, advisers, mortgage keepers, archivists, as well as jailers and executioners. State slaves also existed in Greece, with a classic example being the police officers who patrolled the streets of democratic Athens, who were often Scythians rather than Athenians or Greeks.[20] State slaves, therefore, functioned as operational organs of political power. In the cases of bodyguards and policemen, they had the authority to intervene and act violently against free citizens, as well as to arrest them for their illegal and criminal acts.

The case of the state slaves is merely an example of the fact that there were very significant differences between the different classes of slaves in a way that made it impossible to refer to a general class of slaves with specific characteristics and living conditions. The society of Roman antiquity, like that of Greece, was more multidimensional than that of modern times. Particularly during the explosive period of the transition from traditional Roman polity to imperial power, the class stratification within the Roman state was overly complex.

Apart from the slaves, there were parallel societies in general, which were linked within a single framework but had their own separate class stratification, resulting in very heterogeneous configurations of interests. The conception of society as a bipolar scheme made up of 'exploiters' and 'exploited', rich-poor, bourgeois-proletarian, etc., is simplistic and oversimplified for any era and was in no way valid specifically in the Roman era. That is why slave revolts were in no way class or social revolutions but merely attempts by some groups of people to escape from their terrible living conditions, as well as opportunities for criminals and opportunists. The urban slaves, and many peasant slaves, usually did not only not support them but actively opposed both those that took place in Sicily and that of Spartacus. On the other hand, the latter had some success among desperate free men without even coming close to gaining the elementary mass support of proletarians, who, as an economic class, also fought against it.

Social Structure of the Ancient World

In general, in antiquity, society was not perceived as a set of individuals differentiated by their economic activity and status, as it is today, but rather as a set of families and socio-political categories, which were divided in principle on a political and hierarchical basis. The latter, in many cases, did not correspond to the economic one. Participation in a political and social category was not necessarily aligned with professional activity and economic condition. Being a citizen, a free or freed non-citizen, or a slave, did not mean one had a higher income or a better job. For instance, a person could be wealthy but a non-citizen or even a slave, while one could be a citizen but work in a low-status and low-income job and be poor.[21]

The ultimate unit into which ancient society, and those that followed until the arrival of modern industrial society, was divided was the house, not the individual. The house consisted of the family, slaves, animals and assets, as well as the economic activities associated with them. The head of the family expressed his views in public not as an individual but as a representative of his household, which often involved conversations and consultations with other household members. On the other hand, he exercised control and authority over all other members of the household, including adult sons. Liberation from paternal custody did not occur merely with the attainment of age and the acquisition of political rights, but at a later stage, compared to what happens in modern times. In ancient Rome, a man might take an active part in political power or the administration of the army while remaining legally subject to paternal authority.

That was because ancient societies, like all those that followed, up to the modern era, were not societies of individuals in a state of equality, separated by their attributes, but institutionally hierarchical structures in which people occupied specific positions as part of the whole. The conception of people as independent, self-contained entities, not subject to constraints regarding their social status and position but depending solely on themselves, their choices, their abilities and objective facts, is unique to the modern Western world and has not existed in any other society on the planet.

The individual-centred society was established in modern Western Europe and the United States, where, for the first time, favourable economic conditions for such a development emerged, namely mass industrial production and consumption. In contrast, a similar form of society was impossible in the past, as the vast majority of the population worked in the fields, technical means were minimal compared to those of the industrial age, as were the possibilities of travel and communication, and as a result, the availability of goods was much less than in modern developed countries. Under such objective conditions, free movement and individual choice, as understood today, could not exist.

Consequently, one of the elements of ancient societies, which from today's point of view seems unthinkable, such as the ownership of people by other people, was widely regarded as a normal and intelligible institution, but furthermore, the master's power over the slave was not very different from his powers over his own children, or other citizens and free non-citizens, who were in a position of servitude to him, for example, because of debts.

The above demonstrates how unfounded is the belief of modern liberalism that it is characterised by moral superiority over the ancient Greco-Roman society because it recognises the freedom and the equality of individuals as the highest principle, and it condemns and prohibits slavery – an attitude from which its sympathy for Spartacus and his rebellion derives.

It should also be stressed that the phenomenon of slavery is crucially differentiated between its ancient and modern forms. In modern times, slaves were used almost exclusively for lower-skilled work. The reality of slavery in ancient Greece and Rome was radically different and largely at odds with this picture. As discussed earlier, slaves in antiquity were not relegated to the lowest manual and unskilled level of production; instead, they were actively engaged in every professional field.

Therefore, for the ancient slave, the problem from a professional point of view did not lie in the fact that he was condemned to be active in work of a lower educational level and with lower wages but in the fact that the type of work and his activity was determined by the social status of his owner, as well as by the latter's wishes. However, the price of each slave was judged by the demand for him, and naturally, the more he possessed knowledge, skills and beauty, the more expensive he became, so he ended up in a correspondingly rich house. The slaves sold in the slave markets came into the ownership of a house of a corresponding social level and activities according to their skills and attributes. However, slaves who were not purchased but belonged to a house by birth could also hope for the possibility of being purchased by a wealthier master who would appreciate their attributes and utilise them in a corresponding activity of his house if it turned out that they were particularly intelligent or beautiful and could perform more upscale tasks than those that their original owner needed or could finance.

Also, the slave represented an investment and a cost for the owner, so the owner had every reason to make sure that he or she was put to the best use, which meant that he made sure that he placed each slave in tasks commensurate with his skills and abilities, but also ensured at least tolerable living conditions.

Slavery was, therefore, not decisive for the division of labour, but it was formed mainly in an organic way, in proportion to the existing productive capacities at any given time. Slaves were certainly disadvantaged in that they were not free to seek a better job or a better place to live, and were at the disposal of their owner. However, their survival was generally assured, as was their opportunity to operate in houses much richer and more substantial than those of the average citizen, small farmer or artisan. The slaves of a senator or a wealthy businessman and landowner, who managed to enter the circle of his trusted associates due to their skill and loyalty, were in at least one sense socially and economically superior to most free citizens.

It must therefore be stressed again that it is a fundamental error to try to analyse the economy and society of the ancient world by taking slaves as a class in the sense of economic activity. Slavery in Greek and Roman antiquity had primarily a legal meaning, and often, the financial and professional status of a slave was in complete contradiction with his legal condition as citizen, free or slave.

The basic division of slaves in economic terms was between those who worked in the fields and those who worked in the cities.[22] Within these two categories, there were vast variations; however, in general, the situation of urban slaves was preferable to that of rural slaves. Among the latter were the groups of slaves who experienced the greatest exploitation and oppression,[23] and from whom the ranks of the three great revolts were manned. Their treatment was generally severe, and heavy penalties were prescribed for the lazy and unruly, including flogging and chaining, both during work and sleep.

However, there was also the provision of more food and wine for slaves who performed the most difficult and heavy work, and there were also significant differences between agricultural slaves. The most competent and trustworthy of them worked directly with the owner, occupying positions of stewardship, personnel management and production organisation, and were paid much better and also enjoyed greater freedoms.[24]

The situation was usually considerably more favourable for urban slaves, who carried out tasks related to the house or their master's urban activities.[25] Among the urban slaves, there were almost all the professions of the time: cooks, hairdressers, guards, bodyguards, secretaries, weavers, porters, accountants, librarians, copyists, nannies, nurses, caterers, as well as slaves working in the trades of the sea, fishermen and sailors. Perhaps some slaves were also used in crafts, but certainly, this was limited in Rome, unlike in classical Greece. In contrast to earlier times, when the duties of slaves were more general, the Roman era saw a gradual increase in specialisation, sometimes to the point of excess, which was natural given the expansion in size. The numbers of slaves held by the wealthy houses during the period of Roman rule were much greater than those of previous periods.[26]

In cases of great wealth, there were slaves whose only job was to look after their appearance and accompany the owner in his public appearances or to beautify the place with their presence at receptions and celebrations organised by him: beautiful young men and women in luxurious clothes, through which their master displayed his wealth and power. There were also dancers, singers, jesters, comedians and pipers who entertained the partygoers alongside the sommeliers, winemakers and waiters. Some took care of the physical well-being of their masters and guests in a more direct way, such as masseurs. It is also understandable that gentlemen and ladies often had sexual relations with slaves and servants of the house.[27]

Among the master's followers, especially in the case of politicians, lawyers and business people, there was very often a slave whose job was to remember names, persons and qualities, and to mention them in a low voice or remind his master of them when they met someone in the street or a public place. Other slaves worked as messengers, carrying messages, proposals and threats to their owner's associates and rivals. Others served as informers, gathering information and news to report to their master. Slaves of this kind had great freedom of movement, and some slaves travelled to distant places and could be away for months at a time, promoting their master's affairs and carrying out missions. They were trusted slaves, sent with enough money as agents of their master in trade negotiations and authorised to make selections on his behalf.[28]

In the wealthy houses of hegemonic Rome, one could also meet slaves who worked as 'butlers', announcing and accompanying guests, and were in charge of the jewellery room, bathroom, bedroom, laundry, dinner room, and the decorators, stable boys and gardeners. Also, the house doctor was a slave, and in general, in Rome, doctors were almost always slaves or freedmen. The same was true of the pedagogues, who, in most cases, were Greek. Finally, in the houses of senators and culture-loving knights, some learned slaves taught their masters rhetoric, history and philosophy, as the owner valued them and wanted to keep them close to him, taking care of their living.[29] A classic example of this category of slaves is the Greek philosopher Epictetus, one of the most important representatives of the Stoic school of philosophy.

Another famous example of a talented slave is Tiron, who was born and raised in Cicero's household, eventually becoming the closest assistant to the great Roman jurist, politician and writer. It is believed that Tiron invented a pioneering shorthand method by which he was able to record with precision every word he heard.[30] This is also very important for historical research, given Cicero's central role in the political life of Rome for a long time. It is worth noting that at the time of the Spartacus rebellion, Cicero was in the early stages of his career and had aligned himself with the faction of Gnaeus Pompey, while sharing a mutual dislike with Marcus Licinius Crassus.

Apart from the activities mentioned above, the urban slaves were also active in another sector of central importance: banking. Both in Rome and in classical Athens, banks were operated and managed almost exclusively by slaves and freedmen. Indeed, many of them, after their emancipation, became owners of the banks in which they worked or founded their own, as they knew the profession better than anyone else. Often, their former masters would leave part or all of the property of their bank to their slaves in their wills, provided the remaining property was large enough, as their children had never been in the banking business and could not manage it.[31]

In general, it can be said that slaves, except those who worked in forced labour in the mines and, in some rough cases, in countryside farms, were economically similar to modern public and private sector employees from the lowest to the highest level. The clerical employment relationship was not as common as it is in modern times among freedmen in antiquity. The free man was typically economically private, either as a peasant, like the majority, or as an artisan, craftsman or merchant. Additionally, as mentioned earlier, senior administrative and organisational positions, sometimes even in governmental sectors, were often filled by slaves, who were, therefore, financially equivalent to today's managers and executives in large corporations and governmental organisations.

The primary difference between the modern employee who lives and operates in a free economy and the ancient slave is that in the case of the former, the employer exercises authority over them only in the context of their work. In contrast, the ancient slave owners had authority over their slaves in all aspects of life. In practice, of course, the owner had no reason to degrade the slave's job as long as he was performing satisfactorily, whereas, in our time, an employee who is not qualified to perform a given level of work will, de facto, be forced to seek jobs with lower requirements, hence lower pay.

Moreover, in the communist systems of the modern era, the power of the employer, i.e. the regime, over the worker extended far beyond the limits of the labour process. Coercive and sometimes violent movements and reassignments of workers from above were standard features of the system, depending on the regime's decisions about the types of production to be preferred and promoted. Therefore, in terms of position in production, the difference between the ancient slave and the worker in a communist state is that the former could hope that if he worked satisfactorily and was well behaved, he would gain his freedom, as well as the fact that he often already had a private economic activity as a slave. On the contrary, the latter remained subject to the regime's decisions for the entirety of their lives.

The reason why a servant class of free men with a central role in the economy did not develop in antiquity is not because of the cost but because of the certainty of the continuation of work. The wages of slaves were, as a rule, equal to those of free men for the same work, and in addition, the possession of slaves meant for the owner the cost of food, clothing, housing, training and education, which does not exist in the case of free men. So, the owner's gain from using slaves was not the reduction of production costs but the certainty that he would have sufficient labour for the work he had to perform. Proof of this is that even during the period of maximum slavery development, free seasonal workers were also employed on farms. The slaves were used in positions where steady work was needed throughout the year.

The significant increase in the number of slaves occurred in Roman history in parallel with and in proportion to the concentration of land ownership. When this process was completed, and a large proletariat emerged in place of the old small autonomous peasants, the reverse process began, and the reduction in the number of slaves started, as there were now numerous workers available to be recruited at any time from the large farms. This development was also reinforced by the fact that, by reaching the imperial era and the Pax Romana, slaves became significantly more expensive than in the past, as there were no longer any constant flows of prisoners of war to replenish the supply on the slave market.

Finally, the redistribution of land by the great military leaders, particularly Marius, Sulla and Julius Caesar, as well as the new situation formed and consolidated by Octavian Augustus in the imperial era, played a significant role. These developments essentially led to the restoration of extensive autonomous small landholdings and reduced the number and size of the latifundia. In a paradoxical way and through a broken historical path, Tiberius Gracchus' goal was achieved a century after his death.

Institutions

Apart from the 'unofficial' possibility of autonomous work and ownership of property, as well as the placement of the slave in tasks of high responsibility and freedom of action by the owner, Roman law also provided for institutionalised types of asset disposal in the management of slaves. In general, in the Roman system, slavery had three legal forms, which were not mutually exclusive but could coexist in two or all three together: a) work under the direct supervision of the owner, in the sense that the slave worked in a production unit managed by the owner himself; b) authorised management of the owner's assets by the slave; c) usufruct of the slave over the owner's assets. The first is none other than the classic form of slavery. The second and the third, however, constitute two very important and specific institutions of slavery in Roman times, called, respectively, *praepositio* and *peculium* – the equivalent of the earlier Greek *chrimation* (χρημάτιον).[32]

The *praepositio* was a legal form in which the master entrusted to the slave a productive unit or generally an asset of his property, with the consent of the slave, so that he could manage it as he thought fit, but without acquiring property rights over it. The object of the *praepositio* could be anything, such as a farm, a group of slaves, a bank, a sum of money, or, according to the example of the great third-century CE jurist Ulpian, a ship that the slave was to rule.[33] In the *praepositio*, the owner retained all the profits, and the slave did not receive a direct share of them. However, he was paid for his work and gained the esteem and trust of the owner, which ensured him various benefits in the future, contingent upon successful management.

The slave with *praepositio* was, therefore, a category that can be professionally paralleled with modern business managers, investment managers and general employees in administrative positions, provided that they are not shareholders in the company for which they work and that the owners refrain from managing it, as well as with professional figures such as charter boat captains.

The institution of the *peculium* offered even greater possibilities to the slave, since, in this case, he did not simply manage his master's property but kept the profits for himself. It was, therefore, a relationship of usufruct and semi-ownership, as the slave's owner retained ownership of the asset but had no right to its management and the profits derived from it. He could only regain management of all or part of the asset if he freed the slave.

The *peculium* was the most favourable situation in which a slave could find himself since it made him not just a managerial employee or freelancer but a real autonomous entrepreneur. Moreover, in the vast majority of cases, the choice of an owner to assign a *peculium* to his slave meant that the latter regularly acquired private property since at least part, if not all, of the *peculium* was left by the owner in the ownership of the slave after emancipation. The master benefited from the *peculium*, firstly because in the event of successful management by the slave, his asset acquired greater value, but even more so because the return of the *peculium* reasonably created gratitude and absolute loyalty on the part of the slave to his master, which continued after his release, often with even greater intensity. Freedmen usually continued in the same job they had as slaves and even in collaboration with their former owners, to whom they remained attached.

Praepositio and *peculium* are excellent examples of effective human resource management, which anticipate many centuries of modern notions that staff satisfaction maximises the productivity and profitability of a company rather than relying on cold exploitation. With these two institutions, the Romans ensured significantly greater energy and mobility for their economy, harnessing talents, skills and the will to work and create that would otherwise have remained dormant.

The *peculium* and the *praepositio* created a class of slave entrepreneurs, which gave impetus and dynamism to the economy, increasing the overall power of Roman society and the Roman state. It is evident that the assets assigned by the owners to the management of the slaves were, as a rule, secondary parts of their property, which would otherwise have remained inactive or underperformed, yielding less to the economy of the time than they eventually did, thanks to these two institutions.

Another practice, the cultivation and exploitation of the skills of slaves, which had been established in the Hellenistic kingdoms and continued after the Roman state annexed these regions, was the apprenticeship system. Owners would send some of their slaves to apprentice themselves to skilled artisans, whom they paid to train them in technical tasks. After completing their training, the slaves worked for their owners, but being skilled artisans, they could also engage in private business activities. Additionally, in some cases, the owners did not intend to use their trained artisan slaves themselves but rather specialised them through apprenticeship so that they could hire them out to those who needed their technical work and were willing to pay for it.

Finally, the release of slaves after years of successful and dedicated service was not an uncommon practice. Owners several times freed their slaves in their wills, but just as often freed them while they were alive. Importantly, freed former slaves of Roman citizens automatically acquired Roman citizenship, which was not the case in Greek cities.[34] The benefit to the owner of such an action was, to some extent, financial, as the custom was for slaves to pay for their emancipation to their owners the amount that the owners had spent on their purchase. Most of all, however, emancipation secured in most cases the gratitude and loyalty of the former slave and present citizen, as well as therefore his vote, and also often in terms of economic activity, the situation remained essentially unchanged, since as mentioned, the freedman usually continued to work in the same position as before, or in any case to do business with his former owner.

Thus, in many cases, there were actual liberation agreements in which the slave would agree with the owner to pay him a sum of money or to take over some of his tasks and affairs in exchange for being freed. This type of agreement was initially informal and not binding on the owner; however, it underwent a change in the imperial period when the manumission agreement acquired legal status, becoming a regular contract that bound the owner and imposed penalties on him if he failed to comply with its terms.

Criteria for a Better Understanding of Slavery

Methodologically, excluding other possible biases, the modern misunderstandings about ancient slavery are the result of studying slavery focusing on its formal kind and not establishing broader specific criteria that take into account its actual financial, social and political functioning. In this way, chattel slavery of the modern United States are classified as of the same kind with the slavery in ancient Greece and Rome. However, that parallelism collapses if we examine the actual figure of the slave in the two eras, along with others.

If one wants to draw parallels of modern slavery with other eras and cultures, one can look at South Asia, India and other places, but not in the Roman Empire or classical Athens. The latter two lack the critical traits that connect the other cases, that is, slavery as a condition where a person belongs *collectively*, and limits them to low-status professional activities. The Black slaves in the United States of the nineteenth century had much more in common with the lower caste of India, the serfs of temples in Sri Lanka,[35] medieval Greek-Orthodox serfs under Frankish and Venetian rule, the biblical representation of the Jews under the Egyptian pharaoh, Russians under Mongols, and then other Slav serfs under Tsarist Russians, than they had with the slaves in classical Greece or imperial Rome.

Slavery in the Greek and Roman world, except for cases such as Sparta, was a private legal condition one could sometimes even sell and buy, and in any case, absolutely not something one was a part of with a collective sense and perception based on ethnicity, race, religion, gender and so on, or something destined to keep them at low-status and low-income jobs.

As far as their jobs were concerned, the slaves in Greece and Rome were more similar to modern employees, including CEOs, doctors and secretaries of senators – actually, being a doctor and a secretary of a senator in the empire almost certainly meant you were a slave. Of course, that didn't mean that they couldn't end up getting whipped if their master so decided. However, that could happen also to free people.[36]

That actual condition has nothing to do with slavery in the United States, where the slave was bonded to specific low-skill-intensive and low-income activities for life and social mobility as far as the slaves were concerned was practically non-existent. That's the condition of serfdom of the examples I mentioned above, where there is a collectively perceived servility, restricted roles and lack of social mobility. In the case of the Black slaves in America, there was collective racialisation, as Blackness was perceived as servility, hereditary transmission of status, and near-zero chance of status mobility. Blacks were treated collectively as a servile group, totally unlike the slaves in Greece and Rome, and very similarly to the serfs of medieval Europe, Russia and South Asia, or biblical Egypt.

So, we should study slavery not by legal form as chattel or serfdom, but by a typology that will take into account the social function and collective perception, which will be a far more realistic and deep criterion.

I propose a typology of three models, whereby the first type will be the legal-individualist slavery of the Greek-Roman model; the second type will be the collective-hereditary servitude of the caste, feudal and racialised models; and the third type will be a hierarchical-fluid system, such as the Ottoman and Arab one.

In the first type, typical of the Greek-Roman world, slavery is a legal condition of an individual, not a permanent group identity, there is social mobility and possibility of manumission, and the slave can work at all levels of production, even the high-status and high-income ones.

In the second type, typical of the Indian caste system, serfdom of medieval Europe and Russia, and Black slavery in the US, a whole group is seen as born to serve, with nearly fixed roles, the mobility is extremely rare or impossible, and the slave is limited to menial or degrading tasks. An entire race or ethnicity is perceived as inherently servile.

In the third type, typical of the Ottoman millet system and the Abbasid and Mamluk ones, a communal hierarchy exists but it's not rigidly exclusionary, as individuals from lower groups can rise in wealth and even political power. Group identity matters but there is social mobility – a Greek Orthodox or a Jew is seen as a member of an inferior group, yet he can become rich and socially influent.

Following this typology, which is based on multiple criteria and the actual socio-economic condition of the slave or serf, instead of insisting on the formal type, it becomes evident that drawing parallels between modern racial slavery and Greek-Roman slavery is analytically flawed and misleading.

Scholars who focus on the transatlantic slave trade and racial oppression would find more grounded and meaningful parallels in historical contexts such as caste societies in South Asia, medieval serfdom, or bonded labour systems of the colonial era. Slavery in the ancient Greek and Roman world had very different principles. Slavery was not less brutal, but primarily it consisted of a personal legal status that did not exclude the financial and social rise of the enslaved person, or their liberation, even due to their own financial means. In addition, it usually had nothing to do with a collective condition of certain ethnic, racial or religious groups. As such, it is rather incompatible and not relevant for modern narratives of systemic exploitation.

Epilogue

Throughout history, ideologies, regimes and religions attempted to construct symbolic heroes and events to reinforce their legitimacy and consolidation, often by misrepresenting or distorting historical reality, which must later be corrected by critical historical research.

A classic ancient example is the heroisation by the Athenian democracy of Harmodius and Aristogeiton, the so-called 'Tyrannicides', at a time when it is a fact of historical scholarship that the murder of Hipparchus by the two Athenians was not politically motivated but personal. It is also clear that the contribution of this particular action to the fall of the Pisistratid regime was minimal or non-existent since six whole years intervened between the two events, while in any case, the tyrant was Hippias and not his murdered brother Hipparchus, who was not even particularly involved in the governance of Athens. Although all this is known from the works of no less than Thucydides and Aristotle, the Athenians have long held up the 'tyrannicide' as a supposedly revolutionary political act, thanks to which tyranny collapsed and democracy rose.

A similar use of historical events and persons has been made many times throughout history up to the present day. A typical contemporary example is the figure of the Argentine guerrilla Ernesto Che Guevara, who, being a marginal figure of twentieth-century history with little importance and contribution to its development, if any, ended up becoming a kind of communist pop icon for the youth of the Western capitalist world.

Another example is Spartacus. The popular image of Spartacus is a modern ideological construction. As we've seen, the actual slave revolts did not aim to transform the social structure, nor did they have a reforming mindset or ideology as their base. Ironically, the only uprising of those years that indeed had the intention of creating a new society and a social reform plan, albeit utopian, was the one led not by slaves but by the aristocrat Aristonikos, the Stoic philosopher Blossios, and their followers in Pergamon. Most importantly, the truly transforming event of that period was the Social War, even though it was not enough to address the structural limitations of the Republic that led to the rise of the empire.

The fact that, in popular culture, the Spartacus revolt is celebrated that much shows that an emotional and empty insurrectionalism continues to dominate the popular imagination when it comes to social change. On the other hand, Julius Caesar and Augustus could not complain about the fame they still have, even in popular culture. However, that has more to do with glory and grandeur, which is fantastic, but not with acknowledging their crucial role in addressing the central issues of that time's society inside the Roman state.

In both cases, it is not reason but emotion that shapes popular memory. That's not something new, but it's always helpful to remember it.

The tendency to heroise, at least temporarily, historical figures of limited actual importance exists because reality is always too prosaic to be the sole basis for the propaganda of an ideology, political party or regime, but also because the real protagonists of historical evolution, apart from their admirers and fans, often have equally fanatical enemies, precisely because of their great weight and importance. For this reason, the factions and ideological currents that represent and express the real protagonists of history sometimes need to invent figures and symbols that are as widely accepted as possible to strengthen their influence in society and mitigate hostility towards them.

Spartacus and his rebellion are a further typical example of historical exaggeration and distortion. The only peculiarity of this case is that Spartacus was used as a form of ideological and propaganda reference, not in his time but two millennia later. No philosophical, intellectual, political or ideological current in antiquity viewed Spartacus and the rebellion he led with sympathy. On the contrary, it was registered as a typical barbarian horde of plunder and destruction of the kind that struck the civilised Greco-Roman world, murdering and robbing organised societies and their peoples without proposing or expressing anything new on a social and political level. Spartacus received no support or sympathy from groups within the population that were integrated into Roman social and political life, consisting of either freedmen or slaves, nor from the intellectuals of the time. The free men who followed him were essentially only outlaws, deserters, looters and general outcasts.

Modern ideologies have used and promoted Spartacus as a hero of the struggle for freedom despite the apparent lack of evidence to support such a historical verdict because by condemning ancient slavery, they claim a supposed moral superiority of their own over Greco-Roman civilisation, reinforcing their claim to be considered as eminently historically 'progressive'. That is a claim that would otherwise have no way of being asserted since, universally, the foundations of their political principles derive from Greek and Roman antiquity and not from their other moral and cultural references.

Those who admire and join Spartacus and the servile revolts in good faith consider that opposition and rebellion against the fetters of oppression and exploitation is always by definition justified by its nature and are quick to explain or disregard the unlawful and vile acts that may be carried out within its framework, blaming, in fact, the victims of these actions instead of the perpetrators. However, they are committing a fundamental error, which ends up favouring those they think they are opposing because, on the contrary, one ought to be considered worthy of sympathy and support, as well as of liberation from any shackles, precisely because one's attitude tends to convey qualities superior to those of the dominant ones. It is this condition and presupposition that makes bondage unjust and legitimates liberation and subversion. Without it, the formerly oppressed may merely reproduce domination in new and even worse forms.

Appendix I
Gladiators

This appendix offers a concise overview of gladiators of the Roman era, which is always useful in a book that talks about the revolt of Spartacus. The appendix is drawn from standard modern scholarship and archaeological findings, with some interpretive reflections of mine. It is not intended, however, as a specialist study, but as a general introduction to a subject that is often misunderstood.

Schools and Categories of Gladiators

In Latin, gladiators were called *gladiatores*, a term derived from *gladius*, meaning 'sword'. The origin of gladiatorial fights is unclear, and it is uncertain when they first began to take place in Roman territory. It is reported that the Etruscans organised duels as part of funeral rites in honour of prominent dead people. In contrast, duels between humans and wild animals were common in Eastern cultures.[1] What is sure about Roman society is that duels began to establish themselves as a mass spectacle at the beginning of the first century BCE and were to reach their most extraordinary splendor in the imperial era. The era of Spartacus was among the first decades of mass spectating of duels, when this kind of spectacle was still in a primitive form compared to the images that a modern person can conjure in their mind through cinema and television. Similar images capture the sophisticated form that duels and arenas took at a later historical stage. At the time of Spartacus, there were not yet the impressive stone and concrete amphitheatres of the Colosseum in Rome, but the arenas were wooden and often detached, and the gladiators' appearance was not as spectacular as it became later.[2]

The equipment and appearance of the gladiators were, however, from the beginning intended more to please and impress the spectators than to facilitate and protect the gladiator in his work, as was the case with the weapons and armour of the soldiers.[3] The dress of gladiators in the early period of gladiatorial combat was simple, referencing the armour and uniforms customarily worn by hostile and subjugated nations. In Spartacus' time, the three main types of gladiators were the *murmillones* ('fish fighters' in Latin), the *hoplomachi* ('armed fighters' in Greek), and the 'Thracians'.[4] Some gladiators fought against wild animals, and were known as *venatores*.[5] Spartacus himself, although a Thracian, was not included in the 'Thraex' species, but he was a *murmillo*. The school to which he belonged had many Thracian, Gaul and German gladiators in its possession.

Over time, the appearance of gladiators became increasingly spectacular, creating the impression of a battle between mythological monsters and heroes. In the imperial period, there were classic types of gladiators, such as the *retiarius*, who carried a trident and a net, or the *secutor*, equipped with a trapezoidal shield, a helmet that covered his eyes, and an iron arm.

Gladiators were divided into those who had been forced to enter the field of gladiatorial combat and those who had voluntarily chosen to follow the profession. The first category included prisoners of war and slaves, while the second was made up of free men, even Roman citizens, who were attracted by the thrills of gladiatorial combat and the gladiator's lifestyle.[6]

To better understand the unusual choice of profession for a modern man, it is worth noting that gladiatorial combat was a lucrative activity that could provide substantial income, as well as great fame and publicity. It is no exaggeration to say that the most successful gladiators could achieve a level of public recognition and popular fascination broadly comparable to that enjoyed by major sports or entertainment figures today. The most famous gladiators were well known and loved by the people, having real fans who sometimes showed enthusiastic admiration and adoration for their idols, even writing their names on city walls. But there were often members of the upper and more cultured classes who attended such spectacles and sometimes liked to refer to the gladiators during sumptuous dinners.[7]

For these reasons, even people of relatively good financial standing, who found the life of a gladiator exciting, chose to train and become gladiators in some cases. For the most part, of course, among the free men who had decided to follow this path were people who were financially ruined, as well as marginal people and adventurers who found a way out in the gladiator's profession.[8]

The owners of the gladiatorial schools naturally preferred the free and unfree individuals who came to be trained and participate in the activity voluntarily, as the whole process was much smoother. They were also preferred by the public, as being professional gladiators of their own free will and often enthusiastic about what they were doing provided a better show.

However, the free men were clearly in the minority among the gladiators. The majority consisted of slaves that the gladiator schools had regularly purchased from the slave markets or whom their owners had judged undesirable due to unruly and improper behaviour, resulting in them being resold to gladiator schools.

Gladiators who had been acquired as prisoners of war or slaves were usually under the strict supervision of the school guards. The exception to this rule was, as is understandable, the freedmen who had become gladiators voluntarily, for whom there were no restrictions beyond those imposed by the activity itself. They were allowed to leave the profession and the school whenever they wished, provided they paid a sum of money to the school owner for the damage caused by the sudden cessation of cooperation.

In the time of Spartacus, i.e. in the initial period of the duels, conditions were certainly much worse for the gladiators who were forced to be in the arena compared to those of later times. This was normal since, in the early first century BCE, the internal Roman political and social situation was in turmoil, and very often, the gladiators were newly enslaved prisoners who had just fought against Rome. When gladiatorial combat was established as a regular activity and spectacle, and the general situation normalised with the rise of the empire and the end of the century of turmoil and conflict, the living conditions of gladiators and slaves improved markedly.

In the schools, however, strict discipline always prevailed, and the gladiators were trained in duelling techniques and underwent intensive physical training. In addition to gymnasts and trainers who looked after the gladiators' physical condition and fighting skills, the schools had doctors who looked after their health and diet, in order to improve their physique, strength and endurance.[9] In terms of training, the young gladiators were initially taught the use of weapons and practised against a wooden pole of human height, often in the form of a dummy. The basic training was with wooden weapons, and at a more advanced stage, weapons similar to those used for fighting may have been used, but in no case grinded.[10]

After completing the first phase of training, the new gladiators practised duelling with each other to perfect their technique and prepare for real duels in front of an audience. In the event of an injury, the training duel was interrupted, and the injured person received care from the schools' doctors. The gladiators continued to practise in the schools, and after they began participating in real duels, they used these experiences to train and refine their techniques.

The training and practice area in the schools was designed as a replica of the amphitheatres. It included an elliptical-shaped sand arena and also contained bleachers, but these were much smaller than those of the amphitheatres, as they were designed to accommodate professionals in the field rather than spectators. Instructors and gladiator dealers frequented the schools, as well as show organisers who monitored the progress and condition of the gladiators.[11]

The Life of the Gladiator

In addition to the profits secured by the school, at the end of a match, it was customary for wealthy spectators seated in the front row to pass a tray among themselves, offering extra money, which increased the income of the gladiators. The latter, if they succeeded in becoming famous, received additional gifts from their fans, sometimes consisting of large sums of money.[12]

For the non-free gladiators, the money they collected could secure their freedom after an agreement with the owner of the school, similar to what was the case for other slaves. In general, a gladiator's career usually lasted about five years, and at the end of it, if he had survived, he would gain his freedom.

There was also the institution of the 'wooden sword', called 'rudis', which symbolised liberation. The wooden sword was offered to a gladiator when he managed to impress the public with his skill and courage. However, it was possible for a gladiator who won the wooden sword to refuse it, that is, to choose to continue their career as a gladiator rather than be freed. The case of the Syrian gladiator Flamma is typical; he won the wooden sword four times, but each time refused it and continued to duel, at least according to tradition. When he was finally freed, he became a gladiator trainer, but for a time, he continued to duel himself, and eventually retired from duelling after the age of 30, a mature age for a gladiator.[13]

On average, a gladiator participated in two or three duels against other gladiators per year, as the nature of the sport precluded participation in many more, just as is the case today with professional boxing and martial arts competitions.

The majority of duels between professional gladiators did not have a fatal outcome, and the death of a gladiator in the arena, at least sometimes, was probably more of an accident than a deliberate result of a duel. This was perfectly natural, as the last thing a school owner or gladiator trafficker ('manager') wanted to see was the death of one of his gladiators. Each gladiator was an expensive investment and it was not in anyone's interest to see him die, as the school owner had usually spent money to buy him and had certainly spent considerable sums to ensure his training, nutrition and health.

The usual outcome of a duel was either the victory of one of the two gladiators – meaning that the other had been disarmed, was physically unable to continue, or had surrendered – or a draw, when, after a long time, neither of the two had managed to prevail. When the duel ended with the victory of one of the two gladiators, the audience decided whether the loser should be allowed to live or be executed.[14] As a rule, the spectators decided in favour of the gladiator's survival, except in cases where they were dissatisfied with his performance, considering it too poor. Conversely, for gladiators who had become popular and gained a following, death was thus ruled out.

For example, the famous aforementioned gladiator Flamma from Syria ended his extremely long career with twenty-five wins, four losses, and nine draws,[15] as his tombstone discovered near Emesa (modern-day Homs) in Syria states. This particular statistic of Flamma's performance indicates that draws were not rare (nine out of thirty-eight, or almost 24 per cent of duels in this case). At the same time, the fact that a gladiator was defeated four times and allowed to live all four times is indicative of the fact that, as a rule, the loser of a duel did not die. Probably, many blows that caused deaths during duels did not aim necessarily to cause the death of the opponent gladiator who was eventually mortally wounded.

An exception to the above were the fights to the death (*'sine missus'*), in which the duel continued until one of the two opponents was killed, with no possibility of a draw or a pardon from the public. Such contests were organised during the republican period, when the Spartacus rebellion broke out, but were subsequently banned or drastically reduced by the time of Emperor Augustus.[16] Indeed, the early imperial period was generally the least bloody in the amphitheatres, as it is estimated that in the first century AD, over 90 per cent of duels were completed without a gladiator's death in the arena. The situation had become very different by the third century AD, when at least according to some estimates, the probability of death had increased sharply, reaching about 25 per cent for each gladiator when he stepped into the arena.[17] In the third century CE, it seems that morals had returned to a situation similar or even worse than that of the original era of the gladiatorial spectacles, during the republican period.

Organisers and Duels

Gladiators may have been popular and earned considerable money, but at the same time, their profession was considered undignified and vulgar. It could even be considered an insult, similar to what happened to women and men of low morals or other activities of low social prestige.[18] They were also treated in the same way as artistic or television products, which are often regarded as having low value in modern times but are popular among the people and also higher cultural strata.

In general, duelling as a professional activity initially attracted people who were far from good society, as this particular area bordered on the underworld, and of course, it was considered totally inappropriate for an aristocrat and generally for a respectable and dignified citizen. The owners of the schools and the organisers of the fights were usually freedmen, and often former gladiators who had been successful and earned a substantial amount of money then went on to become businesspeople in the field. One of them was probably Lentulus Batiatus, the owner of the school to which Spartacus belonged.

Similarly to what applied to gladiators, the activity of the owner of a school or a gladiatorial organiser occupied a comparable position, as far as social prestige was concerned, to that of activities of the social fringe and the underworld, such as, for example, that of pimps or bouncers. At the same time, however, duels excited the people and exerted an underground fascination on the aristocracy, with the result that the economic profits from duelling became ever greater. Thus, gradually, businessmen and knights, sometimes even aristocrats, began to deal professionally with the lucrative field of gladiatorial contests, buying or founding schools and groups of gladiators, organising competitions, or participating in the distribution and sale of gladiators, much like modern agents of athletes or artists.

Indeed, sometimes aspiring or active politicians even organised all-day duel shows, not for financial gain, but in the hope of garnering votes and political support from citizens who were pleased with the spectacle and who were allowed free admission.

The fights between professional gladiators were the main event of the day's shows in the amphitheatre and their highlight, but other types of duels supplemented the programme. These were mainly duels between gladiators and wild animals, duels between gladiators and convicted criminals, and fights between groups of gladiators and convicted criminals.[19]

Contrary to the modern cinematic image of the Roman arenas, in reality, they were not essentially a place where professional gladiators clashed but where criminals were sentenced to death and prisoners of war were executed. The vast majority of deaths in the amphitheatres were not of gladiators, who, as has been explained, did not die so often in duels, but of criminals and prisoners of war who had been sentenced to death.

Murderers, rapists, arsonists, temple robbers and others convicted of heinous crimes punishable by capital punishment, as well as enemies of Rome, ended up in the arenas, facing the trained gladiators, without having been trained and without wearing armour, essentially to be ritually executed in front of the people. Their public death served both as a warning about the consequences of severe crime and as a demonstration of the Roman state's repressive power and its claim to uphold public order.[20]

That's why, on levels of elite intellectual reflection, the gladiator shows could be seen as having traits of moral instruction for the people, even though they perceived them merely as exciting entertainment. Moreover, one could similarly see the duels as offering a last chance for convicted criminals to redeem their spirit and status by approaching virtue, even at the moment of their death. That is, to die fighting as brave, dignified and proud men, escaping from the barbaric and humiliating aspect of their lives up to that point.

Suppose the public execution of criminals in an arena seems repulsive. In that case, one should recall that public executions have been a constant and widespread practice throughout the Middle Ages and in modern and contemporary times. In some cases, it continues uninterrupted to this day. Furthermore, the modern rather inconsistent aversion to the arenas of antiquity overlooks the fact that duels to the death were considered an acceptable way of resolving personal disputes over matters of honour until the nineteenth century.

In support of the above, it should be added that in antiquity, as in all periods of history before modern times, the chances of violent death were, anyway, much greater than today. The percentages mentioned earlier regarding the odds of dying in a duel between professional gladiators, especially those of the first century AD, were not much greater than those of the average person dying a violent death, whether as a soldier in battle, by bandits in the countryside, or from other personal conflicts. It is estimated that in the twentieth century, despite two world wars with tens of millions of deaths, less than 1 per cent of people died a violent death, and even if deaths from war-related epidemics and famines are included, the figure is no more than 1–2 per cent. By contrast, in prehistoric times, palaeontological and anthropological evidence shows that 10–20 per cent of people died by being killed by other people. Even if, in ancient times, this percentage had decreased significantly, there was still a greater familiarity with real violence and bloodshed than in modern times.[21]

In any case, the attraction to staged violence and controlled danger is not alien to the modern world, even if modern societies experience and represent it in very different forms. The only difference is that modern technical means make it possible to create images that deceive the brain, producing almost the same sensation as real scenes of violence, rendering the latter unnecessary. Countless successful films contain images of violence and death, and indeed, modern people do not watch them in a specially designed space, in which there is at least a latent sense of law enforcement and the opportunity for moral uplift for the vicious, but without any distinction between this spectacle and their daily lives. Also, a modern boxing or martial arts fight excites the public and is considered more spectacular in proportion to the number and severity of the blows, that is, the more it causes injury and physical exhaustion of the contestants.

In general, sporting spectacles belong to the same broad psychological framework, insofar as they refine and ritualise competitive, aggressive and dominance-seeking instincts that are deeply rooted in human behaviour. Fans enjoy the tension, the suspense, the attempt to prevail over the opponent, the sense of conflict and domination, as well as the physical fatigue and overexertion that the bodies undergo.

It is the activation and satisfaction of the same instincts as those that thrilled the spectators in the Roman arenas. Feelings and sensations that people usually avoid in real life, as they are identified with danger, threat, and the possibility of death, become very attractive and appealing when they can be experienced without danger and threat. This is perfectly natural because these emotions are an integral part of human biology and psychology, and people seek to experience them as much as they seek to avoid the dangers associated with them in reality.

Appendix II

Development of the Roman Army and Marius' Reform

Original Form of the Legions

Initially, the Roman army was organised according to the Greek phalanx and in particular, the Etruscan version of it.[1] The transition from a single phalanx formation to a legion consisting of separate units occurred in the first half of the fourth century BCE. The reason was apparently the significant problems the Roman army encountered in dealing with the elastic, open and unconventional way of fighting the Gauls at the beginning of the century, or similar problems the Romans faced during the wars against the Samnites.[2] These experiences were likely decisive in the Roman decision to break the compact but monolithic and unwieldy phalanx into semi-autonomous, agile and adaptable maniples (*manipuli*), each in turn divided into two centurions.

The spires were not simply subdivisions of the whole, like the companies of the Greek phalanxes. To a certain extent, they constituted tactical units with relative autonomy of movement and their own mission on the battlefield. Thus, Roman troops acquired greater flexibility, mobility and the ability to regroup. These characteristics enabled them to adapt to the conditions of battle without compromising the robust organisation and cohesion for which the phalanx formation was renowned. During these changes, the round shield was abandoned and replaced by the trapezoidal shield. It was probably also at this time that the javelin (*pilum*) was adopted in place of the spear. The primary weapon of the legionaries would now be the sword (*gladius*). In contrast, spears were used more to rush the opponent before the impact of the formations.

During the fourth century BCE, the workforce also increased significantly, through the growth of the population, so that the permanent annual army increased from one to four legions, as the Roman historian Titus Livy, who provides many detailed insights into the legions and their structure, reports.[3] The structure of the legion during the Second Punic War and afterwards is also described by the Greek historian Polybius.[4] Polybius was a close personal friend of Scipio Aemilianus, mentioned in a previous chapter, and was even present at the Roman general's side during the capture and levelling of Carthage in 146 BCE.

The operational formation of the legion in the second century BCE consisted of three main divisions of heavy infantry. The first was made up of the *hastati*, the younger legionaries; the second of the *principes*, who were more experienced soldiers; and the third of the veteran *triarii*. Each category of legionaries commanded ten maniples, each of which was divided into two centuries. In the case of the *hastati* and *principes*, each century consisted of about 80 men, and therefore, the maniple as a whole consisted of 160, while in that of the *triarii*, the maniple consisted instead of a constant 60 men in total. The legion's workforce was supplemented by the *velites*, also called skirmishers. The *velites* were light infantrymen and formed thirty groups of about forty men each, supporting the heavy infantry maniples. Finally, each legion had a cavalry corps consisting of 300 cavalrymen, divided into 10 companies of 30 men, and men of various specialties such as engineers, technicians and doctors.

Unlike what happened in earlier times, during Polybius' time, most legionaries were equipped at the state's expense. Perhaps only a few wealthy individuals paid for their own equipment.[5] However, to be eligible to serve in the legions, it was not enough to be a Roman citizen; one had to own property that exceeded a minimum threshold. Those who possessed assets of less than this minimum or had no property at all could not be called up to the legions and were only used by the army in cases of emergency, forming separate auxiliary units.

The male Roman citizens were considered eligible for military service from the age of 17 to 45. There was no compulsory service of a particular duration at a given age, and recruitment was carried out either to man the permanent legions or to form new ones if needed. Continuous service in the ranks of the legions could last up to six consecutive years. However, the legionary then had to be released from duty. He remained conscripted, nonetheless, and could be enlisted in the legions for a total of an additional ten years. The presence in the legion probably did not necessarily last for the whole year, and its exact duration depended on the degree of readiness and engagement of the legion in operations.

Additionally, after the initial expansion of Roman rule and the significant increase in the population of Roman citizens, participation in the army ultimately became largely voluntary, a preference that the Roman leadership favoured for reasons of social tranquility, given the vast number of available conscripts. In fact, the recruiters, who were sent to various cities whenever it was decided to form troops, usually made a selection from among the citizens who offered themselves. As they needed fewer men, the legion formed from those who expressed interest; they chose the most trained, strong and experienced. If necessary, there was always the possibility of forced conscription using the conscript lists, but cases of compulsory conscription were sporadic. When legions were formed, a detailed record was made of the citizens who made up each legion, and then the legionaries were sworn to obey the officers and carry out their orders.

During the period of service, legionaries were paid well enough to compensate them for the fact that they were absent from their professional activities. However, the life of a legionary was hard, and indeed not inferior in difficulty to that of the gladiator described in Appendix I. In the legions, training was continuous and intensive, and there was strict discipline and severe punishments were prescribed in cases where a legionary did not perform his duties as required or broke the rules. For example, commanders had to impose severe penalties on those who committed robberies and other illegalities while serving in the legion. At the same time, if a man lost his weapons or fell asleep on guard duty, he could be flogged and even beaten to death if it was deemed that his negligence had put the unit in mortal danger.

The fixed military forces that existed at all times in Rome amounted to four legions, and each consul had two of them under his direct command. Of course, as Roman rule expanded to more and more of the Mediterranean and Europe, legions were stationed in numerous parts of the territory, from Asia Minor to North Africa and Western Europe. In particular, at the dawn of the imperial era, the permanent Roman army consisted of twenty-eight legions.[6]

Additionally, the consuls and the Senate could proceed to conscription, in the sense of calling volunteers to arms or compulsory conscription of a specified number of citizens, whenever they deemed it necessary. From a certain point onwards, they could entrust the supreme command of an army not only to the consuls but also to generals elected on the spot. In general, until the end of the second century BCE, officers of any rank were not permanent but were chosen at each period of enlistment and legion formation. The Senate elected generals, and the legionaries of each corps elected the popular assembly and junior officers.

Among the commanders and centurions, who were the direct leaders of each century, six military tribunes were chosen for each legion, who were responsible for maintaining discipline in the troops. The main duties of the military tribunes were to carry the orders of the generals to their subordinates, to receive reports in the morning from the legionaries, and to deliver the cues to the sentries. In addition, each general had a treasurer in their service, who was responsible for the finances of the troops, accounting, and the supply and transfer of materials, supplies and clothing. It is noteworthy and characteristic that the needs of the Roman army were met by private businessmen with whom the treasurer had the authority to deal – the tax collection sector of the state operated similarly.

In addition to the legions formed by Roman citizens, the Roman army had supporting forces from allied or vassal cities and kingdoms. Up to the end of the second century BCE, and particularly before the Social War (90–87 BCE), Latin and Italian allies assembled forces to support the Roman legions, with a Roman praetor at their head and under the supreme command of a subaltern or general. The strength of these formations, called 'allied wings' (*alae sociorum*), as well as their structure, was similar to that of the legions.[7]

Marius' Reform

At the end of the second century BCE, Gaius Marius abolished the property requirement for a Roman citizen to join the legions, calling the landless into arms. This had previously only happened in exceptional circumstances, but after Marius' move, it was established as the new normal for the Roman army. Moreover, the fact that the legionary's salary was quite satisfactory made enlisting in the legions an important professional opportunity and economic outlet for the poor. Thus, by the time of the Spartacus uprising three decades later, the legions were no longer manned exclusively by property owners and the majority of autonomous peasants but primarily by proletarians.

Karl Marx did not know or ignored this fact when he wrote to his friend and colleague Friedrich Engels in 1861 that Spartacus was a great leader of the 'ancient proletariat', in a phrase that gave rise to the propagandistic idealisation of Spartacus and his rebellion by communist parties and regimes. In reality, the Roman and Italian proletariat manned the legions and fought against Spartacus and his army during the uprising, and also saw the slaves as antagonists rather than allies.[8]

Marius' reform pushed the Roman army further towards professionalism. It also strengthened the personal bond between soldiers and commanders, creating a class of professional soldiers and legionaries who were not particularly concerned with politics as such but rather supported their commanders' ambitions and expected them to distribute arable land to them at the end of their careers as legionaries. Moreover, the command of the army ceased to be strictly identified with the consuls, as more and more praetors and prefects could be nominated as supreme commanders of armies during wars.

Gaius Marius also made key changes in the structure of the legions, the most significant being the establishment of the cohorts as the basic unit of the legion rather than the centuries. The cohorts consisted of 500–600 men each, and in the case of the first cohort of each legion, 800–900,[9] which made them large enough as corps to operate autonomously, as self-sufficient tactical units. Thus, for example, a general could move one or more cohorts and use them for missions even over a relatively long distance without moving the entire legion to which they belonged. This was not the case in the past with maniples, which had some tactical autonomy on the battlefield but always acted in direct connection with the rest of the legion and did not carry out separate missions and operations. Each legion consisted of 10 cohorts, each with its own commander, for a total of about 5,500 soldiers on average, supported by cavalry and light infantry, usually from the provinces.

In addition, differences in the equipment of legionaries were abolished. In the cohorts, there were no longer separate classes of legionaries with different weapons, as had been the case in the past for the *hastati*, *principes* and *triarii*. Instead, the equipment of the legionaries was uniform, and the unit was unified. The element retained from the earlier form of the legion was the formation of three ranks. When the legion was fully arrayed, the ten corps always lined up in the following pattern: four in the first line and three each in the second and third.

Another change that Marius made was that he removed the numerous slaves and servants who had hitherto followed the troops and carried the soldiers' weapons and baggage during their movements. Marius stipulated that the legionaries had to carry their own stuff and operate the unit's transport vehicles, ensuring greater speed and flexibility in the movement of the troops. Finally, it was Marius who also established the classical eagle as the unique symbol of the legions. Until then, in addition to the eagle, the wolf, the bull-headed man, the wild boar and the horse had been used.

After the Social War and the granting of Roman citizenship to all inhabitants of Italy, they could enlist in the legions as Roman citizens. This further increased the Roman army's pool of recruits, but the legions no longer had the support of the allied wings. Consequently, in the last period of the Republic, the temporary formation of military units from the inhabitants of nearby areas to those where the Roman troops were operating was applied. Numidians, Gauls and Germans were primarily used as cavalrymen, while mercenary archers from Crete and slingers from the Balearic Islands were also recruited. Especially for campaigns in the East, Roman troops were supported by forces provided by local rulers who were allies of Rome.[10]

Political and Cultural Contribution of the Roman Army

Over the centuries of Roman rule in the Mediterranean and most of Europe, the Roman army played a pivotal role in homogenising the territory, linking the various regions and peoples, and spreading the Greco-Roman culture.

The function of the Roman army was significantly broader than that of most other armies and was not limited to military boundaries. The legions often performed policing and tax collection functions, but they also undertook very important construction projects, such as paving roads and erecting buildings. The projects that the legionaries carried out, executing the plans and instructions of the army's architects and engineers, were not always of military use and importance but often consisted of temples, markets, trade routes and even private houses in the provinces.

The legions brought to the provinces the great Roman achievements in engineering, especially the excellent aqueducts and irrigation and sewage networks, as well as roads, improving the living standards of the populations.[11] In addition, the Romans often took care to upgrade to a decisive degree the comforts and luxuries available to the upper classes in each region, in order to tie them more closely to the Roman order and consolidate it. Often, architectural and construction techniques, such as wealth in general, were indirectly transferred in this way, which could later be disseminated further down to the grassroots of local society. It should be noted that the level of Roman architecture and engineering was so high that, in various cases and regions, it took many centuries to recover elements that had been lost after the end of the Roman era. In Great Britain, for example, amenities such as those found in villas built by the Romans, such as permanent hot baths and central heating, did not reappear until modern times.[12]

The importance of the legions to Roman politics was even greater, as political and military offices were often identical, especially during the republican period.[13] Political leadership was also closely tied to the military, and citizens who owned property were always members of the armed forces. In the Roman, as in the Greek civic tradition, civil rights were directly linked to military service. It's telling that in Rome, the work of the popular assembly, such as elections and various votes, took place on the Campus Martius ('Field of Mars'), the site of military training.

When the Romans voted for the elections or to pass a law, it was not the individual votes that counted but the total votes of each century. The electorate, the *populus*, for the Roman Republic was not made up of individuals but of centuries, that is, of groups of men united by the fact that they had stood under the same banners and would fight under them again if necessary. The vote of each century was equal to that of the others. However, the centuries of the two richest classes consisted of far fewer members than those of the lower classes, resulting in the centuries of these two classes being marginally more numerous than those of the other four classes combined. The attitude of the first class and the knights was, therefore, decisive for the outcome. Yet, there was often disagreement between the first class and the knights, but also, at other times, the two classes were divided within themselves, so that the vote of the lower classes became decisive.[14]

Notes

Introduction

1. Marx & Engels 2010, p. 265.
2. Ronald Reagan Presidential Library & Museum, 'Address to Members of the British Parliament', 8 June 1982. https://www.reaganlibrary.gov/archives/speech/address-members-british-parliament
3. Ancient Latium was a bit smaller than the current Lazio province of Italy, but not that different.

Chapter 1

1. Livy, 32.26.4–18.
2. Ibid., 33.36.1–3.
3. Ibid., 39.8.3–9.1; 17.4–6; 18.7.
4. Ibid., 39.29.8–9.
5. Ibid., 39.41.6–7.
6. Rostovtzeff, p. 119.
7. Geraci-Marcone, p. 116; Rostovtzeff, p. 119; Alföldy, p. 92.
8. Rostovtzeff, pp. 119–20; Grant, p. 210.
9. Alföldy, p. 65; Mackay, p. 146.
10. Geraci-Marcone, pp. 114–16; Rostovtzeff, p. 118; Alfodly, p. 92; Grant, p. 210.
11. Brizzi 2012, pp. 152–3; Geraci-Marcone, pp. 114–17.
12. Ibid.
13. Brizzi 2012, pp. 125–8.
14. Ibid., p. 153.
15. Appian, *Civil Wars*, I. 9. [All the citations of Appian refer to the *Civil Wars* unless otherwise specified.]
16. Ibid., I. 7.
17. Rostovtzeff, p. 120.
18. Poma, pp. 57–9.
19. Rostovtzeff, p. 120; Geraci-Marcone, p. 116; Mackay, p. 146; Grant, p. 213.
20. Appian; Plutarch; Geraci-Marcone, p. 116; Grant, pp. 213–14.
21. Plutarch, *Tiberius Gracchus*, 19.2–3; Mackay, p. 147; Rostovtzeff, p. 119.
22. Rostovtzeff, pp. 119–20; Geraci-Marcone, p. 117.
23. Appian, I. 12; Rostovtzeff, p. 121; Geraci-Marcone, p. 117; Grant, p. 215, Mackay, p. 148.

24. Rostovtzeff, p. 121; Grant, p. 215; Mackay, pp. 148–9.
25. Appian, I. 14; Rostovtzeff, pp. 122–3; Mackay, p. 149; Grant, pp. 215–16; Geraci-Marcone, p. 117.
26. Plutarch, *Tiberius Gracchus*, 19.2; Appian, I. 16; Brizzi 2012, p.155.
27. Appian, I. 2.
28. Drokalos, 2025.
29. Diodorus, 34.2.27.
30. Florus, II. 7.3.
31. Diodorus, 34.2.28–29.
32. Ibid., 34.2.1.
33. Ibid., 34.2.2.
34. Ibid., 34.2.3.
35. Ibid., 34.2.4.
36. Ibid., 34.2.38–40.
37. Livy, *Summaries*, 56.
38. Posidonius, *Histories*, mentioned by Athenaeus, *Deipnosophistae*, 12.542b.
39. Diodorus, 34.2.5–7.
40. Ibid., 34.2.5.
41. Ibid., 34.2.6.
42. Florus, II. 7.5.
43. Diodorus, 34.2.8.
44. Ibid., 34.2.9.
45. Ibid., 34. 2.11–12.
46. Ibid., 34.2.14.
47. Ibid., 34.2.15.
48. Ibid., 34.2.13.
49. Ibid., 34.2.16.
50. Posidonius, *Histories*, mentioned by Athenaeus, *Deipnosophistae*, 12.542b.
51. Diodorus, 34.2.14.
52. Florus, II. 7.5.
53. Diodorus, 34.2.15.
54. Strabo, *Geography*, 6.2.6.
55. Ibid.
56. Livy, *Summaries*, 56.
57. Ibid., 34.2.18.
58. Ibid., 34.2.17.
59. Orosius, V.9.4.
60. Florus, II. 7.5.
61. Ibid.
62. Livy, *Summaries*, 56.
63. Diodorus, 34.2.18.

64. Livy, *Summaries*, 56.
65. Orosius.
66. Valerius Maximus, 2.7.9; translation from Shaw, p. 104.
67. Valerius Maximus, 4.3.10.
68. Florus, II. 7.6.
69. Diodorus, 34.2.16.
70. Which I wrote about in my first book published by Pen & Sword. Look for *The Wars Betweeen Greeks and Carthaginians* by Sotirios F. Drokalos.
71. Diodorus, 34.2.19–20.
72. Appian, *Iberia*, 96.
73. Diodorus, 34.2.21–23.
74. Valerius Maximus, 2.7.3.
75. Diodorus, 34.2.20.
76. Valerius Maximus, 9.12.1.
77. Diodorus, 34.2.21.
78. Strabo, *Geography*, 6.2.6.
79. Orosius, 5.6.1–6; 5.9.4–9.
80. Diodorus, 34.2.22.
81. Ibid., 34.2.22.
82. Ibid., 34.2.24.
83. Ibid., 34.2.23.
84. Florus, II. 7. 5.
85. Diodorus, 34.2.23.
86. Florus, II. 7.7. We'll see that again later in the case of Crassus' victory over the Spartacus revolt.
87. Orosius, 5.6.1–6; 5.9.4–8.
88. Diodorus, 34.2.19.
89. Orosius, 5.6.1–6; 5.9.4–9; Julius Obsequens, 27.27b.
90. Shaw, p. 97, cit. 10.
91. Orosius, 5.6.1–6; 5.9.4–9.
92. Ibid.
93. Diodorus, 35.10.
94. Heraclitus, Fragment 92.
95. Cicero, *Against Verres*, 2.2.5–15.
96. Ibid., I. 18.
97. Strabo, 14.1.38.
98. He is more often called 'Aristonicus' in English, following the Latinised version of the name. However, I tend to adopt the version that resembles more the original Greek, when the historical figure is not so famous for the name to be established, such as Aeschylus, Epictetus, Epicurus, and so on. Every time there is a Greek name ending in -us, that's a Latinisation of a name that ends in -os in its original form. Just like mine, which would sound 'Sotirius

Fotius Drokalus' in its Latinised version, or better, 'Sotirius Fotius Angelicus Psilus Drokalus', if I add also my mother's name and surname as well as my father's. Fantastic, isn't it?

99. Geraci-Marcone, p. 121.
100. Paleothodoros 2006. In Greek, it is called Κύμη, just like Cumae in Italy. However, in English, they are more often called by different names, Cumae the Κύμη of Italy, and Cyme the Κύμη of Asia Minor.
101. Plutarch, *Tiberius Gracchus*, 8.4.
102. Mackay, pp. 150–1.
103. Strabo, 14.1.38; Frontinus, 4.5.16; Orosius, V. 10.3; Valerius Maximus, III. 2.12.
104. Strabo, 14.1.38; Orosius, V. 10.3.
105. Velleius Paterculus, 2.4.1.

Chapter 2

1. Appian, I. 21; Geraci-Marcone, p. 118.
2. Grant, p. 217; Rostovtzeff, p. 124
3. Rostovtzeff, p. 127; Mackay, pp. 154–5 considers this opinion false; Brizzi 2012, pp. 158–9, says that Gaius' ultimate goal was overthrowing the aristocracy and the Senate.
4. Rostovtzeff, pp. 124–5; Mackay, p. 155; Grant, pp. 220–2 – this case is more complex than described here.
5. Appian, I. 21; Rostovtzeff, pp. 123–4, Mackay, p. 153; Grant, p. 218, says this practice was common in Greek cities.
6. Appian, I. 21; Rostovtzeff, pp. 123; Mackay, p. 154; Grant, pp. 218–19; Brizzi 2012, pp. 158–9.
7. Appian, I. 24; Grant, p. 217.
8. Mackay, p. 155; Grant, p. 217.
9. Rostovtzeff, pp. 125; Mackay, p. 155; Grant, p. 222.
10. Appian, I. 24; Rostovtzeff, p. 125; Brizzi 2012, p. 159.
11. Appian, I. 25–26; Mackay, p. 156; Grant, p. 222.
12. Mackay, p. 150; Geraci-Marcone, p. 115.
13. Plutarch, *Marius*, 1–2.
14. Grant, p. 225.
15. Plutarch, *Marius*, 7; Mackay, p. 159; Geraci-Marcone, p. 122, says that the Metelli family had helped Marius before, when he became tribune in 119 BCE; Brizzi 2012, p. 160 confirms.
16. Plutarch, *Marius*, 7.3–5.
17. Plutarch, *Marius*, 7.6, 8.9; Grant, p. 225.
18. Plutarch, *Marius*, 9. 3–4.
19. Sallust, *Jugurtha*, LXXXV, 12–14.
20. Sallust, *Jugurtha*, LXXXV, 32; Plutarch, *Marius*, 2.2.

21. Plutarch, *Marius*, 9.1; Rostovtzeff, p. 130; Mackay, p. 160; Grant, p. 225; Geraci-Marcone, pp. 122–3.
22. Plutarch, *Sulla*, 3; Plutarch, *Marius*, 10.2; Geraci-Marcone, p. 123; Brizzi 2012, p. 161.
23. Mackay, p. 171.
24. Geraci-Marcone, p. 123.
25. Plutarch, *Marius*, 11 and following.
26. Plutarch, *Marius*, 21, 27; Rostovtzeff, p. 130; Mackay, pp. 161–2; Grant, p. 226.
27. Plutarch, *Marius*, 28.2–5; Brizzi 2012, p. 168.
28. Geraci-Marcone, pp. 124–5, mentions the Saturnino case.
29. Diodorus, 36.2.
30. Ibid.
31. Ibid., 36.2b.
32. Diodorus, 36.3.1.
33. Ibid., 36.3.2.
34. Cassius Dio, *Histories*, 27, fragment 101 (93.1–3).
35. Diodorus, 36.3.
36. Ibid., 36.4.
37. Ibid., 36.4.
38. Ibid., 36.5.
39. Ibid., 36.5.
40. Ibid.
41. Ibid.
42. Ibid., 36.7.
43. Ibid.
44. Ibid., 36.8.
45. Ibid.
46. Ibid., 36.9.
47. Florus, 2.7.9–12.
48. Diodorus, 36.9.
49. Cassius Dio, *Histories*, fragment 104 [93.4].
50. Diodorus, 36.9.
51. Modern scholarship identifies Florus' use of the name 'Titus' here as an error; the correct form is Manius Aquilius (Moore 2013; Schmuck 2001).
52. Florus, 2.7.9–12.
53. Ibid., 36.10.
54. A satyr is a mythical creature, a hybrid of human and animal, who makes mischief in the woods and countryside.
55. Diodorus, 36.10.1–3.
56. Florus, 2.7.9–12.
57. Cicero, *In Defense of Flaccus*, 39.98.
58. Diodorus, 36.11.

59. Ibid., 36.11.
60. Athenaeus, *Deipnosophiste*, 6.272.d–f.
61. Cicero, *Against Verres*, 2.2.136.
62. Ibid., 2.3.66.
63. Ibid., 2.3.125.
64. Florus, 2.7.1–8.
65. Cicero, *On the Agrarian Law*, 2.83.
66. Cicero, *Against Verres*, 2.5.8.
67. Ibid., 2.5.7.
68. Shaw, pp. 128–9.
69. Ibid., p. 127.

Chapter 3

1. De Sanctis, pp. 8–10.
2. The *alae sociorum* were large formations composed of conscripts from the Italian tribes that were allies of Rome during the Republic. They had the same size as Roman legions and practically the same structure and weapons. For each legion, there was an *alae sociorum*, so their contribution was equal to that of the Romans themselves, yet they were not considered to be Roman citizens.
3. Velleius Paterculus, 2.15.
4. De Sanctis, p. 12.
5. He was the son of Marcus Livius Drusus we saw in Chapter 2, the tribune of 122 BCE. See E. Badian. 'Marcus Livius Drusus', *Encyclopedia Britannica*. https://www.britannica.com/biography/Marcus-Livius-Drusus-Roman-tribune-died-91-BCE
6. Ibid., pp. 13–14.
7. Ibid., p. 14.
8. Matyszak, p. 62.
9. Ibid., p. 63.
10. De Sanctis, p. 16.
11. Rostovtzeff, pp. 131–2; Mackay, p. 167; Grant, pp. 229–30; Gèraci-Marcone, p. 126; Brizzi 2012, p. 162; De Sanctis., p. 17.
12. De Sanctis, p. 18.
13. Ibid., p. 19.
14. Ibid., p. 20.
15. Ibid., p. 21.
16. Ibid., pp. 22–3.
17. Ibid. p. 49.
18. Ibid. pp. 50–1.
19. Ibid., p. 53.
20. Ibid. pp. 54–6.
21. Ibid. p. 56.

22. Ibid. pp. 57–60.
23. Ibid. pp. 60–2.
24. Matyszak, p. 89.
25. De Sanctis, pp. 62–4.
26. De Sanctis, p. 65; pp. 73–4; Matyszak, pp. 99–100.
27. Matyszak, p. 99.
28. De Sanctis, pp. 76–7.
29. Ibid., pp. 78–9.
30. Matyszak, p. 106.
31. De Sanctis, pp. 80–1.
32. Ibid., pp. 82–4.
33. Ibid., pp. 85–7. Quintus Caecilius Metellus Pius was the son of Quintus Caecilius Metellus Numidicus, the consul of 109 BCE, whom we saw in Chapter 2.
34. Matyszak, p. 105; De Sanctis, p. 89.
35. De Sanctis., pp. 98–100.
36. Ibid., pp. 92–3.
37. Appian, I. 35–54; Rostovtzeff, pp. 132–4; Mackay, pp. 168–9; Brizzi 2012, pp. 164–5.
38. Plutarch, *Sulla*, 6.1–4; 6.18.
39. Appian, I. 55.
40. Grant, p. 232; Brizzi 2012, p. 165.
41. Plutarch, *Sulla*, 8; Livy, *Periochae*, 77; Appian, I. 55; Dio Cassius, fragment 102.4.
42. Appian, I. 56; Plutarch, *Marius*, 34.1–2; Grant, p. 232; Geraci-Marcone, p. 132.
43. Plutarch, *Sulla*, 8–9; Appian, I. 57–59.
44. Appian, I. 59; Plutarch, *Sulla*, 10.1; Livy, *Periochae*, 77.
45. Appian, I. 60–61; Grant, p. 235; Geraci-Marcone, p. 132.
46. Appian, I. 71; Plutarch, *Marius*, 43; Rostovtzeff, p. 135; Mackay, p. 173; Brizzi 2012, p. 167.
47. Appian, I. 75; Plutarch, *Marius*, 46.6; Mackay, p. 173; Geraci-Marcone, p. 133; Brizzi 2012, p. 168.
48. Mackay, p. 176; Geraci-Marcone, p. 133.
49. Appian, I. 65.
50. Plutarch, *Marius*, 35.5.
51. Appian, I. 77–78.
52. Plutarch, *Sulla*, 31–32; Appian, I. 95; Geraci-Marcone, p. 134; Brizzi 2012, p. 170 mentions thousands; I have still to find where that 4,700 comes from.
53. Plutarch, *Sulla*, 33.1.
54. Appian, I. 3, I. 103; Plutarch, *Sulla*, 34–35; Geraci-Marcone, pp. 134–5; Brizzi 2012, p. 171.
55. Rostovtzeff, pp. 137–9; Grant, pp. 238–9; Geraci-Marcone, pp. 134–5, Brizzi 2012, pp. 170–1.
56. Appian, I. 96; Geraci-Marcone, p. 134; Brizzi 2012, p. 172.

57. Appian, I. 100; Mackay, p. 178. According to Rostovtzeff, pp. 139–40, the freed slaves were as many as 40,000.
58. Rostovtzeff, p. 142; Mackay, p. 182; Grant, pp. 240–1; Brizzi 2012, p. 174.
59. Geraci-Marcone, p. 136; Brizzi 2012, p. 174.
60. Appian, I. 108; Rostovtzeff, p. 143; Grant, p. 241.

Chapter 4

1. Appian, I. 14. 116.
2. Strauss, p. 15.
3. Ibid., p. 17.
4. Ibid., p. 22.
5. Plutarch, *Crassus*, 8.2.
6. Appian, I. 14. 116
7. Plutarch, *Crassus*, 8.1.
8. Strauss, p. 16.
9. Ibid., p. 19.
10. Plutarch, *Crassus*, 8.1; Appian, I. 14. 116.
11. Florus, 2.8.3, says that thirty or more escaped; Plutarch, Crassus, 8.1, says that seventy-eight managed to escape; Orosius XXIV mentions seventy-four; Frontinus, I. V.21, mentions seventy-four; Livy, 95.e, says seventy-four; Eutropius, VI. VII, says eighty-four.
12. Appian, I. 14.116; Orosius, XXIV.
13. Orosius XXIV says that they were both Gauls; Florus, 2.8.3, does not mention ethnicities; Eutropius, VI. VII, does not mention ethnicities.
14. Livy, 95e, but actually it is rather common in the sources.
15. Florus, 2.8.4.
16. Appian, I. 14.116.
17. Plutarch, *Crassus*, 8.
18. Appian, I. 14.116; Florus, 2.8.4.
19. Appian, I. 14.116.
20. Florus, 2.8.4; Frontinus, I. V. 21, mentions that they plaited ropes of osiers from the woods; Strauss, pp. 50–1.
21. Orosius, XXIV.
22. Florus, 2.8.3.
23. Appian, I. 14.116.
24. Sallust, *Histories*, 3.64.
25. Ibid.
26. Ibid.
27. Sallust, *Histories*, 3.66.
28. Strauss, p. 59.
29. Ibid., pp. 64–5.
30. Sallust, *Histories*, 3.66.

31. Ibid.
32. Ibid.
33. Florus, 2.8.5.
34. Appian, I. 14.116; Florus, 2.8.7.
35. Appian, I. 14.116; Sallust, *Histories*, 3.66.
36. Florus, 2.8.5.
37. Ibid., 2.8.4–5.
38. Orosius, XXIV.
39. Florus, 2.8.6.
40. Orosius, XXIV.
41. Appian, I. 14.116.
42. Strauss, p. 81.
43. Florus, 2.8.6.
44. Plutarch, *Sertorius*, 16–21; 23–27; Appian, I. 110–112.
45. Appian, *Mithridatic Wars*, 72–74; Plutarch, *Lucullus*, 5 & 8; 30,000 foot soldiers, and 2,500 horsemen says Plutrarch (8.5).
46. Eutropius, VI.10.
47. Appian, I. 14.116.
48. Ibid., I. 14.117.
49. Ibid.
50. Appian, I. 14.117; Orosius, XXIV.
51. Appian, I. 14.117.
52. Florus, 2.8.10.
53. Orosius, XXIV.
54. Florus, 2.8.10; Orosius, XXIV, also mentions a battle against the proconsul Gaius Cassius, from which Spartacus and the slave army emerged victorious and Cassius was killed.
55. Appian, I. 14.117.
56. Eutropius, VI. VII.
57. Appian, I. 14.117.
58. Florus, 2.8.9.
59. Orosius, XXIV.
60. Gunther, p. 24.
61. Appian, I. 14.117.
62. Florus, 2.8.11.
63. Strauss, p. 59; p. 92.
64. Appian, I. 14.117.
65. Ibid.
66. Orosius, XXIV. 360.
67. Eutropius, VI. VII.
68. Appian, I. 14.118.
69. Ibid.

70. Appian, I. 14.118; Livy, 96.e.
71. Plutarch, *Crassus*, 2.2–4.
72. Strauss, p. 105.
73. Ibid.
74. Plutarch, *Crassus*, 2.3.
75. Ibid.
76. Ibid., 3.3.
77. Ibid., 2.6.
78. Ibid., 3.3.
79. Ibid., 4.1.
80. Plutarch, *Pompey*, 13.3; *Crassus*, 6–7.
81. Plutarch, *Crassus*, 7.5.
82. Plutarch, *Pompey*, 42–46; *Crassus*, 6–7.
83. Appian, I. 14.117.
84. Ibid.
85. Plutarch, *Crassus*, 10.1.
86. Appian, I. 14.117.
87. Plutarch, *Crassus*, 10.1–2.
88. Ibid., 10.2–3.
89. Appian, I. 4.118.
90. Ibid.
91. Florus, 2.8.2; in 2.8.12 he adds that he is ashamed to give them the title of enemies of Rome.
92. Appian, I. 4.118.
93. Plutarch, *Crassus*, 9.
94. Orosius, XXIV; Appian, I. 4.118.
95. Plutarch, *Crassus*, 10.
96. Appian, I. 4.118.
97. Plutarch, *Crassus*, 10.
98. Ibid.
99. Plutarch, *Pompey*, 25–26.
100. Plutarch, *Crassus*, 10; Florus, 2.8.13.
101. Plutarch, *Crassus*, 10; Appian, I. 4.118.
102. Plutarch, *Crassus*, 10.
103. Appian, I. 14.119; Plutarch, *Crassus*, 10.
104. Plutarch, *Crassus*, 11.3.
105. Appian, I. 4.120.
106. Ibid.
107. Plutarch, *Crassus*, 11.
108. Frontinus, I.V. 20.
109. Plutarch, *Crassus*, 11.

110. Appian, I. 4.119. Appian puts it after the supposed first victory of Crassus over Spartacus; he says that the Romans slaughtered 6,000 slaves in the morning and 6,000 in the evening; Plutarch, 11, says to the mountains of Petelia in Lucania.
111. Plutarch, *Crassus*, 11.3.
112. Appian, I. 14.119.
113. Frontinus, II. V.34.
114. Livy, 97e; Frontinus, II. V.34.
115. Orosius, XXIV.
116. Frontinus, II. IV.7.
117. Ibid., II. V.34.
118. Plutarch, *Crassus*, 11.4.
119. Ibid.
120. Appian, I. 4.119.
121. Ibid., I. 4.120.
122. Plutarch, *Crassus*, 11.
123. Ibid.
124. Florus, 2.8.13–14.
125. Plutarch, *Crassus*, 11.
126. Livy, 97.e.
127. Orosius, XXIV.
128. Plutarch, *Crassus*, 11.
129. Plutarch, *Pompey*, 21.
130. Plutarch, *Crassus*, 11.
131. Plutarch, *Crassus*, 11.11; *Pompey*, 22.
132. Orosius, XXIV.

Chapter 5

1. Alföldy, p. 72; Małowist, p. 29.
2. Andreau-Descat, p. 70.
3. Ibid., p. 37.
4. Małowist, p. 44; pp. 46–8; pp. 62–5.
5. Dalla-Lambertini, pp. 55–6, 59.
6. Ibid., pp. 57–9.
7. Hunt 2018.
8. Małowist, pp. 153–4.
9. Andreau-Descat, pp. 66–7; Małowist, p. 71.
10. Finley 1979.
11. Kay 2016, Carla-Marcone 2011, Scheidel-Von Reden 2010, Manning-Morris 2005, Ward-Perkins 2005.
12. Małowist, p. 162.

13. Ibid., pp. 48–56.
14. Ibid., pp. 68–9, p. 71 and following; also see cit. 90.
15. Andreau-Descat, pp. 45, 68.
16. Ibid., pp. 52, 92–4.
17. Kamen 2023.
18. Małowist, pp. 71–93.
19. Ibid., pp. 99–100.
20. Ibid., pp. 104–105.
21. Ibid., p. 139.
22. Andreau-Descat, p. 68.
23. Ibid., p. 74
24. Ibid., pp. 72–4.
25. Alföldy, pp. 72–3.
26. Małowist, p. 81.
27. Andreau-Descat, p. 108.
28. Małowist, pp. 98–9.
29. Małowist, pp. 83–8; Hunt 2018.
30. Małowist, p. 86.
31. Małowist, pp. 88–93; Andreau-Descat, pp. 79–80.
32. Andreau-Descat, pp. 82–7.
33. Digest, 14.1.1.15, Ulpian.
34. Andreau-Descat, p. 152.
35. Wickramasinghe 2016.
36. Notably, the judges in the Olympic Games had established a drastic solution against cheating by starting to run before the signal in the races: the cheater was whipped. That might sound too much today, but it probably didn't look that way in a time where cameras and photocells weren't invented yet, and you had to defend the integrity of the games from able cheaters who trained to begin a few tenths of a second faster than they should. A tough anti-incentive could work better than pure theoretical moral education.

Appendix I

1. Epplett, Chapter 1: 'Origins and Early Development'.
2. Ibid.
3. Wisdom, pp. 22–3.
4. Epplett, Chapter 2.
5. Wisdom, pp. 11, 13.
6. Epplett; Wisdom, p. 6.
7. Wisdom, p. 6.
8. Strauss, p. 19; Wisdom, p. 13.
9. Wisdom, p. 13.

10. Ibid., p. 21.
11. Epplett, Chapter 4.
12. Wisdom, p. 45.
13. Ibid., pp. 45–6.
14. Strauss, p. 13.
15. Wisdom, p. 46.
16. Ibid., p. 58.
17. Ibid., p. 59.
18. Ibid., p. 13.
19. Ibid., pp. 49–56.
20. Ibid., pp. 5–6.
21. Morris 2014, pp. 7–8.

Appendix II

1. Southern, p. 87.
2. Brizzi 2008, pp. 33–4; Southern, p. 89.
3. Southern, pp. 89–90.
4. Polybius, *Histories*, 6.19–42.
5. Southern, pp. 91–3.
6. Ibid., p. 98.
7. Ibid., pp. 93–4.
8. Alföldy, p. 97.
9. Southern, pp. 100–101.
10. Ibid., pp. 95–6.
11. Ibid., pp. 103–104.
12. Sowell, p. 27.
13. Southern, p. 125.
14. Poma, pp. 66–75; Grant, pp. 218–20.

Bibliography

Alföldy, Géza. *Storia sociale dell'antica Roma*, Il Mulino, Bologna, 2012 (1975).

Andreau, Jean and Raymond Descat. *The Slave in Greece and Rome*, University of Wisconsin Press, Wisconsin, 2011 (2006).

Aristotle. *Politics*. Loeb Classical Library, 1932.

Athenaeus of Naucratis; Charles Burton Gulick (trans.). *The Deipnosophists*, Loeb Classical Library, Harvard University Press (Vols. I–VIII), Cambridge, MA & London, 1927 (translation completed by 1931).

Biscardi, Arnaldo. Αρχαίο Ελληνικό Δίκαιο, Εκδόσεις Παπαδήμα, Αθήνα, 1991 (1982). [*Ancient Greek Law*, *Original title: *Diritto Antico Greco*]

Brizzi, Giovanni. *Il Guerriero, l'Oplita, il Legionario. Gli eserciti nel mondo classico*, Il Mulino, Bologna, 2002.

Brizzi, Giovanni. *Roma. Potere e identità dalle origini alla nascita dell'impero cristiano*, Pàtron Editore, Bologna, 2012.

Canfora, Luciano. *Giulio Cesare. Il dittatore democratico*, Editori Laterza, Bari, 2006 (1999).

Canfora, Luciano. *Il mondo di Atene*, Editori Laterza, Bari, 2011.

Carlà, Filippo and Arnaldo Marcone. *Economia e finanza a Roma*, Il Mulino, Bologna, 2011.

Cassius Dio Cocceianus; Earnest Cary (trans.); Herbert Baldwin Foster (rev.). *Roman History*, Volumes I–IX, Harvard University Press (Loeb Classical Library Nos. 32, 37, 53, 66, 82, 83, 175, see volumes I–IX), Cambridge, MA & London, 1914–1927.

Cicero, Ingo Gildenhard (ed. & trans.). *Against Verres, 2.1. 53–86*, Open Book Publishers, Cambridge & Minneapolis, 2011.

Cicero, Gesine Manuwald (ed. & trans.). *Agrarian Speeches: De Lege Agraria contra Rullum and Pro Flacco*, Oxford University Press, Oxford & New York, 2018.

Cipolla, Carlo M. *Introduzione alla storia economica*, Il Mulino, Bologna, 2003 (1988).

Cipolla, Carlo M. *Storia economica dell'Europa pre-industriale*, Il Mulino, Bologna, 2002 (1974).

Dalla, Danilo. *Introduzione a un corso romanistico*, Giappichelli, Torino, 1997.

Dalla, Danilo and Renzo Lambertini. *Istituzioni di Diritto Romano*, Giappichelli, Torino, 2001.

Dionigi di Alicarnasso. *Antichità Romane*, Einaudi, Torino, 2010.

Drokalos, Sotirios F. *Σπάρτακος. Οι Δούλοι της Ρώμης Διεκδικούν την Ελευθερία τους* (73–71 π.*X*.), Γνώμων Εκδοτική, Αθήνα, 2018. [*Spartacus. The Slaves of Rome Fight for their Freedom (73-71 BC)*]

Epplett, Christopher. *Gladiators: Deadly Arena Sports of Ancient Rome*, Skyhorse Publishing, New York, 2017.

Eutropius, Harold W. Bird (trans.). *The Breviarium ab Urbe Condita of Eutropius*, Translated Texts for Historians 14, Liverpool University Press, Liverpool, 1993.

Finley, Moses. *L'economia degli antichi e dei moderni*, Editori Laterza, Bari, 2008 (1979).

Florus, Lucius Annaeus (trans. & ed. J. Wight Duff & Edward S. Forster). *Epitome of Roman History*, Harvard University Press (Loeb Classical Library No. 231), Cambridge, MA & London, 1984.

Frontinus, Sextus Julius; Charles E. Bennett (trans.); Mary B. McElwain (ed.). *The Stratagems and the Aqueducts of Rome*, Harvard University Press (Loeb Classical Library No. 174), Cambridge, MA & London, 1925.

Gibbon, Edward. *History of the Decline and Fall of the Roman Empire* (7 volumes), George Bell & Sons, London, 1891 (e-book).

Grant, Michael. *Ιστορία της Ρώμης*, Σύλλογος προς διάδοσιν ωφέλιμων βιβλίων, Αθήνα, 2011. (*Original title: *History of Rome*)

Gschnitzer, Fritz. *Storia sociale dell'antica Grecia*, Il Mulino, Bologna, 2010 (1981).

Gunther, Rigobert. *Η Εξέγερση του Σπάρτακου, Σύγχρονη Εποχή, Αθήνα*, 2013 (1984). [*The Revolt of Spartacus*, *Original title: *Der Aufstand des Spartacus*]

Heraclitus, Thomas M. Robinson (ed. & trans.). *Heraclitus: Fragments*, Phoenix Presocratic Series No. 22, University of Toronto Press, Toronto, 1987.

Hunt, Peter. *Ancient Greek and Roman Slavery*, Wiley-Blackwell, Hoboken, 2018.

Jacques, François and John Scheid. *Roma e il suo Impero. Istituzioni, economia, religione*, Editori Laterza, Bari, 2010 (1990).

De Jaeghere, Michel. *Gli ultimi giorni dell'impero romano*, LEG Edizioni, Gorizia, 2019 (2014).

Joshel, Sandra R. *Slavery in the Roman World*, Cambridge University Press, New York, 2010.

Justinian I (compiler, based on jurists including Ulpian); Alan Watson (ed. & trans.). *The Digest of Roman Law*, University of Pennsylvania Press, Philadelphia, 2009–2011.

Kamen, Debora. *Greek Slavery*, De Gruyter, Berlin, 2023.

Kay, Philip. *Rome's Economic Revolution*, Oxford University Press, Oxford, 2016.

Livy, Titus. David S. Levene (ed. & trans.). *The Fragments and Periochae. Volume I: Fragments, Citations, Testimonia; Volume II: Periochae 1–45*, Oxford University Press, Oxford, 2024.

Livy, Titus. John C. Yardley (trans.). *The Dawn of the Roman Empire: Books 31–40 of History of Rome*, Oxford World's Classics, Oxford & New York, 2007.

Livy, Titus. J. C. Yardley (trans.). *History of Rome, Books 23–25*, Harvard University Press (Loeb Classical Library), Cambridge, MA & London, 2020.

Livy, Titus. Aubrey de Sélincourt (trans.). *The Early History of Rome: Books I–V*, Penguin Classics, London & New York, 1960.

Livy, Titus. Aubrey de Sélincourt (trans.). *Rome and Italy: Books VI–X*, Penguin Classics, London & New York, 1965.

Livy, Titus. Aubrey de Sélincourt (trans.). *The War with Hannibal: Books XXI–XXX*, Penguin Classics, London & New York, 1965.

Livy, Titus. Jane D. Chaplin (ed.). *Rome's Mediterranean Empire: Books41–45 and the Periochae*, Oxford World's Classics, Oxford & New York, 2010.

Mackay, Christopher S. Αρχαία Ρώμη. *Στρατιωτική και πολιτική ιστορία, Εκδόσεις* Παπαδήμα, Αθήνα, 2013 (2004). (*Original title: *Ancient Rome. A Military and Political History*)

Małowist, Iża Bieżuńska. *La schiavitù nel mondo antico*, Edizioni Scientifiche Italiane, Napoli, 1991.

Manning, J. G. and Ian Morris (eds.). *The Ancient Economy: Evidence and Models*, Stanford University Press, Stanford, 2005.

Marcone, Arnaldo. *Augusto. Il fondatore dell'impero che cambiò la storia di Roma e del mondo*, Salerno Editrice, Roma, 2015.

Marx, Karl & Engels, Friedrich. *Collected Works Volume 41* (*Letters 1860–64*). Lawrence & Wishart, 2010.

Matyszak, Philip. *Cataclysm 90 BC: The Forgotten War That Almost Destroyed Rome*, Pen & Sword Books, Barnsley, 2014.

Meyer-Zwiffelhoffer, Eckhard. *Storia delle province romane*, Il Mulino, Bologna, 2011.
Moore, Lee Christopher. *Ex Senatu Eiecti Sunt: Expulsion from the Senate of the Roman Republic, c. 319–50 BC*. University College London (UCL), PhD, 2013.
Morris, Ian. *War: What is it Good For?*, Profile Books, London, 2014.
Paleothodoros, Dimitris. 'Aristonicus' Revolt (133–129 BCE)', Encyclopedia of the Hellenic World, (6/22/2006).
Plutarch, *Roman Lives: A Selection of Eight Roman Lives*, translated by Robin Waterfield; introduction and notes by Philip A. Stadter, Oxford University Press, Oxford & New York, 1999.
Plutarch, Rex Warner (trans.). *The Fall of the Roman Republic: Six Lives*, Penguin Classics, London & New York, 1972.
Polybius, Robin Waterfield (trans.); Brian McGing (intro.). *The Histories*, Oxford World's Classics, Oxford & New York, 2010.
Polybius, W. R. Paton (trans.); revised by F. W. Walbank & Christian Habicht. *The Histories*, Volumes I–VI, Harvard University Press (Loeb Classical Library Nos. 128, 137, 138, 159, 160, 161), Cambridge, MA & London, 2010–2012.
Poma, Gabriella. *Le istituzioni politiche del mondo romano*, Il Mulino, Bologna, 2009 (2002).
Poma, Gabriella. *Le istituzioni politiche della Grecia in età classica*, Il Mulino, Bologna, 2003.
Rostovtzeff, Michael Ivanovitch. *A Large Estate in Egypt in the Third Century B.C.*, Forgotten Books, London, 2012 (1922).
Rostovtzeff, Michael Ivanovitch. *Ρωμαϊκή Ιστορία*, Εκδόσεις Παπαζήση, Αθήνα, 1984 (1928). (*Original title: *Rome*)
Rostovtzeff, Michael Ivanovitch. *The Social and Economic History of the Roman Empire*, Sandpiper Books Ltd, Midsomer Norton, 1998 (Oxford University Press, New York, 1957).
Rostovtzeff, Michael Ivanovitch. *Caravan Cities*, Lavergne, 2012 (1932).
Sallust, J. C. Rolfe (trans.). *The War with Catiline; The War with Jugurtha*, Harvard University Press (Loeb Classical Library No. 116), Cambridge, MA & London, 1921 (rev. 1931).
Sallust, Josiah Osgood (trans.). *How to Stop a Conspiracy: An Ancient Guide to Saving a Republic*, Princeton University Press, Princeton & Oxford, 2017.
De Sanctis, Gaetano. *La guerra sociale*, La Nuova Italia Editrice, Firenze, 1976.
Scheidel, Walter and Sitta von Reden (eds.). *The Ancient Economy*, Routledge, New York, 2002.
Schmuck, Hilmar (compiled by). *Biographical Index of the Classical World 1 (A–E)*. K.G. Saur Verlag, Munich, 2001.
Shaw, Brent D. (ed. & trans.). *Spartacus and the Slave Wars: A Brief History with Documents*, Bedford/St Martin's, Boston & New York, 2001.
Bassanelli Sommariva, Gisella. *Lezioni di storia del diritto romano*, Edizioni Nautilus, Bologna, 2003.
Southern, Pat. *The Roman Army: A Social and Institutional History*, Oxford University Press, Oxford, 2007.
Sowell, Thomas. *Conquests and Cultures: An International History*, Basic Books, New York, 1998.
Sowell, Thomas. *Black Rednecks and White Liberals*, Encounter Books, San Francisco, 2005.
Storici latini: Cesare, Cornelio Nepote, Sallustio, Svetonio, Tacito, Newton Compton Editori, Roma, 2011.
Strabo, Sarah Pothecary (trans.). *Strabo's Geography: A Translation for the Modern World*, Princeton University Press, Princeton & Oxford, 2024.
Strauss, Barry. *The Spartacus War*, Weidenfeld & Nicolson, London, 2009.

The Cambridge History of Greek and Roman Warfare, Vols. I–II, Cambridge University Press, Cambridge & New York, 2007.

The Cambridge History of Greek and Roman Political Thought, Cambridge University Press, Cambridge & New York, 2006.

Valerius Maximus; D. R. Shackleton Bailey (ed. & trans.). *Memorable Deeds and Sayings*, Vols. I–II, Harvard University Press (Loeb Classical Library Nos. 492–493), Cambridge, MA & London, 2000.

Velleius Paterculus, A.J. Woodman (ed. & trans.). *The Histories of Velleius Paterculus*, Harvard University Press (Loeb Classical Library No. 152), Cambridge, MA & London, 2025.

Veyne, Paul. *L'Impero Greco-Romano*, Rizzoli, Milano, 2007.

Walbank, Frank W. *Ο ελληνιστικός κόσμος*, Εκδόσεις Βάνιας, Θεσσαλονίκη, 1999 (1981). (*Original title: *The Hellenistic World*)

Ward-Perkins, Bryan. *La caduta di Roma e la fine della civiltà*, Mondolibri, Milano, 2008.

Whittaker, C.R. *Frontiers of the Roman Empire: A Social and Economic Study*, The Johns Hopkins University Press, Baltimore, 1994.

Wickham, Chris. *The Inheritance of Rome: Illuminating the Dark Ages 400–1000*, Penguin Books, London, 2010.

Wickramasinghe, Chandima S.M. *Slavery from Known to Unknown: A Comparative Study of Slavery in Ancient Greek Poleis and Ancient Sri Lanka*, BAR Publishing, Oxford, 2016.

Wisdom, Stephen. *Gladiators 100 BCE–AD 200*, Osprey Publishing, Oxford, 2001.

Index